# RIDING
# WITH THE
# LION

Also by Kyriacos C. Markides

THE MAGUS OF STROVOLOS

HOMAGE TO THE SUN

FIRE IN THE HEART

# RIDING
# WITH THE
# LION

## In Search
## of Mystical
## Christianity

Kyriacos C. Markides

VIKING ARKANA

VIKING
Published by the Penguin Group
Penguin Books USA Inc., 375 Hudson Street, New York, New York 10014, U.S.A.
Penguin Books Ltd, 27 Wrights Lane, London W8 5TZ, England
Penguin Books Austrlia Ltd, Ringwood, Victoria, Australia
Penguin Books Canada Ltd, 10 Alcorn Avenue,
Toronto, Ontario, Canada M4V 3B2
Penguin Books (N.Z.) Ltd, 182–190 Wairau Road,
Auckland 10, New Zealand

Penguin Books Ltd, Registered Offices: Harmondsworth, Middlesex, England

First published in 1994 by Viking Penguin,
a division of Penguin Books USA Inc.

1   3   5   7   9   10   8   6   4   2

LIBRARY OF CONGRESS CATALOGING IN PUBLICATION DATA
Markides, Kyriacos C.
Riding with the lion: in search of mystical Christianity/
Kyriacos C. Markides.
p.   cm.
Includes bibliographical references.
ISBN 0-670-85780-7
1. Markides, Kyriacos, C.   2. EREVNA (Organization)—Biography.
3. Occultism—United States—History—20th century.
4. Occultism—Cyprus—History—20th century.   5. New Age movement.
6. Mental healing.   7. Reincarnation.   8. Occultism—Religious
aspects—Orthodox Eastern Church.   9. Athos (Greece)   10. Orthodox
Eastern Church—Doctrines.   I. Title.
BP605.E73M375   1995
299'.93—dc20      94–12867

Printed in the United States of America
Set in Janson
Designed by Brian Mulligan

*To the memory of my father, Kostas K. Markides. To my son, Constantine, and to the most important women in my life: my late mother, Melpomeni; my wife, Emily; my daughter, Vasia; my sister Maroulla; and my aunt who raised me, Myrophora*

# AUTHOR'S NOTE

READERS OF MY EARLIER WRITINGS WILL DISCOVER THAT THE first two chapters of this volume will serve as summary and review of the central ideas that I have previously elaborated in great detail. Yet even in these two introductory chapters they will also discover that there is considerable new material and will realize too that although there is continuity between my other books and this one, the latter is a marked departure from the former. This study stands on its own independently of what I have written before. Therefore the first-time reader need not familiarize himself or herself with my other works before reading the present volume.

The dialogues were constructed from real conversations based on real encounters and real experiences. However, for the sake of protecting the anonymity of the persons involved, I used mostly pseudonyms and on occasion changed certain details in the flow of the described events.

As before, I have chosen to use the Greek idiom when directly addressing Greek males. For example, Socrates is addressed as "Socrate," Maximos is "Maxime," Kostas is "Kosta," Kyriacos is "Kyriaco," and so on. Names of Greek females do not pose such linguistic peculiarities.

I am extremely grateful to all the wonderful people of this book who have become part of my life and of my own exploration into the fundamental questions and dilemmas of our human existence. Without their generosity of time, mind, and heart I obviously could not have written this book.

I would like to express my appreciation to the University of Maine for a sabbatical leave in the spring of 1991 to pursue this study. I would also like to offer my deepest gratitude to all my colleagues in the Department of Sociology who have consistently and generously supported me in my research adventures: Stephen Marks, Susan Greenwood, Sandra Gardner, James Gallagher, Kathryn Gaianguest, Steven Cohn, Valerie Carter, and Steven Barkan. I consider myself very fortunate to have such congenial colleagues. Our chairperson, Steven Barkan, and administrative assistant Sue McLaughlin have been exceptionally obliging in creating a most hospitable and supportive atmosphere for teaching, research, and writing.

Special thanks to my superb editor, David Stanford, his assistant, Kristine Puopolo, and my literary agent, Marlene Gabriel, for their determined interest, personal involvement, and faith in the importance of the content of this book and for their first-class professional expertise. I would also like to express my thanks and appreciation to the Bishop of Paphos Chrysostomos and the Church of Cyprus for permission to use the image on the jacket design. Thanks also to Mr. Miltos Miltiadou of the Cyprus embassy in Washington for his assistance in getting the permit.

The list of people that I am indebted to for the completion of my present work is too long for me to mention each one by name. I have already pointed out the many characters that unfold in the pages of this study: my friends in Cyprus, in Maine, in New York, in Greece, and elsewhere. One individual, however, I must especially acknowledge for his pivotal contribution to the quality of this study, my friend and colleague Michael Lewis, professor of art at the University of Maine. He and my wife, Emily, were the first to read each chapter as I completed it. Their insightful feedback, editorial comments, and long conversations on the substance of this book not only sustained my faith and interest in what I was doing but made the final outcome much better than it otherwise would have been. Needless to say, whatever shortcomings one may find in the following pages are mine and mine alone.

As always the last word goes to my wife, Emily, whose extraordinary energy and zest for life kept me moving on into realms of experience that, without her nurturing support and intellectual and emotional stimulation, I would probably not have ventured on my own.

# CONTENTS

*xi*

# RIDING
# WITH THE
# LION

# 1

# SECRET
# KNOWLEDGE

THE SNOW WAS A FOOT DEEP AFTER A MAJOR STORM IN THE
middle of January 1990. The entire state of Maine was blanketed
white, and for the first time in my eighteen years of residency in
this "vacationland" I discovered the pleasures and exhilarations of
cross-country skiing. Colleagues at the university persuaded Emily
and me that sliding through the woods is a more profound experience than just walking. Once I tasted the experience I understood
why so many New Yorkers and Bostonians travel to this sparsely
populated region of the Northeast. They do so for skiing, ice fishing, and for temporary relief from the high anxieties and tensions
of metropolitan life.

Diana, a psychotherapist from Boston, had contacted me a week
earlier and asked whether I could meet with her. She was driving
up to Maine with friends that January weekend for some downhill
skiing at the Sugarloaf resort. Since route I-95 passed by the University of Maine, she thought it was an opportunity to stop for a
while at Orono and clarify certain issues that were of great concern
to her. She had followed my field research and work with a group
of reputed psychic and spiritual healers on the island of Cyprus and
was deeply affected by the three books that I wrote on the philos-

ophy and teachings that came out of my more than ten-year involvement with them as a participant observer. During that time I
was a witness to miraculous cures, and I heard fantastic stories of
out-of-body adventures and alleged detailed memories of past lives.
Most importantly during that period I engaged these mystics in deep
philosophical and theological discussions ranging from the nature
of reality, mind, self, and after-death states to the properties of the
Absolute and the role of archangels in the construction of the various "universes."

Diana dropped off her companions at the Bangor Mall and followed the directions that I gave her to our house. As soon as she
arrived I filled up the woodstove and we sat in the living room,
packed with Emily's plants, and overlooking the Stillwater River.
Emily was with Vasia, our eleven-year-old daughter, cross-country
skiing on the nearby university trails. The day was just brilliant with
sunshine and the fresh snow on the ground and the lush vegetation
created an enchanting, magical setting. A day like this made me
temporarily oblivious of Cyprus. My incurable yearning for the
streets and neighborhoods of my youth and the hidden coves where
I spearfished with my friends receded for a while to the back of my
awareness.

"What is a person like you, having grown up on a Mediterranean
island, doing in a frigid place like Maine?" Diana asked jokingly as
she looked out the bay window at the half-frozen river where, along
its edge, some teenagers were foolishly ice-skating.

"Oh, it must be a form of initiation," I said cryptically. "You see,
God placed me here so that I would overcome my ethnocentric
obsession with Cyprus. He wanted to give me a lesson that the
beauty of nature is not confined only to a sunny Mediterranean
island. It is found everywhere in His Creation, but particularly here
in Maine. Just look," I said, pointing at the window.

"I see what you mean," Diana said lightheartedly; then with a
more somber tone she proceeded to open up the issue that had

prompted her to pay me a visit. "So it is true that there is a split," she said.

Over the phone I had already confirmed her worst fears, that the rumors she had heard in Boston were true: Kostas and Spyros Sathi ("Daskalos"), the two central figures in my previous books, had split up and no longer had any relationship one to the other. It was a shock to many, because the two practicing mystics and masters of esoteric wisdom were considered to be extremely close. In fact Kostas, as the younger of the two, was presumably being groomed by Spyros Sathi to become his "successor." Furthermore, I myself no longer had any association with Spyros Sathi.

"How could this be possible? I mean, it is so sad. What went on that led to this breakup?" Diana asked, with anguish in her voice. "I was under the impression that truly spiritual people are beyond all that."

"Let me tell you, it was not easy for me," I said. "In fact I went through a kind of psychic inferno. But now I feel fine, more experienced and wiser, I hope. Perhaps 'liberated' may be the right word. I found my peace. I learned about certain truths and realities concerning gurus and masters, that in my more innocent years evaded my attention. You see, while writing those three books* I assumed that people who do great healings and are sources of great wisdom are necessarily impeccable, saintly characters with hardly any trace of ego. I thought that any rough edges that may have appeared in their personality were of no significance considering that other, shining side of them. I was wrong. Gurus and reputed masters are human beings like ourselves with weaknesses, flaws, and human passions like the rest of us. None of us is perfect, gurus notwithstanding. This is what most people have a hard time recognizing.

"You see, Diana," I went on to say, "when I was carrying on my research with Spyros Sathi I focused exclusively on the most glit-

* *The Magus of Strovolos, Homage to the Sun, Fire in the Heart.*

tering, most positive side of him and underplayed, as well as un-derestimated, the more human side of him. I thought that what was important was the teachings and a faithful description of what I heard and what I witnessed. I assumed that what appeared as minor rough edges and flaws of the ego were inconsequential. The details of his personal life that were not related to his reputed status as a teacher of metaphysical knowledge were of no interest to me and I left them unexplored. Rightly or wrongly I excluded them from my attention and kept them out of the portrait that I painted."

I stopped for a moment and then I went on in a joking tone. "Who knows? Sometimes ignorance may indeed be bliss."

Diana pondered what I said and then she asked what I expected her to: "What about Kostas? Do you have the same problems with him?"

"On the contrary," I replied. "I have an ongoing, close relation-ship with Kostas. The problem is with Spyros Sathi, not Kostas." I went on to repeat to Diana what I brought to the attention of my readers in the last chapter of *Fire in the Heart*, that Kostas remains the head of Erevna, the nonprofit foundation that was set up for the exploration and dissemination of this esoteric wisdom—Erevna meaning "Research," research for the Truth.

I pointed out to Diana that it is not the first time that this phe-nomenon has happened in the history of esoteric groups. In fact, as I am told by many knowledgeable people, it seems as if it is more like an archetypal pattern. Just think, I added, what happened with Gurdjieff and Ouspensky, Krishnamurti and the Theosophists, Ru-dolf Steiner and the Theosophists, Freud and Jung, and on and on.

"The catalyst that brought about the split was the formation of Erevna. Originally Spyros Sathi supported the effort and then turned against it, preferring to have his own family-based operation. But the rift over this matter brought into the forefront other issues that I prefer to let go and not discuss," I said.

"I understand," Diana said.

I had in my possession a formal statement, "To Whom It May Concern," that was sent out by the Erevna foundation in reference to this matter and Kostas' split with Spyros Sathi. To further clarify the issue for Diana I went on to read excerpts.

"Well, Diana," I said, as I folded the paper, "I know this will not fully satisfy you but I hope it partially answers some of the questions you and others have. It is not with any sense of satisfaction that I am saying these things to you. But events do happen that continue to lead us to deeper truths."

"What do you see as a deeper truth in these developments?" Diana asked with a sad look on her face.

"The truth that I learned from this is one that Spyros Sathi himself often stated, namely that the teachings come from the spiritual realm, whereas the master or teacher is a human being with faults. No one is beyond reproach. We all can make serious mistakes and blunders, gurus and followers alike. Perhaps this is in fact the last lesson."

"But wouldn't this split between Spyros Sathi and Kostas and you have an effect on the teachings themselves?" Diana asked.

"I believe that whatever is grounded on Truth will survive. Whatever is founded on fantasy and ego will eventually wither away. It is my conviction, however, that the credibility and validity of these teachings will not be affected by these developments. If they are part of the esoteric wisdom, then their truth value is independent of personalities. In fact I am discovering that these teachings are found in many other sources. For example, I am fascinated at the convergence between these teachings, that I wrote about, and the lectures given at the turn of the century in Chicago by a yogi named Ramacharaka. The thirteen volumes of his talks published by his disciples in 1903 have great similarity with what I have written in my three books.[1] Of course you find similarities between what I wrote and the works of Rudolf Steiner, the Rosicrucians, Tibetan Buddhists, Christian mystics, and many other spiritual traditions. So the Truth does not rise and fall with the rise and fall of various masters and gurus that happen to tap into it."

I went on to tell Diana that my passion for pursuing the research for the truth has not been diminished by these developments. On the contrary. My efforts will be to continue to write and help expand my own awareness and that of others on these fundamental issues and teachings on human existence of which Spyros Sathi and myself as well as Kostas play only an insignificant part.

"Our paths," I said, "converged at a certain point and it was a very creative and life-enhancing encounter. I will never forget those years. In a sense they marked me for life, radically affecting my consciousness and the direction of my work. As I was told many times, the law of cause and effect works in mysterious ways. At this point it is leading us in different directions. Perhaps it had to be that way for some reason that is beyond my comprehension.

"For as long as our relationship was intact," I went on to say, "I tried as faithfully as I could to record my encounters with Spyros Sathi and his immediate circles. Unfortunately when we are not dealing with the teachings but our everyday realities, differences arise between people, differences in values, strategies, appropriate behavior, and so on. These can create complications that often get out of control. So the breakup seems in retrospect to have been almost inevitable. From now on I will simply focus on what is authentic spiritual teachings and philosophy independent of the personality of particular individuals and teachers." We remained silent for a few seconds and watched the ice-skaters from our window.

"A few days ago," I continued, "I received a letter from a very sensitive young man that I liked from the moment I met him in Cyprus last summer. Let me call him John. At that time John told me that he was working on a doctoral degree in physics. His real passion, however, was psychical research and spirituality. In fact he told me of many psychic experiences that he had had over the years and that his long-term plan was to combine the study of physics with psychical research. That is why he joined the circles of Erevna. During his visit to Cyprus John met separately with both Spyros Sathi and Kostas, and learned about the problems. Like most of us he agonized over it for a long time, trying to find some answers that would make sense to him. In the letter he wrote to me he described an extraordinary dream that he believed revealed to him a certain profound truth about this matter. Would you like me to read it to you?"

"Oh yes, please," Diana replied.

I went upstairs to my study and pulled John's letter out of a file. "Here is what he considered his revelational dream on this issue," I said and began reading:

The dream I told you about followed many days of agonizing and soul searching. That day, I had just had an extremely painful discussion with a member of our circle on the question of Daskalos. The dream itself was as follows: Walking around a small, deep lake, I was trying to make sense of what was going on. I felt that the answer lay at the bottom of the lake, but as I walked around it, I could only see the light reflecting off the surface—I could not see to the bottom. Daskalos himself appeared by the side of the lake, and we exchanged a friendly greeting. Then I noticed a tall stone tower in front of me, right by the side of the lake. I reasoned that if I could climb to the top and look down, I would be able to see to the bottom of the lake without the diversion of the reflected light on the surface. Daskalos went off in the other direction, and I climbed the many flights of steps to the top of the tower. When I got to the top, I was dismayed to find that all of the windows had been painted over so that I could not see out. As I stood there, totally disappointed, a voice spoke which seemed to be coming from all around, and yet sounded within me. It said that Daskalos' public teachings were among the best. He himself recognizes his own flaws that cause him extreme pain. Yet at the same time, he teaches total compassion for those who have succumbed to similar human weaknesses and shows great willingness to help those who wish to be healed. His personal predilections, this voice said to me, were really no concern of mine. Upon waking up, I was filled with a strong, quiet peace regarding this subject. Even though I still have an interest in the workings of the circles and the personal and karmic relationships among the people involved, that peace has really never left me.

"That is some dream!" Diana exclaimed. "The voice that John heard in his dream makes a lot of sense." She paused for a second and then she went on.

"Perhaps at a deeper level," Diana said thoughtfully, "you are still connected with Spyros Sathi and your differences are only in regard to this life."

"In fact," I said, laughing, "this is what a Brazilian psychic told me when she entered into a trance. She said that within the spiritual realms Spyros Sathi and I are very close and that our differences are only on the gross material level. Well, only God really knows the deeper meaning of all this and the mysterious karmic forces that brought us together. I hope the Brazilian psychic has tapped into some deeper truth that is beyond our grasp at the moment. So may God bless us all."

"Amen," Diana murmured with a pensive look on her face.

Within my limited awareness I knew that my association with Spyros Sathi was over. I had to turn past that chapter of my life and move forward to where the karmic forces were destined to take me. When Diana left to rejoin her companions I pondered this issue further and made a promise to myself that I would never raise it again. Chapter closed.

I went to my study and reflected on an upcoming lecture and

workshop that I was to offer in Manhattan at the New York Open Center, a nonprofit holistic center in Soho that organizes and sets up lectures, workshops, and conferences dealing with issues related to the mind/body connection, alternative healing traditions, Eastern philosophies, and cross-cultural spirituality in general. The brochure published by the Center titled my workshop "Consciousness, Spirituality, and Healing: A Western Path." The first paragraph read:

> Contemporary interest in spirituality has often been exclusively preoccupied and identified with non-Western traditions such as those springing from Hindu, Buddhist and Tibetan mysticism as well as native American shamanism. In this workshop Kyriacos C. Markides, author of *The Magus of Strovolos*, *Homage to the Sun*, and *Fire in the Heart*, will introduce participants to a living spiritual tradition and practice that springs from within the Western Judaeo-Christian civilization and culture.

I flew to New York on Friday. The following morning at ten o'clock we began the workshop. There were twenty-eight people, primarily professional men and women in their thirties and forties whose spiritual and intellectual life could no longer be satisfied either by mainstream religion or by a conventional science that has exorcised all spiritual traces from its enterprise.

We sat around in a circle, name tags glued on our chests, and began. I first introduced myself and thanked everybody for getting together on that sunny Saturday morning at the Open Center. I then asked everyone to say a few things about themselves and, if they wished, the reasons that prompted them to come to the workshop. I prefer to do this right at the start of a workshop, not only for each participant to get a feeling of who is in the room but also to give me a few extra minutes to overcome the initial nervousness that I always carry with me whenever I face an audience for the first time.

"My name is Mary Ann. I am a therapist, a Jungian therapist," a woman in her late forties informed us. "I have been involved with esoteric teachings for the past ten years. I am interested to hear more of the work you wrote about. They fit well with what I am doing myself."

"I am Susan, a photographer by profession," the woman next to her said. "I am interested in healing. Some day I would like to photograph thought forms or what you call elementals."

"That would be quite an accomplishment," I marveled.

"My name is John," a tall slender man said. "Professionally, I started out in mathematics and physics, then went into the business world and became an accountant. I have been to India and studied with many teachers there for five years, but I am searching for a teaching from within the Western tradition."

"My name is Mary. Professionally I am an artist. I am here to learn more about the teachings."

"My name is Don. I earn my living as a computer programming expert for the state. I have been trained in the sciences and I am also a Christian pastor. I am looking toward the integration of science and religion."

As the introductions moved around we discovered that among us there was a great diversity of professions and personal backgrounds. There was a high school teacher, a biochemist, a Broadway actor, a commercial artist, a radiologist, a professional astrologer and numerologist with a psychology degree from New York University, a retired city engineer who had decided that he wished to explore his "inner world," a taxi driver with a degree in Asian history, a nun, a massage therapist, a nurse, a medical doctor, several psychotherapists, and so on.

I was pleased. The audience, unlike some of my introductory

sociology classes, was extremely motivated, alert and eager to participate. My nervousness evaporated when, fifteen minutes later, my turn came to speak and begin the workshop.

"Before I proceed," I said, "let me start with a warning. I am no master of esoteric knowledge. I will simply discuss with you my own personal adventure into these matters, what I heard, what I read and what I experienced with people who are reputed to know more than ordinary people like ourselves. Yet even these people who are considered to be masters of esoteric knowledge themselves claim that in reality they are also students, researchers of truth."

I paused for a moment and then continued as I looked around the circle. "Perhaps you have heard this story. There was once a Zen master who was invited to give a talk on the nature of Reality. He stood in front of his eager audience for half an hour uttering not a single word. Then he stepped down and left the room. The stunned sponsors rushed outside to ask for explanations. 'I *did* give my lecture,' he reassured them. 'Silence.' "

After the laughter I went on. "Just remember what Lao-tzu said in the *Tao Te Ching:* 'Those who know do not speak and those who speak do not know.' Alas, I do a voluminous amount of speaking." There was more laughter. "So remember, be aware of Greeks bearing words!" I felt at ease, and after more laughter I proceeded in a more serious tone.

"Please realize that what I have just said is not out of modesty, or false modesty for that matter. It is a brute fact. I personally take very seriously what all the great mystics, saints, and teachers of all the great spiritual traditions warn us, that true knowledge of Reality cannot be talked about. It can only be experienced, in silence. This is what the great masters are telling us. But our technocratic, rationalistic, materialistic, linguistically noisy civilization has exorcised experience as irrelevant and relegated it to the 'merely subjective,' therefore 'unreal.' What one experiences cannot be real unless subjugated to rigorous, experimental 'objective' controls. This is what I was taught to believe as an academic sociologist over the many years of training and practice—and conditioning, if I may add.

"So what happened that led to my change of heart over the last thirteen or so years? What happened that let me realize that true knowledge of Reality can only be experienced and not talked about. That Knowledge with a capital $K$ is trans-logical, trans-scientific, trans-linguistic. Please notice that I am saying trans-scientific and trans-logical, not anti-scientific, irrational, or non-logical. You see, I do firmly believe that science, given our existential ignorance, is our most powerful tool to understand the material world that we confront through our five senses. But that is as far as science can go, the study of the laws that govern the material universe. If there are universes that are inaccessible to either the senses or to our mathematical formulations, then science cannot be much of a help.

"Those of you who have read my other books know where I come from and the circumstances that led to the above realization. For those who have not I would like to say a few words about my background as a way of entering the substance of today's workshop, an exploration into the nature of our existence using, alas, the most imperfect tool at our disposal, language." I paused for a few seconds to make certain that I had the small audience with me. Then I continued.

"We are all unique. Millions and billions of human beings have lived and are now living on this planet. We are now over five billion self-conscious souls living on this endangered planet. Yet it is an existential fact that no two human beings go through life having identical experiences. No two human beings look exactly alike, have the same fingerprints, let alone have identical experiences, identical emotions, identical thoughts or personalities. And the more complex our societies become the further apart we move from each other in terms of uniqueness of life's experience. Realization of this fact can be exhilarating and frightening at the same time. At least it was so for me when I discovered that I could not find anyone like myself. That is, someone who was born a Greek Cypriot, came to America to study accounting, ended up ten years later at the University of Maine as professor of sociology with a specialization in political sociology, and finally got involved with research on mystics, psychic healers, and spiritualists of all sorts.

"For a while I assumed that the way I personally went through life was singularly abnormal and I often envied the life of 'normal' people and longed for the normal life that I entertained in my fantasies. And normal life for me was living in Kyrenia, the northern part of Cyprus, by the sea, spending blissful weekends spearfishing and strolling with friends up and down the promenade as we watched the sun set into the Mediterranean sea. When the Turks took over that part of Cyprus, along with our house in Famagusta (the eastern port) during the terrible invasion of 1974, that dream was shattered and I was forced to live what I thought was the abnormal life of a half-refugee academic deep in the Maine hinterland, which, I must hasten to add, I came to deeply cherish and appreciate.

"Of course after a more careful and sober reflection I recognized that all human beings go through analogous experiences and must feel these same unsettling emotions. That we all go through life in very unique pathways. We are all uniquely abnormal." There was the expected laughter when I spoke the last words.

"For me, coming to America was not only a movement into another continent, a movement in space, but also a movement in time. The culture and politics of the island I grew up on were dominated by the Greek Orthodox Church. The intellectual environment was not that much different from the cultural environment that prevailed in Europe during the time of Saint Augustine." I knew of course that I was exaggerating but I continued. "All existential questions were answered by the parish priests, who knew everything about the beyond and what happens to the dead. So when my mother died a few months before I turned five, the Church was there to provide the answers and soothe the pain. My mother went to sleep. One day I will meet with her again. But my father was unimpressed and unconsoled and was furious at both God and the priests. 'How could a good God allow such a tragedy?' he would repeat. It was the age-old question. How could a good God allow such evil? It took my father ten years before he could set foot in a church again. But he never questioned the reality of God. He only questioned His justice and ultimate goodness that the deacons and priests eulogized in their incantations.

"The doctrines of the Church enjoyed an unchallenged authority. There were no secular intellectuals around to question those notions, nor any other religions, with the exception of Islam whose presence fortified the Greeks' devotion to their Church.

"Coming to America was a radical shock for me and the beginning of my own secularization. Every sacred idea that I cherished came under attack. First, I lost faith in Greek nationalism. I went through the Greek Cypriot rebellion against British colonial rule, and when I arrived at my relatives' in Ohio to study business administration I carried with me an overinflated sense of Greek pride that was injected into me by furious theologians and philologists in high school. When I discovered that Americans were also under the spell of the same patriotic sentiments I began losing faith in the inherent value of my own patriotism—'the last refuge of scoundrels,' I read in a book assigned for an English class. I was beginning to learn the meaning of cultural relativity. Absolute values were nowhere to be found. Beliefs and values were 'socially constructed.'

"Religious values, like patriotism, suffered a similar blow in my consciousness. My professor of psychology impressed upon me that belief in God was the product of unconscious fears and weaknesses. My English instructor mocked the Church, and the sociology professor revealed to us that religion was in reality the divinization of society. And all of them had sterling credentials, doctorates of philosophy. Wide-eyed, I assumed they knew. . . .

"It was not difficult for me to overcome nationalism. Deep down I knew that it was indeed a form of 'false consciousness.' In fact I felt liberated when I would no longer be under its violent sway. I could easily point my finger at nationalism as the culprit of the great suffering in Cyprus and the impossibility of me enjoying weekends of fishing and sunset watching in Kyrenia.

"With religion it was an entirely different matter. I could easily live without nationalism, but without religion? 'God is dead,' my English professor announced triumphantly one morning as he read a passage from *Thus Spake Zarathustra*. I couldn't understand why he looked so happy about it. Had he gone mad? I wondered. After all, normal people mourn when someone dies. That professor looked so enchanted with the death of the only God we've got. I shivered and vehemently rebelled against this notion. It was not easy to overcome the psychological security that the Church provided for me being an altar boy in my early teens, offering me a strong sense of identity and helping me overcome the pain of my mother's loss. The chants and the rituals were deeply ingrained in my subconscious as I confronted the formidable challenge of modern secular education. My logic at the time was telling me that the existence of an ultimate divine principle, a God if you will, was absolutely necessary as a foundation for all possible values. The death of God would unavoidably lead to nihilism. This is what I thought at the time. This is what I learned later that Nietzsche, the author of that frightful declaration, felt. That the death of God was bound to unleash in the coming twentieth century unheard-of demoniacal forces. He was prophetic in his vision and paid for it with his sanity.

"There emerged a struggle within me to find satisfying answers to these questions. The dissonance in my thoughts drove me from the study of business administration to sociology. I assumed that there I would find some answers. That decision brought me a sense of direction and personal satisfaction. God may be dead but I could leave that as an open question. Notions about God, the nature of ultimate meaning and human destiny were beyond our capacity to understand, I concluded. Therefore it would have been an unwise expenditure of both time and energy to be preoccupied with such matters. Those issues should remain the province of theologians. Yet I knew in the back of my mind that the work of theologians could not be taken seriously. Their cultural legitimacy had already been swept away by the forces of secularization and scientific rationality. I went along with the subtle position that theology was in reality, like astrology, a leftover of the Middle Ages. It was of marginal utility, having very little to offer in our understanding of the human predicament. Let the theologians spin out their improbable and unprovable assumptions about God. Let them consume their energies trying to calculate how many angels can dance on the head of a pin. I knew better than that as to how to use my precious time.

"Step by step I became a convert to rational science and philosophical agnosticism. Yet I was not a cheerful agnostic like so many fellow students and professors I met. I was an agnostic out of intellectual necessity, not out of any psychological propensity. I thought I had no choice. I certainly did not need to rebel against the Church, because in my personal experience the Church was not an oppressor. In fact the beauty of its liturgy, the sounds of the ceremonies, the smells of the burning incense and candles made of beeswax remained an integral part of my cultural subconscious. I may have become an agnostic but I remained culturally a Greek Orthodox in the same way that an agnostic Jew remains culturally a Jew. The scientific, intellectual, and cultural verdict was too overwhelmingly in favor of atheism and agnosticism. The God taught to me in catechism after class during my elementary school years was by now nothing more than a comforting illusion useful for the childhood of my existence but an irrelevant embarrassment for a grown-up, mature Western intellectual.

"I made peace with myself. In the final analysis whatever I or anyone else believes is immaterial and inconsequential. Whatever is *Is* and I can do nothing to change it. I will accept whatever is true in Nature. Whether death will annihilate me or not is not up to me to decide. With this understanding my serenity was restored. I resolved to just focus my attention on that which I thought I could understand, at least to some extent, and that was society.

"I accepted sociology not only as a profession but also as a new secular frame of existential orientation, as a new calling. It replaced religion and in the process it liberated me from both society and the religion of my youth. I realized later as I read the work of Alan Watts[2] that a central tenet of the Eastern concept of 'liberation' was in fact liberation from cultural conditioning. As long as we exclusively identify ourselves with our tribe, our nation, or our religion we can never truly discover our real Self. I was beginning to entertain the idea that modern secular culture and education may in fact help masses of humanity to overcome this cultural conditioning which although necessary in the earlier stages of our development can become an obstacle to true spiritual experience and liberation. Imagine what it would imply if we understood modern education, particularly the social and behavioral sciences, and all sciences for that matter, as vehicles for liberation that could lead to true enlightenment." I stopped for a few seconds to make certain that I did not bore my audience with my life's story.

"A turning point in my experience of America was coming to Maine in the early seventies to teach sociology. The second day after our arrival, I noticed a sign outside of the office of a colleague who'd gotten his appointment the same year I did. The notice said 'Please do not disturb. Meditation in process.' I had never heard the word meditation before nor did I know what it was all about. But I was intrigued. I asked Stephen, my colleague, questions about what he was doing locked up in his office with that strange sign pinned on his door. He explained to me in great detail the nature of TM meditation and gave me articles to read on the bodily effects of this Eastern practice. I was impressed with the scientific evidence on its beneficial effects. Two months later I was sticking notices outside of my door, so as not to be disturbed: Meditation in process.

"Now, I became a meditator for pragmatic reasons, to overcome stress and become more effective in what I was doing. The pressures for tenure loomed large. With meditation I could work harder, be more productive, publish more papers. Perhaps the senior professors in our department and the dean would be impressed enough to offer me tenure. It worked.

"My life took an interesting and unexpected twist, however. As I reached the pinnacle of a secular training, as I felt liberated from the fetters of nationalism and religion, as I completed my assimilation into the tenets and values of the modern American academic scene, and as I began feeling very comfortably established within it, I started flirting once more with my earlier preoccupations.

"The very exposure to Eastern meditation practices gradually sensitized me and brought me into contact with the thought of the East and, like so many other Westerners, I became enamored by it. More and more I began to reconsider the possibility that perhaps there may be answers to be found on the nature of our existence. That after all we may not be just helpless creatures on an insignificant planet at the edges of the Milky Way, as our Western philosophies and sciences led us to believe. That perhaps wisdom and a deeper understanding of reality may still be possible.

"The speculations of some theoretical physicists on the possible convergence of the teachings of Eastern yogis and modern theoretical physics stirred in me primordial yearnings for the unity and absolute meaningfulness of knowledge and the search for it. For I often questioned the ultimate value of pursuing knowledge, or anything for that matter, if in the final analysis there was only death waiting for us and an utter void, a nihilistic Abyss.

"I flirted with these ideas for several years after my introduction to Eastern philosophies and practices, but it was an after-work preoccupation, so to speak. I never would have imagined that the involvement with esoteric philosophies would become the focus of my research activities.

"Those of you who have read my books are familiar with how I got involved with the small circle of esoteric practitioners that I accidentally discovered on a trip to Cyprus in the summer of 1978. There is no need here to repeat the coincidences and encounters that prompted me to shift my academic research from the study of political violence to the study of practicing mystics and healers. It is important, however, to point out that my exposure to Eastern philosophies, meditation practice, and the writings of physicists with an interest in esoteric matters allowed me to listen without the temptation to explain away what these Greek healers, mystics, and psychics had to tell me about their experience of reality.

"You see," I continued, "had I been an anthropologist entering that field in the fifties, for example, most probably I would have followed the theoretical fashions of the time and assumed that shamans and so-called mystics were people suffering from some kind of either personal delusion or, even worse, schizophrenia. After all wasn't Jesus explained away by a psychiatrist in the early part of this century as a 'paranoid schizophrenic suffering from delusions of grandeur?'

"Had I followed this line of approach I would have offered very eloquent and seemingly persuasive and erudite explanations to account for the extraordinary tales that the mystics I studied revealed to me. After all, what sense can a reasonable person make if otherwise sane human beings would claim in all sincerity that they abandon their bodies at will, traveling to other dimensions of reality, meeting and consulting there with beings at higher levels of existence, and so on?

"But my encounter with the Cypriot mystics and healers took place in the late seventies. By that time long-cherished prejudices on the study of alternative healing traditions were beginning to be challenged. Some anthropologists were beginning to look at shamans not as lunatics but as authentic therapists of their respective societies. The dogmatic and uncritical acceptance of the older ethnocentric perspectives was being replaced by models that emphasized tolerance and a nonjudgmental approach to exotic cultural realities. That is the type of perspective that I have tried to employ in my more than ten-year involvement with the mystics and psychics of Cyprus. I simply let these unusual people speak for themselves and explain their world as they themselves experienced it. With such an approach I was able to gain their trust and consequently I was able to sit in meetings and proceedings at which presumably only the most trusted members of the inner circles were allowed to be present." I stopped and paused for a few moments.

"Well, this is what I wanted to say as a background to the issues that we will be exploring today. But before we proceed with the substance of the workshop I would like to inform you about certain developments." I then went on to explain the issues that I discussed with Diana. After the clarifications I asked them to shift their attention to the teachings and the subject matter of the workshop.

"Why don't we begin with questions that you may have, other than what we have just discussed," I said as a way of shifting our focus.

"How did you end up in Maine and how did you manage to survive in academia given your interest in these matters?" Mary Ann, the Jungian analyst, asked.

I laughed. Those were questions that people usually ask me. "As far as your first question," I replied, "I can only say that a series of what appeared to me in retrospect as incredible coincidences brought me to this American outpost. As I said before, the life of each one of us is extraordinarily unique. The coincidences that bring us to a certain point are, once we reflect upon them, truly incredible. Study that in yourself and you will find out what I mean. Chance or apparently chance encounters with people or circumstances shift the trajectory of our lives in a radically different direction.

"But Maine, you see, suits me just fine. At the periphery you always have greater freedom and independence than at the center. The University of Maine has been very generous with me regardless of the unusual nature of the type of research that I have been doing. I doubt whether I could have written the books that I have written had I taught at the urban centers of academic orthodoxy. The pressures would have been just too powerful to conform to mainstream-type research.

"On the other hand, my approach in working with this material has been quite academic—that is, I am not preaching on the absolute validity of these esoteric teachings. I am simply raising questions and letting people explore these ideas for themselves and discover whether they have any validity. My job is to bring these hidden and unknown traditions to the wider public, and Maine has served me well in that endeavor. I can see why Henry David Thoreau was so enchanted with the place and was inspired to write *The Maine Woods* in the 1860s. For me, Maine is an ongoing spiritual retreat. It has what mystics could call 'good energy.' "

"I am sure you must have been asked this question many times, but are you a believer. I mean, do you accept that there are realities and dimensions other than the one that we are familiar with?" Mary Ann asked again. "In short, do you accept the view of the world as presented by the mystics you wrote about?"

"People who accept only the reality of gross matter call me a believer and people who claim to be psychic and clairvoyant consider me too much of a skeptic, a Doubting Thomas," I said with a chuckle. "But look. I believe what I have seen and experienced myself and what I have concluded based on my own reason and level of understanding. For example, I have witnessed healings that could not be explained, at least as far as I know, in any conventional way. I cannot therefore deny my own personal experience because of some a priori assumption that such phenomena are impossible. Furthermore, the teachings themselves, as we shall see in this workshop, have internal logical consistency and are almost identical with all the esoteric teachings of all the great religions.

"In addition, what I have discovered over the years," I said further, "is that many people who have read my books either tell me personally or write to me that the world they live in is identical to the world I describe in my books. This really impresses me. And these are quite rational people, capable of distinguishing this world from the world of other dimensions that they claim they enter at will. So phenomena such as the voluntary out-of-body experience, what in Greek is called *exomatosis* or *exosomatosis*, is a very real experience to a large number of people that contacted me thanks to my books. Therefore, I can state as a fact that people *do* have these experiences and they are not schizophrenic or mentally abnormal experiences, as the uninitiated observer may have concluded."

I reached into my briefcase. "In fact," I said, "here is a letter that I received a week ago from a practicing New York healer that I met a year ago. He claims he had visited the healers in Cyprus in an out-of-body state. Do you want me to read it to you?"

As I expected, everybody showed keen interest, so I proceeded to read the letter without, of course, identifying the author:

> I decided to see if I could visit one of the Cypriot masters in the astral realm. . . . I found myself in a sort of alleyway that led from the street toward a series of rooms, perhaps just slightly below street level. Before I could enter the rooms themselves, I met a man mostly bald, with hair on either side

of his head. He was also wearing glasses, and stood perhaps five foot seven or eight. I asked him if he was a master. He nodded yes. I was surprised, since he looked more like an accountant to me (no slur on accountants intended: my family contains two of them!). I then asked him if he was one of the masters in your books. He said no, and indicated that one of the masters was inside past a right turn into another room, where he sat on a throne or high chair. I could go no farther. The feeling (though not clear) was that either the old master of your book . . . was no longer on this plane, or that I could not visit him in the psychic realm. . . . Could the man in the corridor have been Kostas?

After explaining who Kostas was to those students who had not read my books, I continued: "The experience of this healer does not seem to have any direct and literal relationship to the gross material environment of the Cypriot psychics that I know. No one sits on some high throne, nor is Kostas a bald-headed accountant, although there is a bald-headed accountant who is close to Kostas. What shall we make of this? We may choose to dismiss it as pure fantasy. But I think it would be a mistake. He underwent an experience which for him was very real. It was definitely not of the gross material level and probably he made no contact with the Cypriot healers. But Kostas would say that he probably did make contact with some beings or masters living on higher levels of vibrations who may have presented themselves in a way to which the New York healer could relate.

"But what is more interesting is what he wrote at the bottom of his letter in the form of a P.S.," I said, and proceeded to read further:

While working with one of my patients—who has a degenerative disease of the retina—I decided to use dematerialization as described in your first book. I had previously used a similar technique on other patients, but always with the assistance of Guides. As I began to work on this person's retina, a very strong presence filled the room: The Master. He said, "Let me do it. You are not ready for this yet," and accomplished the procedure while I watched in awe. The patient was unaware of this, and told me upon rising from the table that she had had the image of an old man looking at her. The results were impressive as well: she was able to see better out of her ailing eye. Needless to say, I was very moved. During a subsequent meditation a week or so later, I asked the Master if I could learn from him. He said: "Write me a letter. The rest will follow."

I folded the letter and put it back in my briefcase. "You see, I cannot say whether the experience of that person was real and 'objective,' since I have not entered into a voluntary out-of-body state myself nor have I subjected this man to some kind of scientific testing. And scientists would not accept anything as real unless it is subjected to the controls of science. Therefore, a conventional scientist or skeptic would dismiss such experiences as fantasies. Do I accept it as real? All I can say is that it is real to the person having the experience and we have no way of judging one way or another. This does not mean that the experience is necessarily not authentically real. This is my difference with conventional scientists and skeptics. They would dismiss as unreal whatever does not conform to their beliefs about reality. On the other hand, by inclination I cannot accept as necessarily real claims to reality which I have no access to. I am, however, willing to listen and suspend judgment. But what I do know for a fact is that people do have such experiences and these experiences may be as real as the reality that we happen to be in at this very moment. And healings like the one reported by this person do take place in very mysterious ways."

"I know people who have such experiences," Susan, the photographer, said, and others joined in to point out that they themselves also know individuals who have similar experiences. "What I want to know," she went on, "is the significance of this fact, that is, that there are human beings among us who have these types of extraordinary experiences."

I waited a few seconds for a volunteer but the question was addressed to me, so I offered an answer. "I believe the empirical fact of the presence of such individuals in our midst should alert us to the possibility of alternate realities that may be all around us that we are normally totally unconscious of. Perhaps by becoming conscious of realities that mystics, healers, shamans, and people like them talk about will help us transcend the narrowness of our consciousness and vision within the three dimensions. It may open a real breakthrough in the evolution of our species. We have become so thoroughly conditioned by the underlying beliefs of conventional science that we have assumed that the only real world is the world that can be studied by orthodox science. As a civilization we have become enchanted with *scientism*, the uncritical belief that *only* through science can we know anything. We have forgotten what the philosopher Huston Smith has called the *primordial tradition*[3] or what Huxley called *philosophia perennis*, 'the perennial philosophy.' "

I explained that the primordial tradition is that philosophical tradition that one can detect at the core of all the great religions and philosophies. It is a tradition that is essentially unaltered and unaffected by the fashionable currents of thought, be it philosophical, scientific, or religious, that happen to prevail in any particular culture or historical period. Furthermore, I went on to say, this tradition has been hidden from the masses and been preserved in secret societies and brotherhoods throughout the ages.

"I have with me a book," I said, "written at the beginning of this century by the Russian mathematician P. D. Ouspensky, which I believe is one of the earliest statements in this century by a European thinker on the reality of 'hidden knowledge.' "

I pulled Ouspensky's *A New Model of the Universe* from my briefcase[4] and read a few passages:

The idea of a knowledge which surpasses all ordinary human knowledge, and is inaccessible to ordinary people, but which exists somewhere and belongs to somebody, permeates the whole history of the thought of mankind from the most remote periods. And according to certain memorials of the past a knowledge quite different from ours formed the essence and content of human thought at those times when, according to other opinions, man differed very little, or did not differ at all, from animals. . . . In our time theories which deny the possibility of hidden knowledge have become predominant. . . . They have become so only very recently and only among a small, although a very noisy, part of humanity. . . .

Believing in the possibility and existence of "hidden knowledge," people always ascribed new properties to it, always regarded it as rising above the plane of ordinary knowledge and stretching beyond the limits of the "five senses." This is the true meaning of "hidden knowledge," of magic, of miraculous knowledge and so on. If we take away from hidden knowledge the idea that it goes beyond the five senses, it will lose all meaning and importance.

"I believe Plato's 'parable of the cave' is an allusion to the reality of this secret knowledge. That a few brave souls after heroic personal struggles manage to escape the shadowy world of the cave into which they were chained on a pole. When they reach the outside they experience the sunshine of enlightenment. After that experience they are compelled by compassion for those left behind to return to the cave and help their fellow humans to escape from the shadows of their ignorance."

"How does one discover this secret knowledge, how does one get out of the cave to become enlightened?" someone asked.

"Well," I replied, "according to Erevna, the primordial tradition, and in fact according to all the authentic esoteric teachings, you don't need to travel to central Asia or anywhere else for that matter. The primordial tradition or secret knowledge is discovered through deep meditation and contemplation by anyone advanced enough spiritually. Therefore, the primordial tradition is deeply buried in the psyche of every human being awaiting discovery by initiates and contemplatives of all cultures and historical periods. The primordial tradition is not a philosophical system that has been invented or constructed by intellectuals. It is therefore beyond time and space. It is the very essence of wisdom itself. For this reason Huston Smith and other contemporary thinkers caution against the hitching of the primordial tradition to contemporary quantum physics, as it is fashionable today among a growing number of 'New Age' thinkers.

"It is of course fascinating to explore the apparent similarities and seeming convergence between the visions of the mystics and what theoretical physicists like Fritjof Capra[5] teach today. Nevertheless what Huston Smith says is that whereas the primordial tradition is unchanging as it springs from sources beyond time and space, science is part of the ongoing historical development of humanity and therefore subjected to constant change and transformation. What was true in science yesterday is not necessarily true today. And what is true in science today will not necessarily be true tomorrow. The primordial tradition is called precisely so because it is not subjected to the transformative law of time and space. Therefore, to link this tradition with science is to relativize the former, which in its true nature is timeless and transhistorical. It is immortal Wisdom itself."[6]

"So the various mystics, gurus, magi, and shamans of history are expressing this primordial tradition," Jerry, the retired engineer, said thoughtfully.

"The Great Ones, yes. Not necessarily those who think of themselves or are thought by others as 'great,'" I responded. "By the Great Ones I mean the likes of Krishna, Buddha, Pythagoras, Socrates, and so on. Others also throughout the ages have been tapping into and expressing fragments of this tradition, expressed always through the lenses of their culture and their own level of awareness.

"The experiences of shamans, prophets, mystics, magi, and gurus are really at the very heart of all cultures and civilizations," I went on to say. "The foundations of all the great civilizations started with the teachings based on the direct experience of the primordial tradition of masters like Buddha, Jesus, Moses, Mohammed, Krishna. And these historical personalities have exemplified extraordinary, call them 'supernatural' abilities. It may sound ironic but our Western civilization, which in the last two hundred years has become thoroughly secularized, thoroughly technocratic, thoroughly mechanical and materialistic, has its roots and origins in the teachings and paranormal visions of the great prophets and shamans of history. Shamans, mystics, and prophets have always been with us. Their presence on this planet has not been confined exclusively to the deserts of Palestine two millennia ago. Their existence among us today suggests the possibility that there may be realities within realities, that where we are in terms of our individual and collective awareness is perhaps only at the basement of our consciousness. It seems as if we are stranded here. Don't take me wrong. I greatly value the importance of science. It is the most powerful method for unlocking the mysteries of the three-dimensional reality within which our consciousness is focused at this stage of our development. But science has become so successful in this task that it has literally enchanted us like the sorceress Circe who bewitched and turned into swine Odysseus' companions. We have assumed that there are no other realities except those studied by science. The yogis, shamans, mystics, and prophets offer us an alternative vision and challenge us to liberate ourselves from the fetters of our mechanistic enchantment. This is very important today if we are to survive as a culture and as a species, if we are to survive our technology, that is." I stopped my monologue as there were several questions for clarification and comments by the other participants. I suggested that it was time for a break.

"Before our break," I said, "how about a very simple visualization exercise for replenishing our energy, followed by a healing meditation. It will take about ten minutes." Everybody began stretching, trying to loosen their muscles.

"Close your eyes and sit in a comfortable upright position," I said slowly. "Begin to breathe deeply and comfortably. Breathe easily and deeply. Concentrate on your breathing. Nothing else attracts your attention. Visualize yourself inside a white irradiance. As you breathe in feel every particle of your body. Every particle is breathing in energy. See your body breathing energy. Feel it. As you inhale, you inhale white light. As you exhale, you exhale whatever impurities there may be on your aura. You inhale white light. With every breath your aura becomes whiter and whiter. Deep and comfortable breathing. Feel your entire body breathing. You are not only breathing from your lungs and nostrils. You are breathing from every particle and cell of your body.

"White light enters into every particle of your material body," I went on slowly and in a low voice. "Wish good health to your present personality. Wish for full health to your gross material body, to your sentiments and to your thoughts. You are becoming whiter and whiter. With every exhalation you let go of any impurities that stain your whiteness. You feel this energy penetrating you, it revitalizes you. It is life-giving etheric energy. Deep and comfortable breathing.

"As you see yourself," I continued, "becoming whiter and whiter, notice that this room is filled with light. We are all inside this luminous sphere. White light permeates this room, and we are inside it. We are all white, and this whiteness merges with everybody else's whiteness.

"Extend your hands forward," I said after a minute's pause. "Your hands rest on your knees and face upward. Visualize now two balls of light, one on your left hand and the other on your right hand. They both have a diameter of approximately six inches. Two white balls of light. Feel the warmth of these two balls of light. You can feel the vibration in your hands. As you breathe in energy, this energy now is transmitted to these two balls of light. Feel their weight. You can feel them in your hands. They have acquired concreteness. Give them more energy.

"Now visualize the ball in your right hand gradually moving out of your hand, very slowly, and see it moving in the direction of somebody you love and you want healed from some ailment. See this ball of light moving in the direction of that person. This ball of light eventually goes and lands on the head of that person. See this ball of light now gradually moving downward and filling the entire body of that person. Wish for full health for that person. Visualize that person radiating white light, good energy, full of health.

"Concentrate now on the ball of light that you have on your left hand," I went on after a minute. "Feel it in your hand. As your left hand holds this ball of light move it upward toward your heart and visualize this light entering inside you, spreading throughout your body. Visualize yourself in full health, in your body, in your thoughts, in your feelings. Visualize that you have only healthy thoughts, only loving feelings and that your gross material body is in full health.

"With a few more breaths," I said, "come out of your meditation, at your own pace."

# 2

# PERENNIAL
# QUESTIONS

DURING THE BREAK SANDRA, A MASSAGE THERAPIST, REVEALED
to me in private her ordeal with her former guru. She was abused
by him, she claimed, not only mentally but also sexually. With some
help from a spiritual psychotherapist she was beginning to heal herself and repair the damage inflicted on her by this unscrupulous
yogi. When we resumed the workshop Sandra raised the question
of the authenticity of masters and how to protect oneself from possible abuses.

"The problem that I face personally, and I know others are facing," she said, "is how to identify an authentic master. How can
one recognize a real teaching that springs from the sources of the
primordial tradition from that which is fake and even dangerous?
Do you have any ideas on this issue?"

"You are pointing at a very important problem for which I am
not sure I can offer you a very satisfactory answer. There seems to
be a number of impostors who roam around seducing the innocent
by presenting themselves as gurus and yogis. There are also others
who, although honest and sincere in what they do, have neither the
wisdom nor the qualifications to be considered real spiritual teachers. So then, how can we measure authenticity? In the end you will

*31*

reach a point when you will be able yourself to distinguish the real from the questionable, analogous to the way an experienced jeweler can authenticate a real gem from a fake. But since we are not at the stage to distinguish the two we need to follow perhaps certain suggestions offered by people who have explored this issue in some depth.

"Ken Wilber[1] offers, I believe, some useful guidelines on how to recognize an authentic tradition and teacher. He made these suggestions for contemporary Westerners who are shopping in the contemporary bazaar of spiritual cults and gurus. Wilber says that a positive authentic group will likely be 'trans-rational' rather than 'pre-rational' in its orientation. That means among other things that the teachings do not advocate the abandonment of reason but its enhancement and eventual transcendence to higher levels of consciousness. These transcendent states will incorporate the rational and not destroy it, as is suggested by some pop mystical groups. Authentic teachings generally involve disciplined practice, concentration, and will and they are explicitly grounded on moral foundations. The discipline required is often as arduous as that involved in getting, let us say, a doctorate.

"Furthermore, Wilber suggests that a set of teachings will be less problematic if they are anchored within a long-established legitimate tradition, such as Christianity, Sufism, Buddhism, Judaism, Hinduism, and so on. That means the teachings will be less dependent on the idiosyncrasies of a single individual but will be instead the product of practice for centuries or even thousands of years by many practitioners who over time play a corrective role.

"Another point that Wilber emphasized," I continued, "is that the freedom and individuality of the disciple or the researcher of the truth must never be compromised. Mystical groups that demand submission to some guru are suspect, particularly when that master is presented as some kind of a perfect being. Guru worship is what prompted Krishnamurti to reject his own divinization, which the early Theosophists had tried to cast upon him since childhood, and which led to a lifetime of teaching against that tendency. Guru worship reduces the individual to a childlike dependent state and transforms the master in the eyes of the devotee into someone who is incapable of committing any wrongdoing. When that happens masters may behave in singularly unbecoming ways. The inexperienced devotees often either become thoroughly disillusioned and abandon the spiritual path, or rationalize the master's unethical behavior as hiding some esoteric teaching that the uninitiated simply do not understand. For example, I have heard of an American guru considered to be a self-realized master within his commune, who was expected to sleep and copulate with every prospective bride among his disciples. It was considered a form of blessing. After all, the guru was acting from the vantage point of 'egolessness' and 'perfect knowledge.' I heard that in one case a couple split up before the wedding because the bride refused to go along with this practice in spite of the pressure from her prospective husband, who was a fanatical devotee.

"Finally," I concluded, "the group or mystical circle is not out to save the world. This breeds tendencies of intolerance and dogmatism which are in reality signs of narcissism and egocentrism that are furthest removed from authentic spirituality."

There was a few moments' pause followed by further discussion on how one who is ready and thirsty for knowledge can find an authentic teacher. I pointed out that it seemed to me that in reality we are all masters and teachers to one another and that every human being that crosses our path is offering us a lesson. All we need to do is to focus and pay attention. "And of course," I added, "the esoteric teachings tell us that the best master is within us, our inner Self, the God within. Therefore one is never alone and abandoned."

"My problem is how to come in contact with my inner Self," someone stated, and several others nodded, smiling.

"It is said," I replied, "that contact with our inner Self begins with self-observation, meditation, and the mastery of thought and emotion."

"But how do you do that?" Sandra asked.

"One way is by *studying* our thoughts and emotions," I said with emphasis. "For example, you may do the following exercise. Before you go to sleep spend five to ten minutes exploring an episode during the day's events and explore the thoughts and feelings that you have experienced as a result of that episode. See to what extent your egotism was involved in that episode whether you have felt, say, hurt or flattery. Explore the amount of ego investment you have employed in that particular encounter. As you do that be neither an advocate nor a judge to yourself. Simply study yourself from the vantage point of a totally neutral observer. In time you will learn how to handle various crises in life with greater detachment and greater objectivity. At some point the question will come up. 'Who is doing the observing?' That will be a first step in the direction of contacting the inner 'I.' Sooner or later you will arrive at the realization that you are neither your gross material body nor your thoughts nor your emotions. With experience you will learn that in reality you are the inner observer that monitors the thoughts, feelings, and actions of the lower self. After this exercise becomes routine, then you will discover that the inner observer becomes your constant companion in all your activities under all circumstances and daily provocations."

"Can you be more specific on how this can be done?" Sandra persisted.

"Suppose you had a fight with your spouse or partner. Your ego at that moment will indulge in self-justification. You will tell yourself that you are absolutely right to have those angry feelings and thoughts. That the other person has done you an injustice and on and on. At that very moment recognize that you are angry and that you are angry because your ego has been hurt. Withdraw into a room, sit on a chair, and take some deep breaths. Realize that you are facing a challenge, an exercise if you will, to help you overcome the enchantment of your ego. Think how grateful you must be to the other person in offering you the opportunity to work on your ego. Do not judge yourself. Don't say 'Oh, how bad I must be to have such terrible feelings, such terrible thoughts. I must be no good.' Don't do that. Simply sit quietly and observe yourself as you would observe another person having those feelings. The moment you become conscious of your angry thoughts and feelings you will notice that at that very moment you begin to overcome your anger, you detach yourself from it.

"After this initial calming down of the negative vibrations, or the de-energizing of what we call the negative elementals, the negative thought forms, that you have created, proceed with meditation and do some visualizations that may help your relationship. Close your eyes and visualize that you are covered with an intense vibrant all-white luminosity. Feel every particle of your body absorbing this energy. It will further calm you down. Remember that your anger results in the burning up and the depletion of your etheric energy, the source of your vitality and well-being. Visualizing etheric energy being absorbed by every cell and every particle of your body will tend to restore this energy.

"When you manage to establish a balance within yourself, that is, when you reach a point when you master your angry feelings, visualize white rose color, the color of love and compassion, emanating from the center of your heart and covering the other person. In the event that you feel comfortable within a specific religious tradition and prayer is easy for you, you may begin to pray also. I am beginning to realize myself that prayer has a decisive impact on our emotional state, particularly in overcoming ego centeredness. It is a way of cultivating compassion and humility and therefore it helps in taming the ego.

"With this type of exercise you will learn to quickly de-energize destructive elementals and replace them with benign ones. With practice you will discover that similar episodes, which formerly would have created intense anger and self-justificatory and aggressive thoughts, will have less of an impact on you. In fact you will reach a point when your daily life will be such that it will not generate the conditions that led to the emergence of these destructive thoughts and emotions to begin with. With this method it is possible that you may learn detachment that can lead to compassion."

"Are you saying that by doing this exercise you will discover your real Self?" Howard, the medical doctor, asked as a certain reluctance showed on his face.

"No, of course not. This is only a first step in mastering the three bodies," I replied. Then for the benefit of those who have not read my other books I elaborated on what the three bodies are and their relationship to our state of awareness.

"According to the Teachings we, as present personalities, have three material bodies, not one. Ordinary people assume that the only body we have is the gross material body that we can see in a mirror. Yet we also have a psychic body, which is also material, but at higher levels of vibrations. This psychic body is the body of our emotions, sentiments, desires, likes and dislikes, and so on. The center of this body is located at the heart. When we visualize white-rose color covering the region of the heart we in fact energize the psychic body. In the same way when we visualize white-blue light at the solar plexus we energize the gross material body. We are capable of feelings and sentiments because we possess a psychic body, literally.

"In addition to the gross material and the psychic body there is also the noetic (or noetical) body which vibrates at even higher levels of vibration. This is the body of thoughts and ideas. Again, we are capable of thoughts and ideas because we possess a noetic body, literally. The focal point of the noetic body is the center of the head. Visualizing white-golden light inside and around the head energizes that body. All three bodies are linked together with their corresponding etheric doubles, or etheric energy. Therefore, as present personalities we are made of these three bodies: the material body, the body of feelings and sentiments, and the body of thoughts and ideas. The higher body can exist by itself without the bodies below it. The gross material body cannot exist by itself. Within it there are also the psychic and the noetic counterparts. But the psychic and noetic bodies can exist by themselves without the gross material body. This is why, it is said, we as present personalities survive after death. Whereas the gross material body dies and decomposes, the 'psychonoetic' body continues after death. We survive, in other words, as centers of self-consciousness carrying along with us our sentiments, thoughts, knowledge, memories, and experiences of the life just lived."

"Is the psychonoetic body what we commonly understand as the Soul?" Howard, the doctor, asked.

"According to these teachings the answer is no. The psychic and noetic bodies as well as the gross material body are the garments through which the Soul expresses itself. What we are as present personalities is the sum total of our thoughts and sentiments that we have generated through our gross material existence. We are capable of thoughts and sentiments because we have a noetic and a psychic body."

"In your other books you write about the differences between the Spirit, the Soul, the permanent personality, and the present personality. Can you please explain the differences between them? I am somewhat confused about which is which," Don, the bearded pastor and computer programmer, asked.

"Well, I think that perhaps the best way to explain the differences is to start from the very top of the hierarchy of consciousness of who we truly are. So, let us begin with the Absolute, what we conventionally call God, or what the Chinese understand as the Tao, the Hindus as Brahman, the Moslems as Allah, and so on." I stopped for a few seconds and then proceeded.

"The Absolute is everything that Is and nothing is outside of It. Whatever exists is a manifestation of the Absolute. Now pay attention to the word 'manifestation.' Whatever exists is not the Absolute but a manifestation of the Absolute. This idea is different from the pantheistic notion that everything, including matter, is God and therefore God equals matter and vice versa. No. According to all the high esoteric teachings that I am familiar with, there is an emphasis on this most important distinction. The Absolute in Itself is beyond all manifestation. In Itself the Absolute simply Is. Now what does that mean? Remember what I said at the very beginning. Those who know do not talk and those who talk do not know. Language and intellect are inadequate to comprehend the absoluteness of the Absolute in Its Beingness. According to the perennial wisdom as I understand it, we will know what the Absolute is in Itself only when we reawaken in our Godly condition. This is what Erevna and the Christian tradition call *Theosis* or God realization. But does that mean that we are totally helpless in at least making some feeble inferences on what must be some of the attributes of the Absolute? Not according to the Teachings.

"Here are some of the basic axioms in reference to the Absolute as conceived by great mystics and as handed down to us at these lower levels of consciousness. The Absolute in Itself, in Its static fullness is Self-sufficient, complete. That is, It has everything within It and lacks nothing. Therefore, It wishes nothing. It simply Is.

"Now if that is all, then the Absolute would have no reason to manifest Itself as Creation. It would have simply remained unexpressed and unmanifest in Its Absolute fullness and *Autarky*, or Self-sufficiency. There is an apparent paradox here. Why does the Absolute manifest Itself even though It is Self-sufficient, It has everything within Itself, and lacks nothing? According to the Teachings another basic attribute of the Absolute must be Its Divine Self-expressiveness or what is called in Greek *Thia Evareskia*, the love of the Absolute to express Itself by Itself. How? Through Mind.

"Mind, then, is the means through which the Absolute as *Thia Evareskia* manifests Itself. It is the infinite ocean of vibrations from the most rarefied highest levels all the way down to the gross material. So gross matter is Mind and Mind is not God but the manifestation of God. The Absolute, or God, is in everything, in every single particle of Mind, but everything is not God. The Absolute God is beyond all manifestation, It is Absolute and pure Spirit.

"And so are we in our innermost essence. According to these teachings we are pure spirit that has dressed Itself with Mind to manifest Itself as part of Creation. Therefore, we as pure Spirit have all the attributes of the Absolute, that is, Divine Autarky on one hand and that attribute which propels us to come down into the worlds of Creation and polarity, i.e., *Thia Evareskia*."

I answered a few questions for clarification, and went on. "The Absolute is composed of an infinite number of Holy Monads that in turn are composed of an infinite number of Spirit-egos. When one such Spirit-ego decides to descend, as it were, for the purpose of acquiring experiences of the worlds of Creation it must first develop a human Soul. A human Soul is created once a Spirit-ego passes through the Human Idea, one of the eternal archetypes within Creation. To acquire experience the Spirit-ego as soul now must descend further down, all the way down into the worlds of the three dimensions, of gross matter. The Soul in itself cannot acquire experience. It is the state of Adam and Eve before their departure from the Garden of Eden. The state of Adam and Eve is the state of the Soul just prior to its entrance into the worlds of time and space where experience can be acquired. According to the Teachings Adam and Eve are not being expelled from Paradise, but voluntarily leave the paradisiac state with the blessings of God the Father (or Mother) in the same way that the Prodigal Son (or Daughter) leaves the loving parental palace, the state of Autarky and Self-sufficiency.

Every human being has once been an Adam and Eve and every human being living on the lower levels of Creation is a Prodigal Son and Daughter, I may add."

I continued after making certain that my small audience was following me. "So what we have here is an involutionary process, the Spirit-ego projects itself into the worlds of polarity by first constructing a Soul. Further down the vibrational levels the Soul must be dressed with an appropriate attire to allow it to acquire experiences within the worlds of time and space. This attire is made up of the three bodies that we have talked about. As the Soul extends itself downward it expresses itself first as permanent personality. This is the lower part of the Soul upon which the incarnational experiences will be recorded and transferred from one life to the next as a sum total of experience.

"The present personality is developed last, the final destination of the Spirit-ego in its descent downward. And the present personality is composed, as I said before, of the three bodies. First the noetic body is constructed. This is the body that will allow the Spirit-ego as present personality now to be able to think and construct noetic images. The noetic body lives within the fifth dimension of existence, as compared with the gross material body, which lives within the three dimensions.

"After the noetic body is constructed, then the psychic body is created—the body of feelings, desires, sentiments. This body lives and has its home within the vibrations of the fourth dimension. Finally, with conception and birth the Spirit-ego enters the gross material world of the three dimensions and the involutionary process comes to completion. The Spirit-ego has completed its descent into the grossest realms of existence. I should also point out that all three bodies are permeated with the corresponding etheric energy, or etheric double. It is through this etheric energy that the three bodies are linked together and constantly influence one another. It means, in other words, that our thoughts influence our emotions, our emotions influence our bodies, and so on. This is possible because all three bodies are being permeated by etheric energy and vitality."

I stopped and at the urging of one of the members of my audience I outlined on a small board the involutionary descent of the Spirit.

## The Self

### 1. SPIRIT
[Divine *Autarky*. Prodigal before departure from Palace]

### 2. SOUL
[Beginning of *Thia Evareskia*. Adam and Eve in the Garden]

### 3. PERMANENT PERSONALITY
[Lower part of the Soul upon which incarnational
experiences will be recorded]

### 4. PRESENT PERSONALITY
a) Noetic body (fifth dimension)
b) Psychic body (fourth dimension)
c) Gross material body (third dimension)

"Notice," I pointed out, "that all these levels of consciousness are in reality Spirit in its various phases of manifestation. Our Western psychologies and philosophies have focused only at the lowest level of that manifestation, namely the gross material body. All our conventional, academic notions about the Self are based strictly on the assumption that the only level there is is the gross material level. The primordial tradition, or Research for the Truth, is in fact an attempt to explore and understand, via direct experience and rational deduction, the reality of all the other dimensions."

I paused for questions and proceeded. "Once the first incarnation has been completed with the first birth into the gross material world the Spirit has reached the end point of its involutionary descent. At that very moment an evolutionary process begins. That is, the Spirit-ego as present personality begins now the arduous journey back to the point of its origin."

As I completed my sentence a certain passage from the Gospel of John that I have heard chanted many times in Greek Orthodox liturgies came to my mind. I recited it in Greek and went on to explain its meaning: "Οὐδεὶς ἀναβέβηκεν εἰς Οὐρανὸν εἰμὴ ὁ ἐκ τοῦ Οὐρανοῦ καταβάς, ὁ Υἱὸς τοῦ ἀνθρώπου, ἱ ὤν ἐν τῷ Οὐρανῷ." No one has ascended to Heaven but he who has descended from Heaven, the Son of man, who is in Heaven.

"As present personality, the Spirit-ego does not have any memory of its Divine origin. It does not have memory of its state of Autarky. This is the source of our suffering and our tragedy. It is the Fall, according to the Christian view, the fall from the paradisiac state, that is the Divine state before time and space.

"You see," I went on to say, "according to the Teachings we are part of God that willfully entered into a state of self-imposed exile, a state of ignorance and amnesia of our true nature that descends into matter to gain experience. Intuitively, though, we do know. It is this inner knowledge that eventually will propel the Prodigal Son as present personality to embark on the return journey, the evolutionary ascent back to Spirit."

"Why did we come down to begin with? Why didn't we remain within the Palace, within our Divine Autarky. Why did we have to go through all this trouble?" Jack, the Broadway actor, asked.

"This is a most crucial paradox that has led some mystics to claim that in fact there is no answer to it. That we must take this for granted and assume that we shall never know. But these teachings that we are exploring today do offer a plausible answer. It is up to you to contemplate this explanation and see whether it makes sense to you.

"The Spirit propelled by *Thia Evareskia* descended into the worlds of polarity to gain its individuality and uniqueness within the Oneness of the Absolute God. Before the descent into the lower worlds the Spirit-ego, the 'I AM I,' could not differentiate itself from the All. It could not know what Light is because it had known nothing but Light. When the Prodigal Son leaves the Palace he does so precisely because in reality he wishes to become conscious of the Palace to which eventually he will return. But in the meantime he must experience the agonies and suffering of ignorance, for without this ignorance the Prince could not experience the world outside the Palace and develop his autonomy, individuality, and uniqueness. It is these experiences within time and space through the use of the three bodies, i.e., the present personality, that will provide the Spirit-ego the opportunity to eventually become a self-conscious Spirit at the final stage of God realization, or *Theosis*.

"This final stage of *Theosis*, is contrary to a popular belief that at the final stage individuality is somehow abolished and gets diluted into the All. In more graphic descriptions it is said that 'the dewdrop is lost into the shining sea.' From the esoteric teachings' point of view the dewdrop opens up and accepts within it the entire sea. In other words, the individual ego as *I-ness*, or as the *I AM I*, is never lost. It is that immortal, eternal center of Self-consciousness that undergoes the experiences within time and space but in itself it is immortal. It is never born and never will it die. It is the eternal Spirit within, which is qualitatively identical with the Absolute in its state of Divine Autarky, or Self-sufficiency.

"This is good news to me!" John, the accountant, exclaimed. "I have been a practitioner of a form of Buddhist meditation for a number of years and I always wondered whether in fact I was working and struggling toward my own annihilation or not. I feared that perhaps Nirvana meant eternal oblivion." There was a burst of laughter by everyone in the room.

"Nirvana, or God realization, according to all the great, authentic traditions that I am familiar with, means the infinite expansion of consciousness, not its abolition. It is the return of our memory of who we truly are. It is our awakening to our true nature. This was in fact what happened to Gautama the Buddha as he was meditating under the Bodhi tree. He attained his enlightenment. When he was asked 'Who are you?' his reply was simply 'I am awake.' This is precisely what we are aiming at; to awaken from the stupor of our ignorance, namely the false belief that who we really are is our present personality and more specifically our gross material body. Once we overcome this false identification, once we make conscious contact with our inner self, our Spirit-ego, then we are liberated from the trials and tribulations of the ego as present personality, the part of us that lives in ignorance and pain."

I paused for a moment. Then Julie, a psychotherapist, asked that we discuss the issue of evil and suffering, one of the most difficult issues that she was encountering, she claimed, on her spiritual path.

"From the point of view that we are examining today," I responded, "evil and suffering is real only within the realm of Creation, only within Divine Self-expressiveness or *Thia Evareskia*. Evil exists at the lower levels of existence and consciousness. The lower worlds of existence are the worlds of polarity and without this polarity, experience would have been impossible. For example, without evil we wouldn't know what good is. The Prodigal Son before his departure was beyond the polarity of good and evil. Adam and Eve in the Garden were un-selfconscious. Likewise Gautama the Buddha—while he was still within the protected confines of his father's palace, he was unaware of good and evil, death and suffering. It was only after he decided to abandon the comforts of his princely status that he learned of old age, of suffering, of sickness and of death. It is experience outside of the Palace or the Garden that will develop our awareness as self-conscious beings. It will be the result of our freedom to make choices between the polarities of good and evil.

"The world of our everyday existence is constructed on this separateness and polarity. There is up and there is down, hot and cold, positive and negative, night and day, angels and demons, good and evil. Eliminate this polarity and you have no world as we know it and no experience of these worlds as such.

"The great masters claim that beyond this polarity there is Unity and that is where we are aiming at. At that level of Unity consciousness there is the infinite and eternal love of the Absolute. Therefore, for the great teachers, pain, suffering, and evil are only phenomenal realities and not realities in and of themselves.

"Now, I know that there are theologians who would object to this idea but just think about it for a moment. If we assume that the Absolute is absolute Love and accept Evil as ultimately real, then we must conclude that there are two Gods, one good and another evil. But this is problematic because it would be like saying that there are two Absolutes, which is a contradiction in terms and ultimately illogical.

"All the great teachings from all the great esoteric traditions speak of an Absolute which is total Love, total Power, and total Knowledge and Wisdom. Therefore, suffering, pain, and evil are relatively real—that is, they are real at the lower expressions of Mind. And they do exist there, precisely to offer us experience for the reasons that we have discussed above.

"I would define evil," I went on to say, "as alienation from the Spirit-ego within, alienation from God. The greater the alienation the greater the evil expressed. Now in Western thinking the concept of alienation has been at the center of our philosophical and political preoccupations. And alienation is recognized as some kind of evil. Marx saw it as alienation from the means of production; that the worker does not have any control over his or her work leads to injustice and suffering. Furthermore, monotonous, unpleasant work creates feelings of worthlessness on the part of the worker because the worker does not feel creative. And creativity for Marx is essential to happiness. Others saw alienation as forms of social isolation; the individual in industrial society becomes isolated, an atom among strangers.

"Now all of these approaches to the reality of alienation as a form of evil are valid. However, these secular thinkers fail to recognize that the ultimate root of all forms of alienation and evil is the estrangement and alienation of the individual as present personality from his or her spiritual center within. The further the alienation the greater the tendency of the ego as present personality to abuse thought and sentiment and the construction of elementals that are destructive both to self and others."

"Can you please elaborate a little further about elementals?" Anna, the nurse, asked. "Are elementals what we commonly understand as thought forms?"

"Yes. But let us elaborate on this topic after we do some meditation exercises and after our lunch break."

It was one o'clock in the afternoon when we were through with the meditation exercises. Most of us went to a nearby restaurant that creatively combined a cozy Village ambiance with vegetarianism, a hospitable place for metaphysical discussions that continued along personal lines.

At two-thirty we were back. Thanks to the breaks and the lunch, participants began to form lively small groups of dyads, triads, quartets. The level of what sociologists call "social interaction" increased in a decisive way. People were beginning to get to know one another. There was a feeling of euphoria, greater energy, more laughter as we all shared our ideas and stories about our spiritual struggles. Here we were, a small gathering of very diverse people in the middle of New York City sharing common concerns and passions exploring the perennial questions of our human existence. Within the context of this lively atmosphere I proceeded to tell a brief story before the planned discussion on elementals.

"I have with me," I said, "a short vignette written by a fellow Mainer. It is about 'The Guru in Peoria.' Here is how it goes:

" 'An individual of high attainment was walking with some disciples through Peoria, Illinois. A vicious-looking dog came bounding out from between two houses. It was growling and barking in a most threatening manner, and it rapidly closed the distance between itself and the group of seekers. The teacher quickly took off his belt, and just as the dog came within range dealt it a sharp blow to its side. The dog yelped in pain and surprise and withdrew to a respectable distance. After they had walked on for about another two blocks, one of the disciples, who witnessed the entire incident, mustered up the courage to speak. "Master," he said, "you have always taught us that God dwells in all creatures, and that whatever we do to the lowest we do to him. Knowing this, how could you strike that dog?" "Indeed," said the master. "What you say is true, we are all God. Knowing this, and being so well attuned to the universal mind, I was able to perceive immediately that God would much prefer to be struck with a belt, than be bitten on his leg." ' "[2]

The participants in the workshop burst into uproarious laughter. "Now," I said, "let us discuss this most serious matter of elementals.

"Elementals are thought forms. That is, they are energies that we project outward as we incessantly generate ideas and feelings. And we can do that, as I said earlier, because we have a noetic and a psychic body. Thoughts and feelings have power, literally. Just like everything else within Creation, thoughts and feelings are Mind. In the same way that the Absolute God through Mind creates the worlds (that is, all the worlds, including the gross material, the psychic, the noetic, and beyond), we as present personalities create elementals.

"Elementals have shape, form, and energy. When we think of a car—a Mercedes, for example—we construct the form of that car in our mind. We visualize a Mercedes automatically, without conscious effort, because we know how a Mercedes looks. If we have a desire to own such a car we inject the idea of a Mercedes (the form) with the desire of ownership (the energy). The greater the desire, the greater the energy injected into the form. The strength of an elemental depends on the amount of energy as desire or passion injected into it. You must keep in mind that the material we use to construct these elementals is Mind. Remember, all the worlds of Creation are Mind at various levels of vibration.

"Yogi Ramacharaka insists that we must view thoughts—i.e., elementals—as 'things' having a life of their own. This is what he says." I went on and read a passage from one of Ramacharaka's many books on esoteric wisdom that I carried along in my briefcase.

" '. . . when we say Thoughts are Things,' Ramacharaka says, 'we are not using the words in a figurative sense or in a fanciful way, but that we are expressing a literal truth. We mean that thought is as much a thing as is light, heat, electricity, or similar forms of manifestations. Thought can be seen by the psychic sight; can be felt by the sensitive; and, if the proper instruments were in existence, could be weighed.'³

"Therefore," I continued as I put Ramacharaka's book down, "if we conceive of elementals as objective realities we will be able to appreciate the profound impact they exert on us. When I create an elemental, for example, of strong desire, not only will it be connected with me through my subconscious and be a karmic part of me, but also it will have an existence independent of my consciousness. Even if I overcome my connection with that elemental, the fact that I have created it means that it will exist in the environment and it will have a certain amount of energy for a certain period of time. It is like, for example, having fire in a room. You light a fire. It brings forth warmth. Then you shut the fire off. But there is still the glow of that fire. The stronger the fire, the longer the afterglow will last. The same with elementals. You create them, they have energy, and that energy will remain for a period of time. Depending on the strength of the source that originally projected it, it can affect people's consciousness and awareness. Just think for a moment of the incredible divine energy and power that was unleashed into the world with Jesus' Sermon on the Mount."

"It changed the course of world history," someone interjected.

"Exactly," I said and continued.

"Now it is the nature of elementals that once projected outward they sooner or later return to their source to acquire further energy. Our desire, in other words, will keep injecting this elemental with energy and it will keep it alive until either the desire has been satisfied or the individual has shifted his or her interest, thus de-energizing the elemental. But as long as elementals are alive they have a tendency to move in the direction of fulfillment.

"It is for this reason that in the Hindu religion a basic precept is that what you desire you shall eventually have. In other words, the elementals you have constructed will catch up with you either in this or in successive incarnations. If you craved wealth, wealth you shall have. If you craved power and you stimulated that desire from one life to the next, the karmic forces will bring you into a position when that craving will be actualized. But be aware. What you crave for may not necessarily bring you happiness or self-fulfillment. In fact, the opposite may be true. Again, every elemental has to fulfill the purpose for which it was created. Every desire that you generate within your subconscious will eventually be fulfilled. Remember, our theater of operations, as it were, is infinity and eternity. Within that context there is nothing that will not be fulfilled. Every desire will bring you down to the gross material level, down to earth."

"What about lofty desires, such as love for fellow human beings?" someone asked.

"All forms of desire, even the loftiest of the lofty, will bring us down to earth to be, in this case, of service to fellow human beings," I replied. "This is what the Teachings say and this is after all part of the Christian tradition with the symbolism of the Crucifixion. The Bodhisattva tradition within Buddhism is another example that comes to mind, that you always come down to be of help to others until everyone is saved."

"The elementals you create," I went on to say, after a pause, "are part of your subconscious; they will always be with you. In fact, your subconscious is the sum total of the elementals that you have constructed since your first descent into the worlds of polarity. We are therefore fully responsible for the construction of our present personality because this lowest part of ourself is the product of the elementals that we incessantly create through the utilization of thought and emotion. And the factory, so to speak, of thoughts and emotions is the psychonoetic body.

"The nature of elementals to return to their source," I said further, "is the dynamic that makes possible the law of karma. What you project outward eventually returns to you, good or bad. An evil elemental that we project against an individual or a group will eventually return to us either in this or in a future life. Therefore, when we harm someone, in reality we harm ourselves. Similarly, when we do good to someone, in reality we do it to ourselves.

"It is this knowledge of the mechanism of how the law of elementals and karma works that has given birth to the golden rule which is at the core of all the great religions: 'Do unto others as you would have them do unto you.' There is no patriarchal God sitting above the clouds, some sort of a Director General of Universe Incorporated, that keeps score, eventually punishing us for our transgressions. We simply punish ourselves through the elementals, or thought forms, we constantly create and through the law of karma. It is the law set up by a perfect Absolute God that allows us total freedom to choose whatever elementals we want to create. Here is how Ramacharaka puts it:

" 'Each individual draws to himself the thoughts corresponding to those produced by his own mind, and he is of course in turn influenced by these attracted thoughts. It is a case of adding fuel to the fire. Let one harbor thoughts of malice or hate for any length of time, and he will be horrified at the vile flood of thoughts which come pouring into his mind. And the longer he persists in the mental state the worse matters will get with him. He is making himself a center for thoughts of that kind. And if he keeps it up until it becomes habitual to him, he will attract to himself circumstances and conditions which will give him an opportunity to manifest these thoughts in action. . . . Let one's mind dwell on the animal passions, and all nature will seem to conspire to lead him into position whereby these passions may be gratified.'

"And here is what Ramacharaka says further on: 'On the other hand, let one cultivate the habit of thinking higher and better thoughts, and he will in time be drawn into conditions in harmony with the habit of thought, and will also draw to himself other thoughts which will readily coalesce with his own. Not only is this true, but each person will draw to himself other people of similar thoughts, and will in turn be drawn to them. We really make our own surroundings and company by our thoughts of yesterday or today.'[4]

"To return now to the original question of evil, it follows from what we have said so far that evil is a form of ignorance, the wrong utilization of the divine substance of Mind. And this ignorance is a function of our alienation from the Wisdom that is the nature of our inner Self, our Spirit-ego. This must be what Socrates had in mind when he said that humans commit evil acts out of ignorance. He was, of course, misunderstood because it was assumed that professional, specialized knowledge was the kind of knowledge that Socrates was talking about. In fact, he must have referred to the knowledge of Reality, the knowledge of Wisdom that is the inherent property of the inner Self as Soul and Spirit-ego.

"It is the elementals that we incessantly create that jam our attunement with our inner Self and cut us off from God. Unbridled desires in the form of what are called elementals of desires-thoughts—that is, elementals where desire comes first and thought is subordinate to it—are the source of our alienation from our inner Self, our readiness to engage in various forms of evil and the concomitant source of our suffering.

"This is why the Buddhists claim that to overcome evil and suffering you must first master and transcend your desires. Erevna, too, teaches that the way to master desire—in other words, the way to de-energize the power of elementals, of desires-thoughts—is to engage in systematic self-observation. The exercise that I mentioned earlier will make us aware of the power of our egotism. The more we do that exercise the more we develop mastery over our thoughts and emotions and the more we will begin to recognize that we are something other than our thoughts and emotions. Contrary to the Cartesian notion of 'I think, therefore I am,' esoteric philosophy teaches that 'I AM and then I think and feel.' If so, then we can master as self-consciousness what we think and what we feel, and generate, willfully now, only constructive elementals, elementals of 'thoughts-desires.' It means that conscious concentration motivated exclusively by love and compassion become the source of all the elementals that we generate. Unlike in the past when the young soul incessantly generated elementals of 'desires-thoughts,' now the mature soul constructs only elementals of 'thoughts-desires' for healing and service to fellow human beings."

"What makes for a mature soul?" Agatha, the soft-spoken former nun, asked.

"Experience within time and space. The greater the experience the greater the maturity of the Soul. That means, according to this philosophy, many lives lived, many incarnations. That is how we learn, how the spiritual laws work. For example, when we are children we may not know that fire burns. When we place our hands over a stove and burn our fingers, then we learn that fire burns and avoid placing our hands over a stove in the future. In the same way the ego moving from life to life learns from past experience how to avoid situations that cause grief and suffering to self and others. This is the path of karma, the law of cause and effect.

"At a certain point, of course, when a certain stage of maturity has been attained, the ego may become conscious of its evolutionary destiny toward *Theosis* and embark on a search for the truth, thus bypassing further unnecessary suffering. This is accomplished, for example, through the various paths offered by the yogas of Hinduism, the Eightfold Path of the Buddhists, the Jesus prayers and ascetical practices of the Christians, and so on. What all these traditions have in common is the realization that every human being is on a path of self-discovery and that the various methods are the various spiritual maps on how to get there. So, in reality we want to go beyond the elementals so that we can discover who we truly are."

I paused for a few seconds. There was a question. "Can groups of people create elementals of evil that can endure over time? And how can one deal with such elementals?"

"It is said that groups of people, just like individuals by themselves, do create elementals, in this case collective elementals. The nature of the elementals would be analogous to the collective energy that was injected into the form of those elementals. All cultural and collective beliefs are elementals that have an existence all their own. They could be good, evil, or none of the above. For example, the gods of Olympus were powerful elementals as long as people believed in the reality of those gods. And people at that time could have seen apparitions of those gods under certain circumstances, in the same way that today Christians may see the Virgin Mary appearing to them and offering advice or healing. In ancient Greece people could have seen in visions Asclepius, the god of medicine, freeing them from some disease, thus reinforcing their belief in Asclepius. You may raise the question, And where is Asclepius now? He is a retired elemental inside the Universal Memory. No group of people believes in Asclepius anymore. Therefore, that collective elemental has lost its power and exists only as a form inside the 'collective unconscious.' "

"I suppose," someone pointed out, "if people began believing in Asclepius he would return as a re-energized elemental."

"Precisely. At this time people believe in the Virgin Mary or in some other collective elemental that could do similar things that Asclepius used to do. So various shrines or temples that are reputed to be healing places are so because of the collective beliefs of the participants. But do realize that ultimately the power of these healing elementals rests with the Holy Spirit, which is transcultural and transhistorical. God's love is behind all these healing manifestations. So if you are a Moslem, God's prophet will not appear to you as John the Baptist but as Mohammed. If you are a Buddhist you may see a vision of the Buddha or some other Buddhist deity. Similarly, if you are a Christian you will see visions appropriate to the Christian religion and not of Krishna. God will appear to us either individually or collectively dressed in the image of the culture that we happen to be part of. The Christ that will appear to us will be a Christ that in a sense we have created with our collective beliefs. And that Christ 'elemental' may act in a way that is consistent with our beliefs about Christ, doing miracles, and so on. But do realize that this Christ that we may perceive within our limited human consciousness is linked up and *is* a manifestation of the Cosmic Christ who is beyond time, space, culture, and specific historical conditions. Let me give an example. Let us say you are a pious Moslem, a very good man or woman; from the point of view of the Cosmic Christ you have expanded your capacity for love and compassion. Your 'Christ' chakra has opened up, as it were. You believe like a good Moslem that there is no God but Allah and that Mohammed is his prophet. Your life is an exemplary model of the devout believer. You are also a healer, a Sufi, operating from within Islam. Then when the time comes to meet your Maker it would be a cruel God who will bring you face to face with Jesus or the Buddha. You are going to meet Mohammed or Allah as you understand Mohammed and Allah. If you are an American Indian, you are going to encounter a reality which is appropriate for your own cultural background. God is beyond any particular cultural manifestation, yet can dress within the context of any religious tradition, thus helping each one of us on the path of self-realization, of *Theosis*. This is how I understand this process as it is brought forward through the esoteric tradition."

There was a brief discussion of the meaning of the Cosmic Christ. I pointed out that within the mystical texts of Christianity there is clear reference to the Christ principle. For example, in the Gospel of John Christ is referred to as the light that enlightens every human being that descends upon the earth. "That means in a sense," I said, "that all human beings are deep down imbued with the Christ principle. Kostas often speaks of a 'pre-Christian Christianity,' meaning that the Christ Logos is beyond time and space, beyond history, and has always been. For a powerful elaboration on this theme I urge you to read Matthew Fox's celebrated work, *The Coming of the Cosmic Christ*."[5]

"I suppose," Mary Ann, the Jungian analyst, said, "the same principle would apply for destructive elementals."

"Exactly. In the same way that we can create elementals of healing and goodness we can also create collective elementals of evil that can have deleterious effects on people, particularly on those who create such elementals."

"How can one protect oneself from such destructive elementals?" someone asked.

"The more spiritually advanced we are, the less likely it is that we will be subjected to such kinds of influences," I replied. "Therefore, the best protection against evil influences emanating from the psycho-noetic dimensions is to engage in spiritual exercises that help us cleanse ourselves of the negative vibrations of the noetic and psychic bodies. That is, we must consciously work in the direction of overcoming the power of our egotism. If we are 'pure at heart' we have nothing to fear." I went on to say that in addition to various psychonoetic exercises, I found lately that the reading of inspirational religious literature is very helpful. For some people the habitual reading from prayer books may be helpful as a method of attunement to higher spiritual vibrations.

I then went further and showed the participants how with certain meditations we can protect ourselves from evil influences. For example, visualizing ourselves covered with white light, making strong suggestions to ourselves that no evil elemental can penetrate our aura and do us harm, is a form of protection. Talismans and religious symbols charged with healing energy can also function as protection against negative psychonoetic influences.

"Most important of all, one should not fear such influences, because fear itself is a magnet of such vibrations," I concluded.

"There is something else I would like to add. According to these teachings it is unwise to pursue directly the acquisition of psychic abilities and powers. Such abilities develop within ourselves naturally as we advance on the spiritual path. Trying to develop them without paying attention to our spiritual growth may have disastrous effects."

Mary Ann urged me to elaborate on the possible disastrous effects that I was talking about.

"When you develop your psychic powers without an analogous development of your spirituality you may use that power for selfish reasons, to bring about certain effects and to satisfy the egotistical desires of the present personality. This is a form of black magic that must be avoided at all costs. Psychic power must be employed only for healing purposes and not for the satisfaction of personal desires. If the individual has not mastered his or her desires, then such an individual can easily succumb to the temptation of using psychic power for personal gain. Even unintentionally an individual may succumb to negative magic. If, for example, you have not mastered anger and you tend like ordinary people to assault in your mind those who provoke you, then you unconsciously may create powerful demonic elementals that can strike the other person, the kind of elementals that evil magicians create consciously. And of course these elementals will eventually return to haunt you, sooner or later. It is for this reason that all the esoteric traditions place most of their emphasis on the development of spirituality and warn against the premature awakening of psychonoetic powers."

I noticed that it was close to five o'clock and I proceeded to bring the workshop toward closure. But there was one more question about elementals from Howard, the medical doctor. "When someone, such as a scientist for example, makes a major discovery, is he or she creating an elemental or pulling it out from the world of elementals that populate the psychonoetic dimensions?"

"That is a very good question," I replied. "As we have said many times we literally swim within a universe of elementals that we have created and others have created and are creating incessantly. Therefore, that which we think is our discovery and our idea in reality may be the idea or ideas created by others before us. So a discovery may be simply the opening up of our subconscious to the influences of these elementals that come pouring down through us. We exist within a web of interacting elementals and whatever we think we discover is already there within the world of elementals and the collective unconscious or Universal Memory.

"Here is how Yogi Ramacharaka puts it," I said.

Unexpressed thought, originally sent out with considerable force of desire, constantly seeks for expression and outlet, and is easily drawn to the mind of one who will express it in action. That is to say, if an ingenious thinker evolves ideas which he has not the energy or ability to express in action, to take advantage of, the strong thoughts on the subject which he throws

off will for years after seek other minds as a channel of expression; and when such thoughts are attracted by a man of
sufficient energy to manifest them, they will pour into his
mind like a flood until he seems to be inspired. . . . The astral
world is full of excellent unexpressed thoughts waiting for the
one who will express them and use them up.[6]

"This can explain," I went on to say, "the nature of human creativity. To be creative presupposes in the final analysis to have a
passion to master something. You pour out energy through hard
work. Let us say a medical researcher is struggling to find a vaccine
against some disease. Many years of hard work may have gone into
his or her experiments. Suddenly a flash of insight pours down to
the scientist's mind at a time when he or she is perhaps not working
on the project. A new vaccine is discovered. It is possible that the
discovery simply came from the world of elementals, perhaps from
the work of another researcher. Remember, we are all intercon-
nected and we constantly influence telepathically one another
through the world of elementals."

There were a few additional questions on the subject. Then I
proceeded to bring a closure to the workshop.

"I would like to remind you what I said at the beginning of this
workshop, that whatever we say with words about what God is is in
the final analysis incomplete and probably false.

"We have a saying in Greek that goes like this: 'The most profound human wisdom is foolishness in the eyes of God.' Please remember that.

"I was at a conference in Washington recently and I met this
remarkable woman, Etel De Loach, a clairvoyant and psychic healer
with an international reputation. Among other things she lectured
at the Johns Hopkins University medical school and took part in
experiments and studies with other researchers on nonmedical healing. During the three days of the conference I had a chance to have

prolonged conversations with Etel about subjects of mutual interest. At one point she confided in me a profound visionary experience she had with a short, stocky man who appeared before her. He announced to her, 'I am Saint Thomas Aquinas.' He came to her, he said, in order to offer his blessings and a lesson on the nature of God. She couldn't understand, Etel told me repeatedly, why this would happen to her in particular. When I asked her whether she knew anything or had read anything about Saint Thomas Aquinas, she replied that she'd never heard of him. I was very intrigued with her description. Etel repeatedly mentioned the peculiar shape of her visitor. I knew from my readings that Saint Thomas during his monastic life as a Catholic theologian in the thirteenth century was a short stocky man whom his classmates at the university used to tease because of his obese appearance. As you may know, Saint Thomas Aquinas has been the most influential theologian of the Catholic Church. He was responsible for setting up through Aristotle's philosophy the foundations of Catholic theology that are valid to this day. One of the most important anecdotes of his life was that during a liturgy he entered into a religious ecstasy and remained in that state for quite some time. When he came back to ordinary consciousness he announced that all that he had written about God for all those years was absolutely insignificant compared to what he had experienced. He never wrote another word and died a year later.

"What Etel was told in that vision is, I believe, one of the most powerful short statements on the nature of God that I have ever heard, and I would like to share it with you." I pulled out of my file the page that Etel had given me on that particular channeling. "Here's how it goes," I began.

My blessings to you and your friends. . . . Tonight we will discuss God and some of the reasons you tend to get into difficulty when you try to understand what God is. We can say that God is the Holy Spirit, the source of all creation, and in a sense we will be right. But the difficulty lies in under-standing what the words really mean. There is so much more to creation than meets the eye. Even when we contemplate only the visible, material universe we cannot really get a feel for its immensity.

You will realize that your idea of God will always be limited by your consciousness. But that should not stop you from meditating on the nature of God, as in the process you will attract all the good you will need to live your life in touch with the one infinite source. The more you think about God, the more you will understand about creation, and you will draw around you the energy we call God's Love, and you can use this energy to radiate love to all those around you that are in need of the uplifting and healing that God's love and light can accomplish.

To know God and understand Him completely would in-volve so much energy that you could not possibly contain it, neither could the earth, the sun, the solar system, the galaxy. Only all there is could contain God, but that is so far above your consciousness, that even the means of comparison are lacking. You will now understand why your idea and under-standing of God will always be limited, but at the same time there is no limit to the extent that you can expand your con-sciousness, and thereby your understanding of God. Your ef-forts of attunement are very important for all living on this earth, and will also affect other dimensions. The time you spend in meditation, fasting and in prayer will bring rich div-idends, so persist. Greetings.

We reflected on this channeling for a while and after several meditation exercises for the construction of healing elementals for the New York area, the country, and the planet we concluded the workshop.

# 3

# MYSTERIES

SPRING SEMESTER 1990 WAS OVER. I HAD JUST COMPLETED CORRECT-
ing my final exams and with a sense of relief turned in the grades
to our departmental office. Finally I was free to think about and
plan my upcoming journey to Cyprus, where I was to continue my
ongoing exploration into Erevna and the esoteric Christian tradition. As much as I was eager to get to Cyprus and reestablish contact
with my friends, I also felt a certain apprehension at abandoning
Maine in the summer. Nature was vibrant, coming to life after a
protracted frozen winter of hibernation.

"Surely there is no better place to be than Maine during this
time of the year," I mused with a sense of well-being as I took
advantage of the warm sunny weather and strolled through the im-
peccably groomed grounds of the university. I walked for more than
an hour, out onto the paths in the nearby woods and fields, enjoying
the stillness of pine trees and breathing the uncontaminated air—a
luxury, alas, at the closing years of our tired century. Relatively unspoiled by development, the Maine woods maintain the same authentic charm that enchanted Henry David Thoreau and other
American transcendentalists.

I kept track of time, as I was scheduled to meet with Pascalis, a

Greek physician I'd met a few days earlier at a friend's house. "I would like to tell you of a very bizarre experience I went through while I was a medical student in Italy," he'd told me after he learned of my professional interest in extraordinary tales, the kinds of experiences commonly referred to as "paranormal phenomena," "mysticism," and "the occult." Mindful of his position as a physician and being suspicious of his own experiences and encounters with the paranormal, he wished to see me privately and talk about the matter in some detail. He stressed to me the night I met him that what he experienced contradicted everything he believed in. "To this day, so many years since those mysterious events took place," he said with a certain hesitation, "I still cannot make any sense of them."

Pascalis was now an intern at a Boston hospital after completing his medical education at the University of Perugia in Italy. A man in his mid-thirties he was of an ebullient, pleasant, and humorous disposition much like the stereotyped image that Americans hold in their minds of Zorba-like Greeks and flamboyant Italians. It was easy to become friends with him. Usually physicians are on the whole a conservative lot, enjoying the full benefits of prestige, power, and wealth that modern society generously bestows upon them. But not Pascalis. Like many Greeks of his generation, he was a political radical. Nevertheless, he did aspire to a comfortable upper-middle-class lifestyle in the suburbs of Athens. Unlike the self-denying, fist-pounding angry Marxists that I have known in academic circles over the years, Pascalis was pleasure-oriented. He even toyed with the notion of eventually buying a sailing boat to roam the Aegean and sail from island to island. During our short conversation it seemed to me that ideologically he was like a recovering Marxist-Leninist, unable to completely kick the habit. I was intrigued. A Greek radical leftist physician who confronted the paranormal and who aspired for the bourgeois lifestyle was a sociological curiosity of the first order. I looked forward to talking with him further.

As I returned from my long and invigorating walk the sun was beginning to set over the Stillwater River, which flows smoothly, parallel to College Avenue and the university. It was four o'clock when I spotted Pascalis wandering near the steps of Fogler Library, trying to orient himself to my office in the Department of Sociology at Fernald Hall. We shook hands and chatted for a few minutes in front of the steps of the library, which faced the long open mall at the center of campus. I then invited him to the "Damn Yankee," the cafeteria at the student union, where we could relax and talk. Most students were already gone for the summer and the otherwise noisy cafeteria was mercifully peaceful.

Since I began writing about esoteric matters I've found myself a focal point for people all over the world who have unusual tales to report. I've become a sort of clearinghouse for people who live within a realm of consciousness and reality radically different from most of us. I had soon come to realize that the world as experienced by the Cypriot healers of my books was not unique to them but widely shared by people from very different societies and cultural backgrounds who either kept their experiences to themselves or shared them with only very few trusted friends.

In addition to practicing healers, clairvoyants, psychics, and out-of-body travelers I was approached by ordinary people who had unusual stories to report to me. Some of these people were genu-inely baffled, since what they had witnessed or experienced, like in Pascalis's case, contradicted everything they believed about the world. I remember one day, for example, when a successful con-tractor, the brother of an initiate into Erevna, told us in a small gathering how he found himself, in full consciousness, traveling with incredible speed around the planet. His description of that experi-ence was almost identical to one that Jung reported in his autobiography.[1] Yet, unlike Jung, this man could not accept the reality of his experience because it contradicted his totally materialistic and mechanistic beliefs about the world. His brother tried, to no avail, to introduce him to esoteric philosophy and scientific findings about ESP. Kostas cautioned his friend and student that he should leave his brother alone because the latter was not ready for esoteric knowledge and wisdom. His eagerness to enlighten his brother generated unnecessary friction between them.

"So, Pascali," I said after fetching two cups of coffee, "I am all ears." He grinned nervously as he sipped from his cup and began. I tried to put him at ease as I reassured him that my ears were accustomed to extraordinary tales and experiences. I joked that nothing he wished to reveal to me could lead me to conclude that he was a victim of some kind of mental aberration.

"During the early months of 1973," Pascalis began, "I went to stay with my Italian friend Mario Albini, a student of political science at the University of Perugia. He was originally from Florence."

"Where abouts is Perugia?" I asked, as I tried mentally to visualize the map of Italy.

"In central Italy, in the region of Umbria, a hilly region of high elevation. On just about every hilltop there is an old castle. There were once many barons and counts that lived in the area and to this day their progeny carry their titles. One of my Italian friends, in fact, was a baron.

"Mario Albini and I were desperately looking for work. Finally we found a house to paint. It belonged to a countess. The house was an old aristocratic mansion dating back to the 1800s. Built on the top of a hill, surrounded by pine trees, it had its own private road and a chain across the front entrance. Right next to that mansion there was the castle where the countess lived, which had at least twenty bedrooms. She hired us to paint the house. You see, the previous year that house was rented to some twenty students from a college in California. They smoked pot and threw paints on the walls. It was a mess. In addition to having to paint the house, we were asked to fix the guests' room. The living room was enormous, with a fireplace about five meters in length and three meters in width. Next to it were benches to sit by the fire.

"One night while sitting there trying to rest from our day's work, Mario Albini began to tell me a story of something that had happened in 1966. In that year three Italian friends of his with their Swedish girlfriends went to visit a place nearby, called La Casa del Diavolo. It was about forty kilometers from where we were. Well, they went there to take a look at a church which was considered by Italians to be cursed. All its doors were barred. The front door was cemented from the outside so that it was impossible for anyone to get in. The three friends and one of the Swedish women decided to go and visit that place. Mario didn't know how, but they managed to get inside. At the back they discovered a small room with two tombstones firmly covered with marble stones with iron rings."

"Very spooky," I quipped.

"Just wait to hear what happened next," Pascalis said mysteriously. "Mario Albini could not tell me more details about his friends' visit to that church and what exactly happened there. The only thing he knew was that one of them died at the staircase of the church and another one ended up at a madhouse in Perugia. The Swedish woman who went into the church was in a state of shock for a while but nothing as dramatic happened to her. The police searched everywhere to discover what went on but they found no solution to the mystery and the case to this day remains unsolved. The woman returned to Sweden and Mario's Italian friend is still in the asylum."

I shook my head as I assumed that Pascalis's story was yet another tale of extraordinary demonic energy or collectively created evil elementals causing such tragedies.

"When I heard this story from Mario Albini," Pascalis continued, "I gave it some thought but I soon forgot about it. But months later in the late spring of 1973 this issue came up again. Some friends who lived in a villa outside of Perugia paid us a visit. Among them was a Greek from the island of Ithaca, Mikis Papadopoulos, who was studying at Pavia. He was on his way to Greece and from there he was planning to continue his studies in America. Mikis was accompanied by four female students from San Francisco. In the same house with Mikis there was another friend of mine, Zacharias Markantonis from Salonica, and another Greek student, Demos from Patras. We gave him the nickname 'the Crow' because he had dark long hair and a long pointed nose like the beak of a crow. In the apartment next to Mikis and Demos there lived another group of friends, three Englishmen and a Canadian with their girlfriends, two British and two American. We were all on very friendly terms with this group and we invited them all to come over and eat spaghetti. We lit the fireplace when the entire group arrived. At the time I had a girlfriend from Yugoslavia and Mario Albini had a girlfriend from Chicago. Her name was Susan Smith. We began eating our spaghetti and drinking good red Italian wine. We then began telling various stories to pass the time. I remembered the story of La Casa del Diavolo that Mario Albini told me, and half serious, half joking, I suggested, 'How about visiting La Casa del Diavolo?' 'What is this Casa del Diavolo?' they asked. Mario Albini told them the story in a few words. With great excitement we all decided to drive there right away.

"The time was eleven-fifteen at night," Pascalis went on. "Mario Albini knew only part of the way and gave us instructions—we had to drive from Perugia to the train station and from there continue until we reached the factory of Perugina, which is world-renowned for its chocolates. We then were to proceed to a hilly region covered with olive trees, many dirt roads, farms, and a crossroad. 'Let us reach that point,' Mario Albini informed us 'and then we can ask for further directions because I don't know the way from there. I have never visited the place.' We all got into our cars.

"Oh, by the way," Pascalis said, "I forgot to mention to you something about the cars that is very significant for the story. Susan Smith had a red American car. Zacharias Markantonis, my friend from Salonica, had an Alfa Romeo, almost brand-new. I drove an old Volkswagen that I was planning to buy from Mikis Papadopoulos. Demos the Crow had a small Fiat. So the whole group got into the various cars and we drove off toward La Casa del Diavolo.

"First we got to the main road; we then reached the station and then Perugina. We proceeded on a dirt road and saw a house, a typical village house, with the porch light on. We stopped to ask how to get to La Casa del Diavolo. We said to Mario Albini: 'Since you are Italian and you are familiar with their ways, go knock at the door and ask them.' He climbed up the steps to the small balcony. When he knocked a man wearing a village hat opened the door. 'What do you want?' he asked. 'We are looking for La Casa del Diavolo,' he told him. 'We want to go there.' The villager did not respond at all. He just said 'Oh' and pointed to the road ahead. Then he slammed the door before Mario Albini had a chance to turn around.

"You see, the Italians are usually a very friendly and obliging people. So the behavior of that villager did not make sense. Anyway, we followed the road that he showed us. We went through many narrow roads not knowing where we were going. Finally after driving around over several hills, we arrived at our destination at about midnight. We found ourselves on a high elevation of about four to five hundred meters. In front of us there was an opening covered with marble stones. At the edge of that opening there stood a gigantic, formidable-looking church. Behind it, beyond the flat opening, the hill proceeded further up and at the top there stood a castle. The ruins of one, that is—only the walls remained.

"We parked in front of the church and stepped out of our cars. The front door had been sealed shut with bricks and stones. It was impossible to get in. But we wanted to get in. The church was too

tall, ten to twelve meters high. Actually, I don't remember, it could
have been higher. We searched around and we discovered that the
rear wall had fallen. There was, however, another wall behind it
which looked like the back of a room. That wall was several meters
high. It was possible for us to climb over it.

"Well, first climbed Zacharias Markantonis, who was tall and
powerful. He stepped on our shoulders and reached the top. Then
he started pulling each one of us up. Eight to ten meters higher and
beyond there was the roof of the church. The width of the outside
wall was about one meter. A very solid wall. But at the spot where
it had fallen down we managed to step on the floor of a room which
was not constructed with solid material. Holding our flashlights we
helped everybody climb up there. There were no lights in the area
and no houses within the vicinity of three to five kilometers. We
climbed up. We were asking each other 'How are we going to get
inside the church?' Zacharias said 'Let's get this log' and pointed at
something lying there. We picked it up and started hitting the outside wall from the room that we found ourselves in. Suddenly a
portion of the wall fell down because it was thin at that point, like
the inside of a house. It was made of relatively small, thin bricks.
So we opened a hole that allowed us to get inside. Zacharias went
first. Then I followed with Demos the Crow. When we stepped
inside we entered another room like the one that we were in before.
It had the shape of a parallelogram and had four doors on each wall.
On one side of the room, on the floor there was an old, torn mattress. It looked like a dirty rug. There was also a small fireplace.
We opened one door and we found ourselves in another room. We
then opened another door and we found ourselves in yet another
room. These rooms were many meters high. There were too many
rooms and we were afraid in case we got lost. We decided to return
and tell the others what we found. In order not to get lost we decided to follow only one direction toward the inside of the church
and open only the doors that were lined one behind the other. We

went outside and told the others to follow us. After standing in line, one by one holding each other's hand we followed the direction toward the center of the church. Over us there stood the roof of the church. We reached the last room and when we opened the door we saw in front of us the inside of the church. That was after we passed about five to six small rooms, one after the other.

"We felt something strange that really impressed us. When we would open the door of each one of those rooms there was a current of wind that rushed in with a strange hissing sound. But we did not wish to make too much out of that even though it appeared mysterious. After all there was no wind outside and we could not figure out from which direction the wind was blowing. When we reached the last room we were high up and below us we saw the center of the church. There was a movable wooden ladder, eight meters long, that linked the place where we stood with the ground floor of the church. It was the only way to get down—as I told you the front door was sealed. So all of us climbed down that ladder, and we searched for the graves that we were told were there. Mario Albini, who seemed more knowledgeable than the rest of us, took the lead and we followed him. Shining our flashlights, we walked through the center of the church toward the sanctum and reached the back. On the right side there was a little room where we found the two marble tombs. Susan Smith said that we should open them to see what was in there."

"How did you feel at that point?" I interrupted Pascalis.

"Not well," he replied with a guilty smile. "But just wait to hear what happened next. All of us stood around those tombs. With a lever we managed to open one of them. There was a large void there and at the bottom we found human bones, hands, legs, skulls, and so on. Susan Smith, Mario Albini's girlfriend, got very excited and jumped into the grave searching for a solid skeleton to take along. She took a cranium that was in good shape. It had all the bones. She also gathered some hand bones. She sat there for a minute or two and then someone gave her a hand and pulled her up. We then tried to open the other tomb but it was impossible.

"Zacharias and Demos, who had strong arms, tried in vain to open it. Meanwhile, Susan Smith had gone out onto the main floor of the church and was looking for art pieces. She was from a rich American family and she was crazy about art. She saw the statue of a saint, broke off the head and arms, and took them, along with the bones, to decorate her apartment. I was with Zacharias, Mikis, and the four American women from San Francisco. We just stayed in the middle of the church looking around. I was feeling nervous about what we were doing and I suggested to Mikis that we step out of the church to have a cigarette. He agreed but he said that we should open the front door. With some effort we managed to break open the front door from the inside. It was a metallic door. But as I told you it was covered over from the outside with bricks and stones. We broke an opening and got out exactly in front of the square where we had parked our cars. We went to the Volkswagen—myself, the four women, and Zacharias. In a few minutes out comes Demos and Mikis. They sat in their own car. The three Englishmen and the Canadian with their girlfriends were still inside. Also still inside were Mario Albini and Susan Smith. The rest of us went outside because we felt bad about what was going on."

"What do you mean?" I interrupted Pascalis as I noticed some hesitation in his voice.

"I mean the vandalism of the church. Zacharias didn't like it either. The four women from San Francisco felt likewise. For this reason we moved away from the rest. We lit cigarettes, waiting nervously.

"Suddenly we heard music. It was magical music, incredible. We were going crazy. We asked each other to make certain that we were not hallucinating. All of us were hearing that strange music. It was a flute. I said to them, 'For certain we are going nuts. Who could be playing a flute at this hour in this place? I am going to ask the others whether they hear the same thing.' I asked Demos in the other car. 'Yes, I hear it,' he said. 'It must be some shepherd.' 'But at this hour?' I asked. There was no light anywhere. Well, we tried not to worry too much. But before we finished our cigarette an incredibly powerful wind began blowing. It was the kind of wind that could uproot trees. It was terrible. And then we heard a loud, macabre-sounding howling coming from the castle, which was about two hundred meters from the church, at the top of the hill. We were petrified.

"As I am telling you this story now I still feel the chills running down my spine," Pascalis said, and after a few moments' pause he continued his story. "Zacharias said to me, 'This is not good. We must get out of here.' We rushed to the church to tell the others that we must leave right away. I didn't tell them what was going on outside. Ordinarily they would not have listened because the unofficial rule in that gang of ours was that one did whatever one wished without listening to anyone. To tell them what to do was out of the question. Most of us were relatively immature twenty-year-olds. But as soon as I told them that we must leave it was as if I'd ordered them to fall in line, and one after another they rushed out of the church, running toward the cars. We were all close to panic. That terrible howling went on continuously. We pushed each other to get into the cars. We turned white from fear.

"Incidentally, I forgot to tell you that when we began up the driveway to La Casa del Diavolo, two kilometers from the house, the hood of Zacharias's Alfa Romero flew open by itself, and a piece of the window broke off and hit Demos the Crow, who was in the passenger seat, scratching him on his right cheek.

"So now we drove off in panic," Pascalis continued. "We were panting as we heard the howling all the way as we drove back down through the hills toward the main road. For about ten kilometers the howling and the demoniacal wind was following us. The olive trees were bending down from the incredible power of that wind.

We could hardly breathe from fear. When we reached the main road, and after the wind and the howling had stopped, we all got out of our cars, asking each other 'What was that all about?' The two Englishmen and one of the women were in a state of shock. We could not explain what happened. We decided all of us would go home together and discuss what we had just gone through. We were very anxious and worried. We kept asking each other questions to verify what we heard and what we saw. Those of us who were outside of the church had heard the music and the howling before those who were inside the church. Those who were inside the church and rushed out heard only the howling but not the music. After a while we calmed down, and we even started joking about our experience. It was our way, I suppose, to relieve our fears. We thought maybe there were people who were having some kind of a fight. But Mario Albini was absolutely certain that there was no house around there, no human life anywhere near. We decided to sleep in the same house. All of us were afraid to stay alone. So everyone stayed at our house. Only Demos the Crow said he was not afraid and went home. Zacharias said, 'We are going to sleep next to each other. I am too scared.' We lived in a large house, as I told you, and we could accommodate a lot of people." Pascalis stopped for a few seconds to collect his thoughts. Then he continued.

"What was most frightening and terrible from this experience," he said slowly, "was what followed. All the cars that went to that church were involved in accidents within a week. One got burned completely. Mikis, who owned the Volkswagen, the one I was considering whether to buy, was in a serious accident. My other friend, with the Alfa Romeo, went to Pavia to get his stuff and bring it to Perugia before leaving for Greece. Outside of Florence his engine caught fire. It was a total loss. Only the tires remained. And it was virtually a brand-new car. The Fiat got all smashed up, and the three Englishmen and the Canadian with their girlfriends were all rushed to the hospital with broken ribs. Susan Smith hit a tree as she was driving up a hill coming to our house. She got bruises all over her body. Her car, also, was a total loss.

"The only ones who were spared were Mario Albini, myself, and Zacharias. All the rest suffered some sort of automobile accident."

"Some coincidences," I marveled and shook my head.

"But there is more to the story," Pascalis added. "In the house that I stayed in, as I told you, lived also Mario Albini and Susan Smith. One night Mario Albini went to Ancona to see his mother. So I was alone in my bedroom with my cat, Sylvestro. He slept on my bed. I heard noises of glasses in the kitchen. Susan Smith's bedroom was on the other side of the house, the east side. To reach her bedroom you had to go through the kitchen, which was quite large, and then you had to pass a hallway of about twenty meters. When I heard those noises in the kitchen I thought for a moment that someone might be washing dishes. But it didn't make sense. It was two o'clock in the morning. It was the noise that woke me up. I opened the door to see what was going on in the kitchen but it was too dark. There was nobody there. I went back to bed. I heard noise on the roof, as if rats were walking around. Suddenly I heard a scream, '*Aiuto! Aiuto!*' which in Italian means 'Help! Help!' coming from Susan Smith's bedroom. Sylvestro jumped up and started to move his head round and round like crazy as if trying to catch his tail. I turned the lights on in my bedroom and in the hallway and I ran toward Susan Smith's bedroom. I found her in a state of hysteria. The light was on. She said there was something at the window. 'There is a terrible noise at my window,' she said. 'Please help me.' I went to open the window. I was also afraid and began to tremble. I started shouting, trying to chase away whatever there was at the window as I was opening it up. I opened it all the way." Pascalis stopped his narrative.

"Before I go on," he went on to say, "let me interject something here. There was also the comic side of this. We had a large circle of friends and we had told them what happened. To tease us they came one night—actually it was four o'clock in the morning—and managed to enter the basement from the outside. It was possible for them to do that because the basement was not locked from the outside. We lived, as I told you, in an old farmhouse in the country. The basement was huge. So they got there and while we were asleep they started making noises trying to scare us. But we recognized them immediately even though it was four in the morning and we were still half asleep.

"Well, after I opened the window I saw nothing outside. Susan Smith was so afraid and shocked she did not wish to stay in the room by herself. She moved to my room and slept next to me. When Mario Albini arrived we told him the story. He then confessed to us that he also had heard those noises but did not tell us anything because he didn't want us to think that he was going insane. 'Let's go,' he suggested, 'to ask the Contessa.' We went to the Contessa, who was an aristocrat but did not seem to be very clever. Actually she looked to us rather strange. She had gray, mysterious-looking eyes. 'Contessa,' we said, 'we hear strange noises in the house.' 'Oh,' she said, 'there must be spirits or ghosts. The house is old and historic. There must be such things around here. But why does that bother you?' 'Thank you very much for the help!' I said, annoyed. I had almost dirtied my pants. We told her that the problem was *serious*. 'Don't worry, don't worry,' she said. 'These things are simple. They happen. It's nothing.' 'That's just great!' I said to myself with impatience, and we left.

"About seven hundred meters from where we were, below the hill where our house stood, there was this farmer who cultivated and took care of the Contessa's vast estate. She lived alone, having only one woman who helped her keep up her castle. So we went to that farmer. He was a good man, working the land with his oxen. He had wine, dark bread, turkeys, and the like and we used to buy such things from him. We told him what was happening. We said nothing about La Casa del Diavolo because we were afraid of the police, that we might be arrested for vandalism. 'What can I tell you,' he said. 'You hear such stories all the time in these farming areas. The person that could perhaps help you is a hermit that lives in a small church at the cemetery nearby.'

"I could hear nothing about monks," Pascalis said with an almost angry tone. "I had no desire to get involved either with monks or priests. And I made my position crystal clear to the others. 'I am no longer involved with such matters,' I told them. 'We must accept the situation as it is and just calm down.' We were all very upset. But Mario Albini and Susan Smith went to that monk anyway. They told him everything. It was some kind of confession for them about what they had done. They told him the story with every detail, the way I am telling it to you now.

"Oh," Pascalis exclaimed, "I forgot to tell you that one night while the four of us were in the kitchen cooking (that was just before my Yugoslav girlfriend left for her country), we began hearing the same flute, the exact type of music. We were terrorized and kept asking each other to verify whether we were hearing the same thing.

"Anyway, that monk instructed them to immediately return everything they got from the church to him. 'Place everything in one bag and bring them to me,' he instructed them. 'Then I'll see what I can do.' Susan Smith, as I told you, had taken parts of a skeleton, and had mounted two hands, folded like this, on the kitchen wall." Pascalis folded his hands. "She placed the skull over the fireplace and decorated it with dark sunglasses and a hat. And she placed the various other objects—fragments of statues and pieces of skeletons —all over the house. Now she threw everything in a bag and brought it to the monk.

"Now what can I say?" Pascalis said with puzzlement in his voice. "Since she did that our troubles ended. We have heard neither the music nor the noises on the roof nor the howling. Until then we had reached such a miserable state that we began getting tranquilizers. I don't know what that monk did but it was as if our problems were cut by a knife, so to speak. From then on we began living a normal life again. We found our peace of mind.[2]

"Occasionally we would discuss among ourselves our bizarre experience but it did not create fear and anxiety among us. There were no longer the episodes, such as the music and the like, to stimulate our anxieties. We calmed down." Pascalis sighed and was silent for a few seconds. Then he proceeded.

"Now, I tried to explain what we went through on the basis of the law of probabilities. I raised the question in my mind whether we suffered from some sort of collective guilt because of the vandalism we committed. And then perhaps we experienced some kind of group hallucination. But that explanation was not satisfying to me. It was too real an experience to dismiss it as hallucination."

"Particularly when it was verified by all of you," I volunteered.

"Precisely," Pascalis said with eagerness in his voice.

"A year later," he went on to say, "I told this story to a friend of mine from Athens and to his Irish girlfriend. They lived together in Perugia. 'Oh,' he said, 'this is nonsense. I don't believe in such things. Let's go to find out what is going on.' 'No thank you,' I said. 'I am not going there again. But if you so wish I will tell you how to get there.' He said that would be fine. I said to him, 'I will accompany you up to a certain point and then I will point the way.' It was about ten in the evening. We got into his little Fiat and drove up to the train station so that I could get off. I got out of the car and while he was in the driver's seat I began explaining how to get to La Casa del Diavolo. Just then his car caught fire. Flames began coming out of the hood. They jumped out. The car burned completely. We went back home by train. He never asked again how to get to La Casa del Diavolo. To this day this story is a mystery to me." Pascalis remained silent for a while, waiting to see my reaction.

"Pascali," I said, "I am curious to know in what way that experience affected you."

"Look," he quickly answered with nervousness. "I don't believe in such things. I have never had such an experience before or since. I had heard similar stories before and I used to dismiss them as nonsense. And I still do," he rushed to reassure me.

"I try to explain such things differently," he proceeded thoughtfully. "I wondered, for example, whether there was some shepherd playing that flute." He paused for a second and then went on. "But again that was impossible. All those coincidences, and then the case with the monk . . ."

"Have you visited that hermit afterward to ask for explanations of what he had done?"

"I personally never went to see him," Pascalis reacted with emphasis. He seemed to have deep resentments against Church, monks, and priests. In fact he emphasized that he was a complete atheist.

"So, what happened to Susan Smith?" I asked in a lighter tone.

"I really can't say," Pascalis replied and laughed nervously. "After that episode I got into a fight with Mario Albini. . . . It was really stupid. About women, I mean . . ."

"How was that?"

Pascalis after hesitating for a moment or two went on. "You see, Susan Smith was attracted to me. In fact it was I who first met her. We were together for a while but I had given my heart elsewhere. That was when Mario Albini got together with her. He was a very close friend of mine. He had a lot of Greek friends and we used to drink ouzo and dance, all of us together. He was a wonderful fellow. Now Susan Smith apparently deep down had resentments against me. She was very rich and her ego was very big. In fact she used to get fifteen times more money each month than I did and assumed she could really buy me. So what do you think she did? She told Mario, 'During your absence, when you left for Angona, Pascalis took advantage of me and seduced me.' Of course it was a lie. I was shocked when I later found out about what she said. So Mario told

me, 'Let's go to a tavern.' 'Fine,' I said, 'let's go.' We went there
and we started drinking. Then suddenly he said to me, 'You know
I love you very much but I want to kill you.' 'If you so wish,' I
replied with incredulity, 'let's go outside and kill each other. What's
the matter, what's going on?' He never believed me. We broke off
our friendship and I left that house. Mario went ahead and married
Susan Smith. A year later they got divorced."

"Are you in contact with him now?"

Pascalis sighed. "If he meets me now he will go crazy with ex-
uberance because he must have realized that I was innocent. Alas, I
have no idea where he is."

"What interests me most, Pascali," I said, "is the way in which
this episode at La Casa del Diavolo has affected you personally, has
changed your life."

"It has affected me all right. I have been thinking about this over
and over for so many years without finding any satisfactory explanation. After all, it is for this reason that I wanted to see you.

"Of course I did not get stuck there," Pascalis hastened to add.
"I have never experienced such things either before or after that
episode. It is beyond my logic. Why so many incredible coincidences? As I told you, I tried to explain it rationally but in vain. I
thought that it was perhaps my fantasy. But I could not accept that
so many people who experienced the same things were into some
kind of collective hallucination. So many people experiencing and
seeing the same things at the same time."

"Perhaps your experience can be explained to some extent," I
proceeded to say with some hesitation, "if you are ready to entertain
the possibility that there are other dimensions of reality and existence. . . . But, my friend, you cannot believe in these things and
yet you did have the experience. Your experience and your notion
of reality do not match. I believe this is what you need to resolve
within yourself. You had an extraordinary experience, a negative one

to be sure, that contradicts your cherished assumptions about the nature of reality."

"Look," Pascalis said with a certain agitation in his voice. "Do you know what the reasons are that I cannot solve this puzzle? I would argue that we have not reached that scientific stage that would enable us to explain such phenomena. But I cannot in all honesty change and accept certain fundamental assumptions about reality that are unscientific—that is, that they are not based on experimental controls and so on.

"If I am willing to change my assumptions about reality and accept metaphysics, then of course I would be able to offer an explanation, that there is the spirit world, and so on. My position on this issue," Pascalis continued with a categorical and forceful intonation in his voice, "my philosophy, if you will, is that eventually science will reach a stage that will explain all that. It may happen after my lifetime, but it will happen. That is okay. But we must stay on firm scientific grounds."

"Tell me, Pascali, what are your beliefs about religion?" I asked softly and pointedly.

Pascalis had no problem answering me with the certainty of a man who knows where he stands. "In regard to matters of existence I believe in one thing. I believe in matter. And I say that mind or spirit is nothing more than a codification of matter. I cannot accept anything outside of matter that I can call spirit. No!" Pascalis tapped the table with his right hand. "And that is what science tells me and what my logic tells me."

"I see." I nodded.

"Let us take medicine, for example," Pascalis continued. "Suppose I meet somebody I love that I haven't seen for a long time. I am an emotional person and I am moved by such an experience. If you place at that moment a microelectrode inside my brain, at a certain part of my brain, you will observe that at that part of the brain there are higher rates of electrical currents. That means that such things as emotions, experiences, memories are explained scientifically. And I do believe that everything is matter. What we call spirit or what we create within our bodies—that is, experiences, images, fantasies, everything—are nothing more than a synthesized codification of matter. And I accept neither spirit as a reality in itself nor metaphysics. I believe our existence is not a metaphysical mystery but a product of matter. And matter in itself is energy. You split the atom and you get energy."

"And why don't you believe in matter as an expression of energy rather than the other way around?" I asked teasingly.

"I cannot perceive the energy. And I believe only that which I can apprehend. I can see matter, I can touch it, and therefore I believe in it. You see, I try to be as simple a human being as possible. I know for example that when I follow certain scientific procedures that have been invented through the centuries, and do this and that with matter, I know I will get energy. So far nobody has shown me that from energy you can get matter. Likewise it is through matter that we create that which people call spirit.

"As far as religion goes," Pascalis proceeded, "I believe it is an expression of human weakness. All religions are like that. That which we cannot control and rationally understand we attribute to the workings of gods."

"Tell me, Pascali," I interrupted, "were all your friends who had that unusual experience of the same persuasions as far as religion goes?"

"I don't know. But one thing I do know. They were not churchgoers, nor were they interested in matters of religion. We never discussed such topics. In fact, the reason why we all went to that church was because we assumed all those stories were superstitious nonsense.

"My beliefs about existence are unshakable in spite of that experience," Pascalis continued as if trying to persuade himself. "And my beliefs are strictly materialistic and scientific. I cannot abandon these principles that humanity has developed over so many centuries and replace them with my own simply because I had those experiences. I believe in progress and evolution. In many ways Darwin's theory satisfies me. We evolved out of matter and we were once monkeys."

Pascalis was pensive for a few seconds and looked as if he had second thoughts of what he had just said with so much self-confidence—the idea that he was once a monkey. Then he said with an emotional tone in his voice, "Yes, yes, my friend. I am troubled by what I experienced and what I truly believe on what life and existence are all about. I hope with the progress of science we will be able to explain such things."

"Are you sure, Pascali," I said with reluctance, "that there are no scientific theories that, to be sure, are outside the model of science that you have in your mind, yet that may in fact shed light on what you have experienced in Italy? I mean a science with a broader framework?" Pascalis was set in his beliefs and my suggestion did not seem to register. He believed in "science," period.

We left the Damn Yankee and walked for a while around campus talking about Greek politics and his plans for an eventual return to an Athenian suburb to practice medicine.

# 4

# DEVOTEES

PASCALIS'S STORY FASCINATED ME NOT ONLY BECAUSE OF THE content of the story itself but also because of his own reaction to it. He was a thoroughly secular man. And like a modern secular person, he had an unshakable faith in the redemptive power and efficacy of science, not only to eventually explain all of reality but also to make the world better. It was the same belief that animated the leading thinkers of the nineteenth century, who couched their philosophies within the boundaries of Newton's model of the universe, a universe resembling a gigantic clock operating with determinate laws of cause and effect. Descartes' dictum *cogito, ergo sum* (I think, therefore I am), which had become the foremost cliché among learned circles, provided the metaphysical and only legitimate basis for the study of this mechanical clock. It was pure thought standing on no other foundation except its own promise to unlock the secrets of this mechanistic, lifeless universe. And materialist, "objective" science was the means to do so. Subjective experience, intuition, feeling, values, and ultimate realities had become suspect, unreal, and virtually banished from the intellectual discourse of the West.

Given Pascalis's schooling his position seemed to me perfectly understandable. He had difficulty believing in his experience. He rigidly adhered to his beliefs: The only world there is is the world of our senses and any other notions of supra- or extrasensory realities, realities beyond the reach of our ordinary consciousness, simply do not exist.

Pascalis's response reminded me of Freud's reaction to a paranormal event that took place in his office in 1909. Present was Carl Jung, at the time his friend and presumed successor, who would lead the spread of the gospel of psychoanalysis. Jung had traveled to Vienna to find out what Freud thought of precognition and psychic phenomena in general, a topic of great interest to him, as he had such experiences himself. In his posthumously published autobiography, Jung described in graphic detail what happened during their fateful meeting.

"I asked [Freud] what he thought of these matters," Jung wrote. "Because of his materialistic prejudice, he rejected this entire complex of questions as nonsensical, and did so in terms of so shallow a positivism that I had difficulty in checking the sharp retort on the tip of my tongue. It was years before he recognized the seriousness of parapsychology and acknowledged the factuality of 'occult' phenomena."

What happened after that was a turning point, the beginning of the breakup of their collaboration and friendship. Jung wrote that while Freud was denouncing "occult" phenomena as nonsense, Jung was experiencing a curious sensation. "It was as if my diaphragm were made of iron and were becoming red-hot—a glowing vault. And at that moment there was such a loud report in the bookcase, which stood right next to us, that we both started up in alarm, fearing the thing was going to topple over on us. I said to Freud: 'There, that is an example of a so-called catalytic exteriorization phenomenon.'"

When Freud reacted negatively, Jung insisted that it had been a real paranormal episode. " 'You are mistaken, Herr Professor,' " Jung said to Freud. " 'And to prove my point I now predict that in a moment there will be another such loud report!' Sure enough, no sooner had I said the words than the same detonation went off in the bookcase. To this day I do not know what gave me this certainty. But I knew beyond all doubt that the report would come again. Freud only stared aghast at me."[1]

The case with Pascalis, I thought, was doubly problematic. Not only was he hostile to any "metaphysical" explanations of the phenomena he had experienced, on "scientific" grounds, but he also carried within his mind the traditional Marxist hostility to anything related to religion.

I discussed the encounter with Pascalis with my good friend and colleague, the painter Michael Lewis, the following evening. I was working late in the office preparing for my trip to Cyprus when I noticed the light was on outside of his studio, which happened to be directly over my office, signaling that Michael was inside working. I would often take breaks from my work and go upstairs to chat for a while and comment on his latest painting. I felt the need to "unburden" myself now of Pascalis's tale. Michael was a superb listener, and being an artist with remarkable spiritual sensitivities and insights into human relationships he was just the right person to whom I felt I could reveal what I heard. His studio was a spacious attic which Michael had turned into a haven of plants, paintings, and music. I always felt re-energized just by being there. I sat in a rocking chair and watched him frame a recently completed painting of mythological, ethereal-looking figures against a background of Maine woods and sky.

"It seems that your friend is on his way to overcoming his scientific materialism," he said thoughtfully as he adjusted the glass over his new painting.

"How so?" I asked as I rocked myself a few times.

"The experience is forcing him to reexamine his beliefs about reality. It has created a dissonance in his mind that he will have to resolve somehow. It is a provocation to reevaluate his values."

I volunteered that it was extremely difficult for Marxists to do so. Scientific materialism, I went on to say, was in its heyday when Marx was writing *Das Kapital*. His theories on political economy were presented as "scientific," and Marx's theories on religion are well known—"the opium of the people." Therefore for Pascalis as for most committed Marxists, to overcome his materialism is doubly difficult and problematic. First he had to question his ideological commitment to scientism.

"What do you mean by that?" Michael asked as he carefully hooked together the sides of the frame.

"He has to overcome his total faith in the scientific method as the alpha and omega of all knowledge. That is no small task, particularly for a medical doctor who has been indoctrinated with the notion that the human individual is nothing more than flesh and bones. Scientism as far as I am concerned is a powerful ideological straitjacket in itself."

"I say!" Michael quipped and continued working on his painting.

"For a Marxist, like himself, there is additional ideological baggage. He will have to reexamine his beliefs about religion as nothing more than a pacifier for oppressed classes, 'the sigh of the oppressed' and 'the opium of the people,' according to Marx. Just think how prejudiced he was at the notion of even visiting that monk that he claimed may have been instrumental in liberating them from those negative experiences."

"But that in itself," Michael replied, "is a sign that he may be reevaluating his beliefs in light of his experience."

"Perhaps. But what I mean to say is that, particularly for Marxists, this is extremely difficult. Not only do they have to overcome their scientific materialism but also their ideological commitment to an antireligious philosophical and political doctrine."

"I wonder what is going to happen now that communism has collapsed in Eastern Europe," Michael said as he paused and looked at the finished product.

"You know, I have been thinking about that," I said and then went on to mention how the Marxist vision of reality had for generations captivated the minds of a significant number of gifted thinkers and rebel academics in the West, consumed by the passion for a just world order. Entire volumes, in fact whole libraries, have been written on Marx's life and thought, on every paragraph he had written, every footnote and every commentary of his corpus. And Marxism's basic tenet is that human consciousness, or mind, is the product of material, historical processes. There are no other worlds, no paradises and hells, no spirit world and no gods other than those created by human beings to soothe their worldly pains. Humanity can find its redemption only through the historical, class struggle which will eventually lead to its liberation when the classless society is firmly established. Then humanity will have no need for religion, no need to spin out grotesque theological doctrines about spirits, demons, and angels.

I told Michael that I believed the collapse of Eastern Europe is bound to undermine the fascination with Marxism. It will liberate minds, entrapped by that mold for so many generations, to explore more holistic perspectives in understanding reality, and to act upon their new convictions.

"Perhaps you can say the same about Freudianism," Michael added.

"Oh, absolutely," I replied. Then I told him of a conversation I'd had with another friend, Robert, a psychology professor at a state university, deeply interested and involved with transpersonal psychology and spirituality.

"I was walking with Robert one bright morning in downtown Nicosia last summer discussing psychoanalysis. Half jokingly he claimed that perhaps the whole field is a Luciferian conspiracy. When I asked him to explain, he said: 'Suppose God implanted within the human psyche the spark of divinity that would propel every human being to labor toward self-discovery, to search for the Divine Self within. Then Lucifer in order to sabotage God's plan sent Freud as a diversionary tactic to appropriate this desire of the ego for self-discovery by inventing psychoanalysis as a counterfeit path."

I chuckled as Michael joined me. "What did you tell him? Did you agree with him?"

"Actually I argued that Freud and psychoanalysis were part of God's work. He sent Freud, I said, to awaken us to the reality of our subconscious. I do believe that Freud is a precursor to the contemporary interest in spirituality. Never mind that Freud himself was an atheist. We must look at the unintended consequences of his work. For example, we would not have had Jung had it not been for Freud. And Jung played a pivotal role in the current regeneration of spiritual psychology. God," I said with a chuckle, "works in mysterious ways. He may even be friends with Lucifer. Or rather," I said with some hesitation, "perhaps Lucifer is a manifestation of the Divine working by other means . . ."

I had fresh in my mind a debate on this very issue between two distinguished theologians and philosophers, David Ray Griffin and Huston Smith. In a jointly authored volume[2] Griffin argued that there was authentic evil in God's creation, whereas Smith, grounding his argument on the perennial philosophy and the primordial tradition, argued that evil is only a relative reality nonexistent at the highest levels of consciousness and awareness—that evil is the dialectical mechanism and provocation for the very evolution of human consciousness toward God. Therefore, evil as such is playing a central, functional role within the totality of the divine symphony of creation. To Huston Smith and every other "perennialist," therefore, evil, although it must be fought at all levels, is only apparently real. At unity consciousness, at the highest levels of awareness, evil is transcended, and only the Absolute Love of God remains.

"Huston Smith," I told Michael, "likes to quote Saint Augustine on this matter, whose position is pretty much identical with that of the oriental mystics."

"What did Augustine say?" Michael asked. I ran downstairs to my office and brought back Griffin and Smith's book. While Michael began framing another painting for an upcoming New York exhibition I turned to page 28 and read Augustine's words: " 'I no longer desired a better world, because I was thinking of creation as a whole: and in the light of this more balanced discernment, I had come to see that higher things are better than the lower, but that the sum of all creation is better than the higher things alone.' "

"Sounds pretty much like what Erevna teaches," Michael pointed out.

"Precisely," I said. "Kostas told me once that although evil can and must be eliminated from individual consciousness and from our planet it can never be eliminated from the totality of creation. Good and evil are always absolutely balanced within the worlds of creation, the worlds of polarity and separateness. Had it not been so, he said, Spirit-egos would not be able to acquire experiences for the purpose of developing their uniqueness and autonomy within the oneness of the One and Absolute God."

We went on to further discuss Pascalis's encounter with evil and tried to make sense of it on the basis of the esoteric philosophy that I have been studying for over a decade.

Phenomena of this kind abound all over the world and have been reported by eyewitnesses throughout the ages. But in our modern secular age we dismiss such stories a priori as nothing more than fabrications of the human imagination or projections of unconscious human weaknesses. We have been convinced, like Bertrand Russell, that the world of the five senses is the only world there is, and that somehow it has always been there without the necessity of a creator or an explanation. But if there are other worlds that mystics claim exist at other vibrational frequencies, that interpenetrate and have an effect on the world of our five senses, then phenomena like La Casa del Diavolo should be taken seriously. "Probably," I speculated, "terrible things must have happened within the space of that church or the castle next to it, either before they were built or after. Possibly there was devil worship or mass killings and murders, or even ritual human sacrifices, black magic, and the like. An evil elemental must have been constructed that remained dormant but alive within the etheric worlds. This satanic elemental was often activated under conditions similar to those described by Pascalis. Bad things must have happened to people in the past and the locals believed that the church was cursed. That is why they shut it firmly. Now, that very collective belief reinforced the power of that evil elemental. The very beliefs of the people of that region offered more energy to that satanic presence that became a reality unto itself."

"So when those fellows engaged in vandalism within the church," Michael added, "the elemental attacked them and they suffered the consequences."

"It seems that way," I agreed. "What the monk did was probably some ritual exorcism that is part of the more esoteric rituals of the Church. Formulas for such rituals do exist both in the Catholic Church as well as the Eastern Orthodox."

"The process of creating an evil energy," Michael pointed out, "is the same process that gives birth to therapeutic, benign elementals."

"That's right. Places like Lourdes in France, the Church of the Holy Virgin on the island of Tínos in Greece, and the Madonna of Guadalupe near Mexico City are healing therapeutic spots. The mystics would argue that there are benign angelic energies there, created by human worship and belief. According to this explanation," I went on to say, "such elementals, whether benign or evil, are products of human consciousness but have become realities unto themselves. They acquire an objective existence over and above any particular individual consciousness that may have given them birth."

"Colin Wilson has written extensively about these matters and in one of his latest books[3] he provides, I believe, impressive arguments and evidence on the objective reality of such paranormal phenomena."

"To most people, including most of our colleagues in universities," Michael pointed out, "such matters are just too threatening. They avoid talking about them, for they undermine their worldview."

"They dismiss all that by calling it 'pseudoscience,' " I said with a chuckle.

A week later I drove with Emily and our two children to New York. We visited with relatives and friends before our departure for Cyprus, where I was to continue my explorations for the summer. Emily, Constantine, and Vasia flew on ahead of me with British Airways via London while I stayed to meet with my publisher, literary agent, and some friends that I had made since the publication of my books.

The day after Emily and the children left I had an appointment with Ted, a businessman friend of mine. I was in his office on Fifth Avenue chatting about my work and other matters of interest when the phone rang. It was Julia, a mutual friend and a lifelong and avid explorer of spirituality and mysticism. She was an author herself, and her background included a doctorate in psychology and considerable administrative experience.

"I want both of you to come and meet Baba," she told Ted. "We will have lunch with other friends at one o'clock. Get a taxi and come right over."

Julia had been telling me about Baba for quite some time. She reassured me that he was "incredible." Baba, I was told, had extraordinary paranormal abilities that would literally blow my mind. She said that after meeting Baba her life had changed drastically for the better. She had complained many times to me that her life was full of physical and emotional pain and that no physician, healer, or medicine woman in her fifty years of life had been able to help her. That is until she met Baba, this extraordinary wonder-worker from the south of India. Julia had told me several times in the past that had it not been for her spiritual concerns she would have committed suicide on several occasions. But, steeped in spiritual literature, she knew that suicide was no solution to personal problems. The appearance of this mysterious oriental guru had sealed her quest for purpose and meaning in her life. It was gratifying for me to hear of Julia's transformation toward a healthier, more optimistic outlook on life.

I was curious to meet Baba not only because of Julia's enthusiastic endorsement and his apparent role in her "road to Damascus" transformation but also because of what Julia called his reputed power to make bodies visible and invisible. Being a skeptic by temperament and training as a sociologist I normally would have dismissed such talk as the fantasies of an untamed mind. But I was intrigued because I had known Julia as a hard-nosed scientist with many years on the board of a major research grant institution. I was even more intrigued when in her last letter she claimed that Baba ". . . moves in and out of time and space as easily and as ordinarily as most of us move from one room to another; and he sees a world that is so much more complex and multidimensional that it is endlessly engaging." Julia went on to write that, "If the masters you studied in Cyprus are some of the last great mystics of the Christian era, then I think Baba is the great teacher of the next two thousand years— the next era, whatever it may be called. The chance to be with him, to be close to him, especially now when he is relatively unknown, is priceless."

"What do you say, Kyriaco? Shall we go?" Ted asked me before putting down the telephone.

"Let's go," I said without any hesitation and stood up. Ted himself was interested in spiritual questions and the paranormal. Like myself he was puzzled and curious.

The address Julia gave us was a townhouse in the heart of Manhattan. We hired a taxi and were there in less than twenty minutes. We knocked several times until a smiling woman in her late thirties opened the door. Before she would let us in we had to explain first that we were guests of Julia and that we wished to meet their Indian teacher. We were escorted into the hallway where several others, casually dressed and friendly in their disposition, were waiting for the master to appear. Julia arrived a little later and with her usual ebullient enthusiasm began introducing us to the people in the room. They all seemed to be very alert and intelligent, radiating a sense of well-being. Indeed they looked to us like people who shared a great secret to which only they, the privileged few, had access.

"I must admit," I said to Julia, "that I have never seen you in a better form."

"Oh, I am, I am," she reassured me and beamed with happiness. "I owe it all to Baba. It is just wonderful. This is what I wanted and what I searched for all my life."

When we inquired about the whereabouts of Baba we were told that he was in the other room having a hearing with one of his devotees. We were told that the house was owned by a practicing psychiatrist who, appreciating Baba's work, had offered the first floor, free of charge, for the weekly meetings. She practiced her psychiatry on the second floor.

"Baba is not a human being. Baba is an experience," an attractive woman declared confidently after both Ted and I began asking questions about their master. We were told that we were indeed very lucky that we would have the opportunity to have the experience of meeting such a profoundly advanced yogi. We were also told that Baba had originally been brought to America a few years before by several psychiatrists who had been exposed to his awesome abilities when they visited India and wished to study him. "We can't wait to see him," I said, and I looked at Ted, who nodded with a grin.

I had hardly finished my sentence when the door opened and a handsome, tall, slender man in his early forties made his appearance. Clean-shaven with piercingly intelligent eyes, he wore a colorful blue shirt. I realized immediately that this must be Baba as I saw wide smiles on everybody's faces. Ted and I also smiled and shook hands with the guru as Julia introduced us with a beam of happiness flashing across her face.

We were invited to join them for lunch in the backyard, a small, enclosed space surrounded by tall apartment buildings, yet very pleasant and well kept with grass, greenery, and flower pots. We served ourselves in the kitchen, the food prepared by Baba's devotees, and sat around two circular tables. Ted and I were offered the honor of sitting at the same table with Baba. Julia sat next to me. While eating and without further delay I began asking Baba questions. Julia pressed the button on her mini–tape recorder. It seemed as if Baba expected my questions and with ease he began narrating his personal story.

He told us of his youth in a small town in south India and how very early in his life he recognized that not everybody experienced the world as he did. That he had soon discovered he had extraordinary abilities, which he himself had been taking for granted.

"Baba," I said, interrupting him. "Is it true that you can make bodies invisible to others?" He stopped eating a piece of chicken and turned to Julia with an inquisitive, almost critical, look.

"Did you tell them such a thing?" he asked softly and grinned.

"Well," Julia explained with some embarrassment, "we normally do not talk about these matters. I mentioned it to you because of your work in Cyprus."

"I appreciate that," I said, and signaled to Baba that it was okay. That both Ted and I were not naive about the powers of the human mind and what it can do. Baba did not wish to talk any further about the invisibility of corporeal bodies so I changed the subject.

"Within the context of what kind of mystical tradition do you work?" I asked. I wondered whether Baba was some kind of Hindu yogi, the kind that Yogananda talks about in his *Autobiography*,[4] or whether he was a Buddhist bodhisattva. Or perhaps a maverick guru starting his own school, charting an entirely new path and basing his practice exclusively on his own charisma, discoveries, and psychic inventions and innovations.

I was not certain whether Baba answered my question. He preferred instead to say that his methods were different. That he was not particularly working within any tradition as such and that his primary concern was to bring his devotees to such a state as to "absorb the light directly." In fact in the brochure I was given this was stated very clearly: ". . . by experiencing the light in a session or in my presence . . . it is as if the darkness within you is being dispelled."

I asked Baba whether within his practice there was any room for healing. "Not directly," he said. "Health is a product of your psychic state. If you are healthy psychologically, then you will be healthy physically. We work on the psyche."

"Come with me," he said, after we finished our lunch. Baba wanted to see both Ted and me individually. I waited with the others in the hallway as Ted went in first. When he came out of the room after about fifteen minutes he was shaking his head. "What happened?" I asked. "You will find out soon," he said, and pointed at the room where Baba was sitting. I went in with some trepidation, not knowing what to expect. But I was reassured. Baba seemed to me to be a likable man. Julia earlier told me that the core of Baba's teaching was love and compassion. There were no "dark spaces." A statement on the brochure attributed to Baba was comforting from the point of view of individual freedom. ". . . To become dependent upon something outside yourself like substances or sex, or even to become dependent upon me, is contrary to the natural unfolding of your own awakening . . ."

"Lie down, be comfortable, and close your eyes," Baba instructed as he pointed at a Freudian couch next to where he was sitting. I was reluctant. I had not come there to undergo some kind of psychic experience. All I was interested in was simply talking to Baba, not having him do things to me, particularly when I knew virtually nothing about him except what Julia had told me. But his friendly tone put me at ease and I lay down as he turned the lights off. There was total darkness, no trace of light in the room. I had my eyes closed as Baba sat behind me and put his palms over my forehead. Without saying a word he kept his hands there. I heard him breathe deeply as I lay there not knowing what to expect. Then suddenly using one of his fingers he pressed the center of my forehead. All I could utter after that was "Oh my God what is this! Oh my God!" My heartbeat soared. With the stroke of his finger I saw an explosion of light of various colors, brilliant white predominating. Baba demonstrated his power but I wasn't that certain whether I wished to experience it. I had my eyes closed, the room was totally dark, and suddenly it was as if a sun flashed in front of my eyes. Yet my eyes were firmly shut. This state lasted for a few seconds but it was enough to shake me up. The thought that immediately came to mind was "Why was Baba so ready to demonstrate his psychic powers?"

I went outside where everybody was sitting. I realized by their smiles that they knew what I had just gone through. Then a bearded man in his late thirties went into the room. I saw him lie down as Baba closed the door. Julia told me that he had been an engineer but that Baba had instructed him to give up his job and become a taxi driver. It was a form of spiritual exercise I was told. Mark had become too comfortable as an engineer and needed a challenge. He had to take up something he deeply detested doing.

When Baba opened the door a cool breeze came out of the room. It felt as if he had opened some kind of a deep freezer, like those that butchers use to keep their meat fresh. But there was no refrigerator in the room. And Mark, who had been lying on the couch, was nowhere to be seen. "Baba has just raised Mark's vibrations and made him invisible to our eyes," Julia whispered, matter-of-factly. Ted and I looked at each other in disbelief. "Julia, are you sure you are not pulling our legs, now?" I said half seriously and raised my eyebrows. "Are you sure Mark is not hiding somewhere in that room?"

"No," Julia said emphatically with a giggle. "Come and see." We went inside the room as Baba came out and began casually chatting with the others. We looked around but we could not see Mark anywhere. "Mark is right there on the couch," Julia reassured us, "but his vibrations are higher than ours. And we can sit on that same couch while he is still lying there."

We sat on the couch for a few seconds. "Julia," I said, "are you personally convinced that Baba is not some kind of a magician or trickster? Is it possible that he has colluded with Mark to create this illusion or phenomenon or whatever you wish to call it?" A decade earlier I would have been tempted to say "farce." But my long exposure with mystics and psychics taught me to keep an open mind and prejudge nothing as absurd, no matter how it might appear to my senses at the moment. I followed this rule on principle, a methodological axiom, if you will.

"Look, I have known both Mark and Baba for a long time. I reassure you there is no foul play here. I raised these questions myself at the beginning and thoroughly researched the possibility. Believe me, this is for real. Let me repeat what I said to you many times over the phone," Julia said forcefully as we sat on the empty couch where presumably Mark was still lying. "I have never met anyone who can lead you on and facilitate your ascent toward enlightenment. I have always craved enlightenment and finally I found someone who can really help me out. Here is a man who can make people totally transparent so that the light can permeate them completely. He can also make himself so transparent that you cannot see him," Julia rushed to add.

"This is heavy stuff," I moaned.

"You bet. I have seen him be at two places at the same time. One of him was coming up the stairs and the other was in this room giving a lesson."

"That can tax the credulity of even the most devoted believer," I declared.

"Here is another case," Julia went on, lowering her voice enough so that only Ted and I could listen. "Several days ago Baba came out of this room, stood out there and made a couple of casual remarks. Then he returned to the room. During all that time there was a woman here in this room who was talking to Baba continuously while she was holding his hand. That woman asked him, 'Baba I hear your voice outside.' He just cracked a joke and said, 'Oh, really?'

"He never left the room," Julia said with excitement and had to make an extra effort to talk slowly. "And yet he was also outside and we were all seeing him and talking to him while he was also inside holding the hand of that woman and giving her some lesson.

"You see," Julia went on, "he does that sort of thing. It is not for show. He is giving us lessons. And some of this has the element of fun and spontaneity." Julia said further that light comes out of Baba's body and is visible in the room. His body, she said, literally lights up, and it is strong enough so that you can even read a newspaper, "if you care to read newspapers under those conditions, that is."

"Does he read your thoughts?" Ted asked.

"He does not interfere with our privacy. He sees the entire life's map of every person. But he never says anything to anyone. His principle is not to interfere. Many times I pleaded with him to tell me. He never does. But I do believe he has access to all knowledge, if he wants to get it. Most of the time he says he does not wish to look."

"Why?" I asked.

"Because it is not fun to do so," Julia said cheerfully. "It is better not to know."

Ted and I shook our heads and followed Julia out of the room. In a few seconds Baba came back and closed the door briefly. When he opened it again, on the very couch that we had just been sitting on, Mark had reappeared in a state that seemed to be either deep sleep or some kind of trance. Baba casually closed and opened the door a few more times as we alternately saw and didn't see Mark lying there. But we never actually witnessed him either appearing or disappearing, which naturally encouraged our suspicions. Julia explained that he could not allow us to see the dematerialization and rematerialization of Mark's body directly because the light that fills the room during such a transformation would be too unbearable for our eyes.

Baba opened the door again, and once more Mark's body had "disappeared." He called on Ted to come into the room, and asked him to stand with his eyes closed facing toward the door with hands stretched forward, the couch behind him where, presumably, Mark was still lying, invisible. Baba then closed the door, with himself, Ted, and the "invisible Mark" in the room. After about ten minutes Baba opened the door and the same cool breeze rushed out of the room. Ted was standing, stretched hands forward as before, with closed eyes, and looking alarmingly pale. There was still no one on the couch. Baba came out of the room and shut the door behind him. Two minutes later Ted opened the door and rushed out of the room, looking anxious.

"Oh, you shouldn't have come out," Baba said, and shook his head. Then I realized what was going on. Baba was trying to make Ted invisible! Ted told me later that when Baba left the room and shut the door he panicked, not knowing what was about to happen to him. So he opened his eyes and turned around, and saw Mark lying on the couch without a trace of life in his face.

After rushing out, Ted sat on a chair trying to recover from the shock. "Actually," he told me and Julia as Baba walked back in to the room where Mark was still in trance, "I was feeling a very pleasant kind of energy passing through my body. But I panicked, not knowing where that was going to lead me." Baba had not forewarned Ted that he was planning to make him invisible.

The woman who had told us earlier that Baba was "not a human being but an experience" now asked whether we wished to have a formal "private audience" with Baba.

"It costs one hundred dollars per session." There were a few moments of silence. "You see, Baba has to make a living," she went on to say, "and charges no more than the local psychiatrists." She sounded uncomfortably apologetic.

"Oh, I fully understand, I understand," I said. "New York is a very expensive town to live in."

We thanked them all but we declined. Ted said, and I agreed, that we must have more time to process what we had witnessed and gone through, and couldn't jump onto the experiential bandwagon no matter how exotic and intriguing it may have appeared to us. I felt relief that Ted spoke so forthrightly. I was not in the least ready to place my subconscious in the hands of a stranger, who seemed to me to have considerable psychic power. Baba was a likable man, and obviously a great charismatic healer to his followers, and Julia's recovery was impressive, but I needed time to reflect on the matter. Julia then told us that Baba was not actually the one who caused these phenomena, but was able to summon powerful spirit guides. I must admit that that did not make me feel any less apprehensive.

"So, Ted, what do you think about all that?" I asked as we rode in the taxi toward his office.

"I am not sure what to think," Ted said pensively as he looked at me to see my reactions.

I raised my shoulders, showing the same kind of apprehension, not knowing how to respond to the experience we had just gone through. I had been involved with the study of psychic healers long enough to not just dismiss the entire episode as a prank. Obviously Baba was an extraordinary individual with extraordinary, paranormal skills. If nothing else at least he was capable of creating collective illusions that convinced his followers of awesome psychic powers to make bodies appear and disappear. Yet the esoteric and occult traditions throughout the ages, and particularly those of India and Tibet, report that such phenomena are possible and real and that some individuals are capable of causing such phenomena. Sai Baba,[5] for example, is reputed to have materialized "sacred ash" and all kinds of objects in front of the admiring eyes of his devotees. Many eyewitnesses attested to the authenticity of what they witnessed. Yet I was wary of such stories. Without minimizing the contribution of such paranormal phenomena in sensitizing unbelievers to the reality of other dimensions, the high spiritual traditions warn against the employment of such powers except in extraordinary circumstances and only for the sake of service and healing.

"I am glad you did not become invisible," I said to Ted jokingly. "Otherwise I would have really worried."

"So would I, so would I," Ted replied with relief.

"But just imagine," I said, "the implications for our notions of reality had what we went through been an authentic experience that could be verified. Right here in the middle of Manhattan at this very moment, when hundreds of scientists in this most secular city are sweating in their laboratories to unlock the laws of nature, an unknown yogi makes bodies appear and disappear by the sheer force of his will!

"By the way," I continued, "while you were in that room, in the process of becoming invisible, one of the women told me that Baba teleported a friend of hers from one part of the city to another. She said her friend was getting out of a building on Seventh Avenue and Fifty-fourth Street and when she walked outside she found herself on Thirty-fourth Street and Fifth Avenue. On another occasion a woman who became invisible on the couch was found lying in bed face down in the bedroom of the apartment right above. Julia re-assured me she was present when this phenomenon took place in front of her eyes. When I challenged Julia as to the reality of what she observed, she said that 'the devil's advocate position is only valid to a certain degree and then there is a point that you must abandon it if you are confronted with sufficient evidence.' "

"Indeed, imagine if it were possible for such a phenomenon to be verified scientifically." Ted chuckled and shook his head. I joined him nervously.

# 5

## SKEPTICAL
## INQUIRERS

EACH TIME I STEP INTO AN AIRPLANE I AM ENCHANTED. I FEEL
like an awestruck child encountering for the first time the miraculous achievements of modern science and technology. No matter
how many times I cross the Atlantic I still experience these "Alice-in-Wonderland" emotions.

My uncles, who immigrated to the land of opportunity during
the Roaring Twenties, left Cyprus on a boat that took more than a
month to arrive in New York. They had never been able to visit
their sisters in Cyprus again. At that time the separation from one's
kinfolk was for all practical purposes permanent—when you said
farewell to those left behind it was farewell for life. That is why I
am so grateful to the scientists and inventors of the airplane. It
allows people like myself to live in America and not lose contact
with relatives and friends back in the home country. It also made
possible for me my ongoing research on Cyprus and the Greek
world.

I sat comfortably by the window, tightened my seat belt, and
watched the lights of New York City fade away as the Boeing 747
megaplane roared into the evening sky on its way to London. It
takes about six hours to reach Heathrow Airport. From there to

Cyprus the flight is about four and a half additional hours. I was to meet my family in London where they had been visiting Uncle Akis, Emily's brother. Then from there we were to board British Airways together and head toward our summer stay in Cyprus.

I have rarely been able to sleep for any length of time during a flight, and habitually carry on board a book to keep me company during the long hours. Before I left New York I was attracted by a title, *Not Necessarily the New Age: Critical Essays,*[1] that I found in a book shop not far from the Open Center. The volume, edited by Robert Basil, is a collection of essays sharply debunking what the authors consider "The New Age movement." I thought I ought to read what those critical authors had to say. Browsing through it I realized that it was a relentless polemic by die-hard skeptics against anything that dealt with the contemporary resurgence of interest in spiritual questions and so-called paranormal phenomena. A casual look at the essays in the collection indicated to me that they were written to defend a particular point of view—that the only truth is that which results from scientific research, and that it's impossible to employ the rational mind or science to explore nonexistent spiritual and paranormal realities. Such attempts are nothing more than "pseudoscience," and are deliberate attempts to confuse and manipulate the gullible.

When I noticed Dr. Carl Sagan's name at the top of the list of contributors I shook my head and murmured to myself, "No wonder." I knew that the eminent astronomer, along with luminaries such as the science fiction writer Isaac Asimov, the stage magician Randi ("The Amazing Randi"), and others, had set up the formidably named "Committee for the Scientific Investigation of Claims of the Paranormal." The aim of the committee is to expose what they consider "pseudoscience," which they see as threatening the very foundations of our rational scientific inheritance. Judging from their brochure, which I used as a bookmark, at stake from their point of view was the very heart and soul of Western civilization.

". . . We have been passing through a period of resurgent mysticism. . . . The new committee has the answer. . . . If alchemy and horoscopes gain hold, then why not the mysteries of blood and race and the other irrationalities that have cursed our history? Science is not the be-all of existence, but its enemies can all too easily be the end-all."

As I looked at Dr. Sagan's name I remembered listening on the radio to his National Press Club appearance in September 1986. During the interview he had presented his well-known proposal that we transform our military economies to peace economies, and engage in economic conversion, away from war production, channeling our high technologies and energies elsewhere. One way of doing that, he said, was to redirect such technologies to the exploration of outer space in cooperation with the Russians. A joint mission to Mars, for example, would have sent a very positive message for peace. Fine, I thought. I applauded, although I was not certain of the wisdom of spending our energy and wealth to land a few Russians and Americans on Mars when there was so much that needed to be done here on our wounded and endangered planet.

But what jolted me was Dr. Sagan's answer when a member of the audience asked: "What are your views on the exploration of inner space?" The Cornell astronomer replied in all seriousness something to the effect that, Of course, we have not completely explored the depths of the oceans, and as we explore outer space we must also continue the study of the ocean floor.

What really shocked me was not his answer, but the fact that he did not seem to understand the question. From the tone of his voice it did not appear that Sagan was joking when he made that remark, nor was he being cynical. He simply did not understand that the question was about inner *psychic* space. His answer represented the essence of how mainstream, institutionally funded science approaches spirituality and psychic experience: not at all.

For "objective" scientists, subjective experiences simply do not have a reality in and of themselves. Subjective experience is the opposite of knowledge which is "objective," that is, external to the individual. When we elevate subjectivity to the status of knowledge, according to this group of "Skeptical Inquirers" we are toying with the irrational. Therefore, to counterbalance what they consider the most dangerous watershed of the "New Age movement" they have started an opposite movement, to expose what they consider the charlatanism, fraudulence, irrationality, and pseudoscientific claims of "New Agers." *Not Necessarily the New Age* was part of that effort.

Personally I have thought of myself neither as a New Ager nor as an advocate of "New Ageism." In fact I have always been suspicious of any *ism*. All ideologies are straitjackets within which the mind takes refuge and becomes imprisoned. The problem that I see with the Skeptical Inquirers is their inability to entertain the possibility that their own movement is grounded on an irrational ideological agenda. For example, one of their brochures invited me to join their society "for the scientific study of paranormal phenomena." Yet in that very brochure they denounced belief in so-called paranormal phenomena as irrational and announced that one aim of the society was to start a scientific crusade to expose those interested in the subject as tricksters and frauds. The Skeptical Inquirers have already made up their minds and a priori reached the conclusion that paranormal phenomena are nonphenomena. The ideologues of scientific fundamentalism, like all ideologues, refuse to question their own ideas as to the nature of reality.

Before I began reading the book I pulled out a notebook and jotted down some ideas that had already been provoked. "This is how I see it," I wrote. "There are two general models of reality that we have invented and experienced historically. One is that the ultimate reality is God or the Absolute or some kind of Divine intelligence behind the phenomenal world. Human life from this point of view is meaningful only when it is grounded within this realization of ultimate Divinity. From this perspective this world of the five senses is not the only world there is. If there are other worlds beyond the reach of our ordinary senses, then it becomes a personal and collective goal to pursue knowledge of these worlds. It is our very nature to pursue knowledge because we are self-conscious beings trying to make sense of our lives, to answer the perennial questions of who we are, why we are here, and where we are going at the end of our journey.

"The other model of reality," I went on, "is that which is entertained by materialistic science and the one advocated by the Skeptical Inquirers. For them the only world there is is the world of gross matter, the world which is accessible to our five senses and our rational mind. Any other claims are self-evidently false and a threat to reason itself. This is the perspective that has come to dominate the cultural landscape of the modern world and this is the perspective that is implicit in our educational curricula from elementary school all the way to the graduate programs of Ivy League universities. The only meaningful pursuit from this point of view is to understand gross matter and how it has evolved over time. Science can help us do that. In fact it is the only promise for making the world better, to bring heaven on earth. Any transcendental beliefs are forms of escapism, leftovers of our irrational infantile past, and a threat to the unfettered progress of science.

"Progress through science and technology has replaced the otherworldliness of bygone times. The triumph of rationality, science, and belief in the perfectibility of this material world has been won after long battles with the official spokespersons of the old model or 'paradigm,' the priests and the theologians. It is recognition of the hard-won victory of science over religion that makes the guardians of scientific orthodoxy uncomfortable with the so-called resurgence of New Age spirituality.

"The cause of this discomfort is the alarming trend, perceived by the orthodox scientists, that many of their peers themselves have joined the New Age and, from the vantage point of modern 'quantum' theory, have offered arguments in favor of a fundamentally spiritual interpretation of ultimate reality. This is what makes the orthodox fume with anger, assaulting the New Agers as engaging in pseudoscience. Interestingly, the orthodox scientists have no quarrel with orthodox religion and theology. The latter have been so decisively marginalized by secularism that they pose no threat to the established materialist, technocratic scientific establishment. On the contrary, old-time religion has joined forces with old-time science to fight what they consider the dangers coming from this amorphous, polymorphous, and unorganized 'New Age movement.' "

What is really going on here? I sipped the Bloody Mary that the hostess brought me and let my mind drift back to my graduate years. I remembered my first year as a doctoral student in sociology and my first seminar in sociological theory. The professor asked us to select one major thinker and study him in depth (I say "him" deliberately because at that time there were no women on the list). That was the assignment of the course—a student-centered approach to running the seminar. Each one of us was expected to make a long presentation of the ideas of our chosen master of sociology. It was a first-come-first-choice approach. The professor gave us a day to figure out whom we wished to study.

To my great chagrin I discovered that most of the big guns of sociology had quickly been reserved by more enterprising classmates. Karl Marx, Émile Durkheim, Max Weber, the secular trinity of classical sociological theory, had already been appropriated. "The only ones not claimed as yet," said my professor, "are Auguste Comte, Herbert Spencer, Charles Horton Cooley and Pitirim Alexandrovich Sorokin. Check and see which one you would like to report on." I was depressed, and envied the others who had chosen the right thinkers to expend their energy on. I went to the library and began my search. I was immediately attracted to the Russian Pitirim Alexandrovich Sorokin for primarily nonlogical reasons. A

refugee of the October Revolution, Sorokin had an Eastern Orthodox background like myself and had trouble adapting to American
culture. Being somewhat of a misfit and feeling quite marginal myself at the time I felt a certain affinity both to his ideas and to him
as a displaced person struggling, with defiance, to adapt to a strange
culture.

Beginning with that seminar I became so enthusiastic and engrossed with the ideas of Sorokin that a year after my animated
presentation my classmates teasingly addressed me as "Pitirim." No
one, including my professor, had ever read Sorokin or took his ideas
seriously and I felt whatever they learned was from my presentation.
Yet he was universally acclaimed as a master of sociological thought,
a genius, and a "walking encyclopedia," according to one of his
former students at Harvard. High over the Atlantic, as I pondered
the book on my lap, my involvement with Sorokin's thought suddenly reawakened in my consciousness like the remembrance of an
old passion long forgotten. His ideas seemed to offer some light on
the New Age movement and the reaction of the Skeptical Inquirers.

Sorokin's theories on history and society were formed not only
as a result of his Russian background but also out of his experiences
in the Russian Revolution, when he was very nearly executed by the
Bolsheviks. Sorokin, a social democrat (a Menshevik), valiantly opposed the czarist regime and became secretary to Kerensky, who
headed the interim government after the overthrow of the czar.
When Lenin carried out his October coup and seized the power
that was "lying in the streets," as he put it, Sorokin escaped into
the Russian hinterland. Eventually he surrendered and was swiftly
sentenced to death. But the day before his execution he was released
after one of his former sociology students, a leading Bolshevik himself, persuaded Lenin to save Sorokin's life. Upon his release from
prison, shaken by his experiences in the revolution, Sorokin migrated to America never to return to Russia. In the 1930s, after five

years of teaching at the University of Minnesota, he was invited to Harvard to set up a sociology department.

Sorokin never felt comfortable with the philosophical currents dominant in America at the time: an unbridled belief in rationality, science, and progress. Having gone through the horrors of the First World War and the Russian Revolution himself he had a less optimistic vision of the state of the world. On the eve of the Second World War he embarked on a monumental project to explore the development of Western civilization from its inception in the Homeric period all the way to the twentieth century. The result was a four-volume *magnum opus* of one thousand pages each. Some called his *Social and Cultural Dynamics*,[2] a "classic."

Sorokin began by exposing what he considered the unjustifiable naïveté, shared by people in the streets and the cultural and scientific beacons alike, of assuming that the world is "progressing." How can we possibly speak of social progress, he asked, when there has been so much savagery and mass destruction in this supposedly most enlightened twentieth century? Sorokin was not endorsing the opposite view advocated by a few historians like the German Oswald Spengler, who, after the defeat of Germany in the First World War, came up with a best-selling volume, *The Decline of the West*.[3] Spengler argued that the fate of all civilizations is analogous to the fate of all human beings: birth, growth, attainment of maturity, decline, and eventual death. Most historians were not impressed, but the Germans felt better. After all it was fateful for all great civilizations to decline and die. Therefore the Germans, who thought of themselves as the *crème de la crème* of Western civilization, could not blame themselves for their political disaster and humiliating military defeat. Spengler soothed their pain. Their humiliation was destiny, an unavoidable historical law.

Sorokin endorsed neither the ideology of "progress," nor a "rise and decline" scenario. Instead, after an exhaustive and detailed study of the social and cultural history of the West, Sorokin argued that civilizations do not indefinitely progress in one unilinear direction. And they do not rise with an unavoidable destiny to decline and die. Rather, civilizations, and more specifically the West, undergo transformations from extreme religiosity to extreme materialism, back and forth, back and forth. History for Sorokin is like a pendulum moving between these two poles, these two "ultimate definitions of reality." The West for Sorokin is not necessarily destined to extinction as the historians of doom have prophesied, but it is unavoidably destined to abandon its materialism and move in the direction of a more spiritual definition of reality. Civilization obeys historical laws of transformation from religion to materialism and back to religion. What appears as decline and death in reality is a process of transformation from one pole of integration to another.

Sorokin argued that the nature of a culture or civilization is predicated on the way "ultimate reality" is defined. If ultimate reality is thought to be God, then that civilization will tend to become integrated around that notion. For example, during the peak of the Middle Ages all cultural and social expressions revolved around the idea that the final reality is God. The dominant institution during that period was the Church. All other institutions depended on the Church, whether in the political sphere, the family, economic activity, education, and so forth. The leading thinkers and philosophers of the time were religious philosophers, such as Saint Augustine and Saint Thomas Aquinas. In cultural expression the idea of God predominated: Art was religious art, music was religious music, poetry was religious poetry. Sorokin called this type of culture *ideational*.

On the other extreme of the pendulum swing is the nineteenth century, the climax of the *sensate* phase of Western civilization. During that period ultimate reality was defined in strictly materialistic terms; there was no reality beyond matter. The only reality was the one that could be apprehended by the five senses. The entire epoch was defined and integrated in a manner around this central conception. The Church was no longer the master institution of society. In its place the secular state was firmly established as the defining social reality. Theology was no longer the "queen of the sciences." It was replaced by the natural physical sciences. Religion and religious institutions became marginalized, irrelevant leftovers of the discredited Middle Ages.

Almost all leading thinkers of the period were declared atheists, celebrating the triumph of rationality and science and the liberation of the human mind from the shackles of religious superstitions. The nineteenth-century philosophers discovered the heavens to be empty. Many of them were happy with that discovery and thought of it as a form of liberation. But a few, like Friedrich Wilhelm Nietzsche, himself an atheist, gloomily accepted, prior to his nervous breakdown, the death of God as a historical calamity, and prophesied the unleashing of diabolical forces for the century yet to come. God became either the projection of unconscious and unresolved fears, the tool of ruling classes to keep the oppressed in check, or a projection of society. In any event God was dead forever, irreversibly.

The artists expressed this belief by focusing on the beauty of physical nature, and before photography was invented they tried to portray it in as "objective" and detailed a way as possible. Scientific, objective knowledge became the defining "paradigm" of the age. The nineteenth century reached a high level of cultural integration around the conception of the ultimacy and supremacy of physical, material Nature and the cognitive superiority of the senses.

Sorokin claimed that in between these two poles there was another phase, another form of integration, that combines the two polar opposites. He called this phase of civilization *idealistic*. Its presence is brief but it must also reach a climax and eventually decline, making way for either of the other two poles, the sensate or the ideational.

The best example of the idealistic phase of Western civilization is the Golden Age of Periclean Athens. Reality there was defined as both divine and profane and the preoccupation of the philosopher or the artist was to portray the "ideal form," whether it be an ideal republic or an ideal beauty. What was important for the sculptor was not the creation of a statue of a woman or man but rather the creation of an art piece that would portray the ideal beauty, as if a divine principle of beauty had acquired form and shape in the hands of the artist. The Parthenon was built at the climax of the idealistic expression of Western civilization, a most "perfect" building honoring the goddess Athena.

But what preoccupied Sorokin most was the inexorable movement between the sensate and the ideational poles or the sensate and ideational definitions of ultimate reality. The history of the West, he claimed, was neither the history of progress nor the history of rise and decline. Rather, the West had been oscillating between the ideational pole and the sensate, and it will continue to do so for the indefinite future.

Sorokin started his analysis from the Homeric period of about 1500 B.C. At the peak of that period when the *Iliad* was written human affairs were directly controlled by the gods. Different gods took favor with different heroes and the latter listened to them and saw them leading and guiding them into battle. Nothing of significance in this world was the product of chance. If we accept Julian Jaynes's thesis,[4] the Homeric heroes actually listened to voices in their heads, which they interpreted as voices of the gods. Literally guided in their actions by these voices, ancient humans were like "schizophrenics" listening to voices. Schizophrenics today are throwbacks to that earlier period in human history when listening to voices was normal—or so says Jaynes, of Princeton's Department of Psychology.

The original ideational phase of Western civilization, according to Sorokin, reached its climax at a certain point after which it eventually began to "decline"—that is, it moved away from integration. All civilizations, Sorokin claimed, are under the influence of two axiomatic principles, the "principle of immanent change" and the "principle of limits." The principle of immanent change stipulates that civilizations are constantly changing from within, either toward greater forms of cultural integration or away from such integration. Everything is in a state of flux, nothing stands still.

The principle of limits stipulates that as a civilization moves to higher forms of integration be it ideational, sensate, or idealistic, it will reach a limit beyond which any further and higher form of integration is impossible. Once that limit is reached, then due to the ongoingness of immanent change a reversible trend will begin, away from integration and toward disintegration. But this movement away from the pinnacle of integration will reach its own limit of disintegration at which point a reversible process will begin toward integration, a new phase on the historical pendulum.

Thus when the ideational Homeric period reached its peak, the turn to disintegration opened the way to the new phase of integration, namely the idealistic Golden Age of about 400 B.C. But that period too underwent its own rise and decline and a new sensate period began to emerge, the Hellenistic period of the Sophists, Stoics, and Epicureans that reached its climax and peak during the Roman period. That in its own turn began to disintegrate, lose its cultural integration and thus pave the way for the ideational period of the Holy Roman Empire and the theocratic Middle Ages. After the decline of the Middle Ages there was a brief period of idealistic culture during Dante's time and then the long movement toward the sensate phase of Western civilization with its scientific, industrial, and political revolutions reaching a climax of integration during the nineteenth century.

Sorokin claimed that the twentieth century is at the declining slope of the sensate phase of Western civilization—a position we have in common with the Roman period. He argued that during periods of the disintegration of sensate culture there are excessive expressions of violence, civil disturbances, and wars.

After writing his *Social and Cultural Dynamics* Sorokin devoted his energies to advocating a "smoother transition" toward the ideational pole—a movement he considered inevitable. Right in the heat of the Second World War Sorokin was prophesying the inevitable ascent of a new age of spiritual renaissance.

From the academic citadel of Harvard, Sorokin waged a relentless battle against the materialism of a sensate civilization and, like so many other Russian writers and mystics, never hid his preference for a more spiritual, ideational culture, which he considered the next movement of the historical pendulum. Sorokin thundered like an Old Testament prophet against what he perceived as the rampant sensuous avarice and consumerism of his adopted country. He argued for a mobilization to make the transition to the ideational pole less devastating—human will, by understanding the historical process at work, could intervene to make the transition less painful.

The explosion of atomic bombs over Japan fueled Sorokin's missionary zeal. For the first time it seemed that the historical pendulum might come to a final and irreversible halt. Nero burned Rome but even he could not burn the world. Western civilization had in the past survived and transformed itself toward new forms of cultural integration, but the potential appearance of modern Neros at the helm of nuclear-armed states seemed to put the transition to the ideational pole at risk. He concluded that men and women of goodwill and compassion must be mobilized to work for the increase of altruistic love as the key ingredient for the survival of human civilization—through love and altruism he hoped that the depths of the decline of sensate culture could be navigated.

The social sciences, Sorokin complained, have placed the greatest emphasis on the study of social pathology. All our conceptions of society and the individual are based on these studies. But what was more important, he argued, was the study of what was positive, the study of the ways that love and altruism could transform both individuals and society. After his retirement Sorokin set up the Harvard Center for the Study of Creative Altruism. It lasted only as long as he was alive.

The phenomenon of the New Age movement that has created so much upheaval among so many orthodox scientists and religious leaders may in fact be the transition to a different form of cultural integration. When Sorokin made his predictions in the late thirties and early forties there was no New Age movement as such. The general consensus among historians and social scientists was that the secular age was the climax of an evolutionary process in human consciousness that began from the depths of ignorance, superstition, and barbarism and led to the modern secular, rational scientific age. Works like those of Sorokin, though praised for their originality and historical and philosophical depth, could not be taken very seriously because they were not based on "testable propositions." And when Sorokin thundered that social scientists suffered from the mental malady of "testomania" and "quantophrenia"[5] and were therefore blinded to the most important issues of our times, he was condemned to sociological irrelevance. Yet, a year before his death, Sorokin was elected president of the American Sociological Association, in recognition of his massive contributions to modern thought.

I have often told my colleagues that I consider Sorokin, like Jung, a formidable, yet unrecognized, precursor to the contemporary resurgence of interest in spirituality, a sociological prophet of ideational culture and the New Age. The lack of coherence and integration both for the emerging New Age and the sensate culture that it presumably undermines is a state of affairs that Sorokin predicted fifty years ago. And his concept of the "supraconscious,"[6] as the source of higher creativity and a higher source of consciousness than either the subconscious or the conscious of Freud, predates Abraham Maslow and humanistic psychology, as well as its offshoot transpersonal psychology.

I had been so carried away with nostalgia about my graduate years and my immersion into Sorokin's thought that I had almost forgotten the collection of critical essays resting idly on my lap, and the awesome fact that I was thirty-five thousand feet above the Atlantic speeding through the sky at the unbelievable speed of six hundred miles an hour. Dinner had already been served and most passengers were preparing either to sleep or to watch the in-flight movie, which I had already seen. I turned my light on and immersed myself in reading.

According to the introduction, the so-called New Age movement attained national attention after Andrew Greeley, an American sociologist, published a survey showing that there was some kind of "spiritual revolution" going on in the country. With the assistance of the University of Chicago's National Opinion Research Council, Greeley reported in the January/February 1987 issue of *American Health* magazine that 67 percent of those surveyed reported having experienced extrasensory perception (ESP), 31 percent had experienced clairvoyance, 29 percent had "visions," and 42 percent had some "contact with the dead." Greeley reported that those who experienced such "paranormal" abilities were neither "religious nuts" nor psychiatric cases. On the contrary they were on the whole above average in education and intelligence and somewhat less than average in religious involvement.

I found these findings consistent with my own personal non-quantitative observations of the people who have reported to me on their nonordinary experiences. But for the Skeptical Inquirers such statistics are warning signals of the advance of the irrational into American culture and the fear that because so many intelligent people are reporting such experiences the scientific enterprise itself is threatened. These experiences are "uncorroborated by science" according to the author, and therefore (the underlying message goes) they lack a basis of reality.

"Evidence for . . . psychic powers, reincarnation, telekinesis, trance-channeling, and so forth is weak indeed, certainly no more conclusive than the evidence for Jesus' bodily resurrection: New Age belief grows from faith, not from evidence that the world at large can witness and replicate."[7] This conclusion is highly questionable. The evidence for and the reality of "psi" (from the term psychic ability) has been amply researched and documented by scientific researchers for over a hundred years. Only a true believer in scientific materialism could deny this information. Even *Nova*, the serious and prestigious public television science program, has addressed the issue with a verdict overwhelmingly and unequivocally in support of psi. It is spurious to equate the voluminous material on psi research and the scientific evidence for it with the Christian belief in the resurrection of Jesus' body. Yet this is the position of the Skeptical Inquirers. One gets the feeling that it is a hopeless task to convince the die-hard skeptics. No matter what evidence you may parade in front of them, they will not regard it, like a born-again fundamentalist unwilling to consider the case in support of evolution.

The author went on to assault Shirley MacLaine—as if the celebrated actress represented the top of some hierarchy of the New Age. She quoted MacLaine as saying that she lost interest in politics and public affairs once she found spirituality, that they had become largely irrelevant to her. MacLaine was quoted as saying, "Why vote, or why march, when all suffering serves good karmic purpose, when we'll all be reincarnated, when supernatural entities are coming to rescue us?"

Poor Shirley! I thought. She had become a convenient scapegoat. The perennial philosophy, the Hermetic tradition, the Vedic philosophy of India, Taoism, Buddhism, Christian mysticism, and all the great esoteric teachings of East and West rise or fall on the public statements, personal actions, reputation, and literary productions of an American Hollywood star.

Had the Skeptical Inquirers just directed their assault on the commercialization of spirituality, on the corruption of self-proclaimed gurus, on the spreading of suspect and downright bizarre cults offering instant gratification and effortless enlightenment, they would have provided a badly needed service. But what they assault are all forms of spirituality, authentic or inauthentic, as threats to rationality and Western civilization itself. The tragic irony of it is that they are totally unsuspicious of the irrational foundations of their own self-assured, unbending positivistic beliefs and dogmas.

As I went further into the book I realized the Skeptical Inquirers had little ability to discriminate, to distinguish that which is real and authentic from that which is false and inauthentic. Thus *A Course in Miracles*,[8] the celebrated channeled inspirational work of two Columbia University psychologists, is downgraded and ridiculed in the same breath as some quaint fringe channeler that pours out nonsense in California.

The author goes so far as to suggest that by not having a unified core philosophy the so-called New Age is even more of a threat to modern rational culture. "Having repudiated drugs and politics, the New Age is much less defined than the counterculture. . . . But the movement's amorphousness is the reason it is more, not less, powerful than earlier countercultures were. Slippery and insistent, the movement can co-opt and disown single-issue movements easily; it can disguise itself in order to insinuate itself into mainstream institutions."

This type of reaction reminded me of a newspaper clipping I had in my briefcase. I pulled it out and compared it with what the Skeptical Inquirers were saying. The piece was from the December 1990 and January 1991 issues of the monthly newspaper *Orthodox Observer*, published by the Greek Orthodox Church of North and South America. A Father Philip Armstrong had written on "New

Age—A New Heresy." The most orthodox father wrote with alarm:

"During the past few years, my attention has been captured by a suspect movement which has experienced phenomenal growth and an ever-increasing realm of societal influence. The term most frequently associated with this movement is 'New Age' . . . My first encounter with the New Age Movement took place in an unassuming bookstore in Boston. As I was browsing, I could not help but notice there was an entire section devoted to the title-heading, New Age. Leafing through several of the books in this section, I became horrified by what I read. I discovered . . . the frightful foundation of a new Gnostic religion that would prove dangerously enticing to the easily influenced American populace. After setting the texts down, I began to notice other peculiar objects not usually displayed in bookstores—crystals, pyramids to be worn on chains, and rainbow decals. When I left the store that afternoon, little did I realize how quickly this movement would spread, not only in America, but throughout the world."

The good father went on to sound the alarm.

"Today, the movement has expanded to include the following organizations: The Lucis Trust, Amnesty International, the Stanford Research Institute (SRI), and the Dorian Association. Even the Guardian Angels, a para-military organization, are linked to it. . . . The movement has further infiltrated our society as well as our churches by using vehicles such as Holistic Health Centers, Montessori schools, Waldorf education, Transcendental Meditation (TM), mind-control courses, hunger projects and the Whole Earth catalogue. This movement is also heavily involved in many social causes, as well as research and experimentation in astral projection, channeling, 'Harmonic Convergence,' para-psychology, and psychic predictions. People from all walks of life, including the highest tiers of the corporate world and public service, are found among its ranks. It is difficult to determine how far the tentacles of the New Age Movement have reached because it lacks a formal structure."

The father then went on to outline what he perceived as the dangerous and heretical principles of this movement: belief in one's personal salvation without the need of a church, reincarnation, the universality of all religions, and the creation of a "mandatory New World religion." "Contemplating this agenda sends shivers up and down one's spine. The movement wants complete control over all public and private life under the guise of noble and humanitarian auspices."

I put the paper back in my briefcase and sighed. Finally, I thought with sadness mixed with amusement, mainstream religion and mainstream science are joining forces to fight a common satan, the New Age movement. I wondered what Sorokin would have said had he been alive today. A thinker who was never accused of modesty, Sorokin would have thundered "I told you so!" The New Age movement that has caused so much alarm to orthodox believers and unbelievers alike is symptomatic of the final breakdown of sensate culture and the beginnings of the march toward the ideational pole of cultural integration.

I felt tired. The Skeptical Inquirers had kept me preoccupied for several hours while most of the other passengers slept. London was only an hour and forty-five minutes away. I turned my light off— even fifteen minutes of sleep could inject me with enough energy to be able to function at the airport. I planned to continue with the Skeptical Inquirers while in London.

"Straighten your seat, please, and fasten your seat belt." I felt the gentle tapping on my shoulder as the air hostess tried to wake me up. In fifteen minutes we were due to land at Heathrow Airport.

# 6

## PIONEERS

I SPENT THE FOLLOWING TWO DAYS RESTING IN LONDON AND adjusting to the new time zone at the suburban home of Emily's brother, a Cypriot businessman. He was in charge of the London office of the Cyprus cooperatives for distribution of island produce (potatoes, carrots, grapes, watermelons, lemons, oranges, etc.) into the British and European markets. While Emily visited friends in downtown London I stayed home to complete my imaginary debate with the Skeptical Inquirers before boarding the plane for Cyprus the next day. It was one of those unlikely sunny days that could fool a first-time visitor about the typical weather conditions in that great metropolis. I sat outside in the well-groomed and spacious backyard and returned to the book.

I zeroed in on an article, by Paul Edwards, about karma and reincarnation, a topic of central concern for me, and for mystical religion in general.[1] The editors in their introductory remarks praised the essay as "the most powerful critique of karma and reincarnation ever written." Presumably since these two concepts are at the core of the belief system of the New Age movement, assaulting such concepts undermines the very foundation of the movement. The editors who claimed that they were offering a balanced "objective" collection of essays on this phenomenon inform the reader that "Paul Edwards dismantles this kind of rhetorical turpitude [karma and reincarnation] with immaculate rigor. . . . Edwards finds them empirically unverifiable, logically untenable, and morally insulting." So much for objectivity, I thought.

The author of the article, to his credit, dismisses the crude version of reincarnation that stipulates that some souls may reincarnate into animals or even plants and minerals. Instead he focuses his critique on the most sophisticated version of this doctrine, that a human personality can reincarnate only as a human being. As far as I know this is the position of all the serious esoteric teachings.

But alas, a few paragraphs into his essay Edwards makes a serious error by assuming that the doctrine in its most sophisticated form stipulates that the souls of individuals that inhabit their bodies have no beginning and stretch infinitely into the past. ". . . reincarnationism is opposed to any doctrine of 'special creation' of souls. It denies that 'new souls' are ever added to the world. All souls have always existed. Every birth is a rebirth—the rebirth of a soul that has already existed."

He quotes the Bhagavad Gita, the sacred book of India: "the eternal in man cannot die" and "We have all been for all time: I, and thou, and those kings of men. And we all shall be for all time, we all for ever and ever." Obviously the author makes no distinction between "beingness" and "existence," no distinction between Spirit, which according to esoteric teachings has no beginning and no end, and the Soul, which does have a beginning with the first incarnation into the worlds of polarity. Spirit is the God within, which by definition has no beginning and no end, whereas the Soul, extending all the way to the permanent and present personality, is the way that the Spirit manifests itself within the lower worlds. I was certain that the sages who wrote the Bhagavad Gita, which has inspired hundreds of generations since its appearance, had that in mind. Spirit is the "I AM I" that was never born and will never die, not the individual as present personality.

Further down Edwards noted, ". . . the notion of a disembodied mind seems to many philosophers quite incoherent; but even if it is not incoherent, it seems incompatible with the evidence from neurology concerning the dependence of consciousness on the brain." The author went on to state that "There is not the slightest reason to suppose that in order to explain the extraordinary gifts of men like Mozart . . . we have to go outside the study of the human brain. It should be remembered that in spite of the impressive progress of recent years, brain research is still in its infancy. I think very few brain researchers have any serious doubts that with further improvements in our instruments we will be able to shed much light on these problems. It seems entirely plausible, for example, that Mozart's auditory cortex was in certain ways significantly different from that of people lacking his gifts."

This may be what the Skeptical Inquirers want fervently to be true, but it is not what the greatest philosophers and scientists of history have said or believed. In my mind flashed the names of several of the greatest philosophers of the West: Pythagoras, Plato, Socrates, Aristotle, Aquinas, Kant, Hegel, Schopenhauer, Heidegger, not to mention great scientists like Newton (yes, even Newton), Kepler, Einstein, and David Bohm. All of them took for granted the reality of God and the existence of "mind" independent of bodies. So with the exception of Nietzsche, Russell, and Sartre, who are the "many philosophers" the author has in mind? And what if we take into account the great minds of the East from Shankara and Patanjali to Sri Aurobindo? To my knowledge, we shall not find a single name that questioned the reality of a Reality behind the transient world of phenomena, of *maya*. Alas, the materialists, the positivists, and reductionists who have taken over the leadership of our intellectual and cultural life during the last 150 years have tried relentlessly to convince us that their crippled view of the world is the only legitimate view and anybody who thinks otherwise is a threat to rationality and civilization.

As far as "the evidence from neurology" goes, some leading scientists have drawn exactly the opposite conclusions, that mind cannot be explained by the brain. Dr. Wilder Penfield, the famous brain researcher, pointed out in *The Mystery of the Mind*[2] that for most of his life he was a total materialist believing that mind cannot exist independently of the brain. Yet on the basis of his research he recognized that certain functions of mind could not possibly be explained on the basis of the material brain. That led him to the conclusion that the mind cannot be contained within the brain and that the latter is simply a vehicle for the former. One reviewer of his book stated that "[*The Mystery of the Mind*] . . . is Wilder Penfield's apology for his belated conversion from monism to dualism. That may not sound like much, but Professor Penfield, now at the end of his career as a pioneering neurosurgeon and explorer of the brain, has come to the conclusion that brain and mind are separate entities and that, while the mind is ordinarily dependent on the brain for its activity, it cannot be explained entirely by brain mechanisms. In a field where many workers will not even admit the existence of nonphysical realities like mind, that is quite a conclusion." The reviewer concludes: "I once heard a Hindu yogi tell a group of Western scientists that 'all of the brain is contained within the mind, but not all of the mind is in the brain.' To hear a Western neurosurgeon say something similar is most remarkable."[3]

This is the type of reasoning that is causing the poor Skeptical Inquirers to suffer from apoplexy, I thought, and laughed to myself.

Larry Dossey, a medical researcher and practicing physician, has done us all a great service with his *Recovering the Soul: A Scientific and Spiritual Search*.[4] As a physician, Dossey has often faced events and miraculous cures in his patients that he could not explain by conventional science. Drawing from the latest research, he synthesized the ideas of leading scientists such as Schrödinger, Einstein, Gödel, and Margenau, with the insights of the perennial philosophy. In doing so he presented convincing evidence for a "nonlocal," holistic view of mind, and according to reputable critics "proof of the existence of the soul."

Just before I left Maine my friend Professor Robert Sollod of Cleveland State University sent me a photocopy of the latest *Brain/ Mind Bulletin* (January 1990) with an attached note: "Thought this would be of interest." The *Brain/Mind Bulletin* reports news from the leading edge of research on matters related to that subject. On the first page of that particular issue they reported extraordinary research results on the ability of one individual to mentally affect the physical state of another individual: "Texas researchers using a stringent testing method . . . say that based on a series of introductory experiments, such an effect does indeed exist. William Braud and Marilyn Schlitz of the Mind Science Foundation in San Antonio reported recently that in 13 carefully designed preliminary tests, one person's imagery coincided with another's physiological state vastly more often than chance or known bodily rhythms would predict." That is, under controlled conditions subjects could influence the brain waves of other subjects in another location without any physical contact between the two.

The Texas researchers went on to conclude: "We do think that psychosomatic factors are very important in healing. . . . But since our study was designed to prevent them from playing any part, the results suggest the existence of a separate mechanism through which healing and other kinds of influence work. Obviously, it's hard to explain what we found through traditional scientific means, so we don't understand at this point how it happens. But the effect is clearly there."

Then the authors offered certain tentative conclusions: (a) The ability to produce and receive the imagery must be widespread; (b) the effect can occur at a distance; (c) the recipient need not know attempts are being made; and (d) the effect does not always occur.[5]

A similar pioneer study appeared earlier in the July 1988 *Southern Medical Journal*. It was carried out by the cardiologist Dr. Randolph Byrd, on the faculty of the University of California Medical School at San Francisco. Professor Byrd explored the possible impact of prayer on four hundred heart patients. He divided them into two groups, the control group and the experimental group. The patients in the latter were prayed for, whereas the former were not. The first names and a brief description of their condition were given to several prayer groups in various parts of the United States. They were asked to pray for those patients every day for a certain period of time. The results were statistically significant, an extraordinary phenomenon. The patients that were prayed for were considerably less likely to develop congestive heart failure and five times less likely to require antibiotics. Also, none in the prayed-for group required "endotracheal intubation" (artificial breathing tube) and fewer developed pneumonia. What makes this study so important is the fact that the researcher followed the most stringent scientific procedures, including randomization, and conducted a double-blind experiment in which neither the patients, nurses, nor doctors knew which group the patients were in. Dr. Larry Dossey, commenting on the importance of the experiment, pointed out that "This rigorous study suggests that something about the mind allows it to intervene in the course of *distant* happenings. . . . In this prayer study the degree of spatial separation did not seem to matter."[6] Dossey concluded that the mind is not confined within the brain: the latter is a vehicle for the expression of the former. It is not the mind that is inside the brain: the brain is inside the mind.

Of course these research projects and publications are causing the most severe reaction from the Skeptical Inquirers, who systematically anathematize and dismiss such valiant endeavors with the convenient label of "pseudoscience," undermining the readiness of foundations to support this kind of research and forcing many re-

searchers to shy away from such projects. Alas, the Skeptical Inquirers quite often have the effect of undermining the work of
pioneers who labor at the furthest frontiers of contemporary
thought.

Back to the topic of karma and reincarnation. I plowed further
into the *Critical Essays*. The author refers to and quotes from the
eighteenth-century agnostic philosopher David Hume, who claimed
that when you compare the theory of karma and reincarnation to
the traditional Christian view of eternal hell and damnation, the
former is on balance superior. After all, a loving God could not
possibly send most of humanity to the eternal misery envisioned by
hell-and-damnation evangelists. But the recognition that reincarnation is an improvement over hell-and-damnation beliefs does not
make reincarnation any truer, according to the author. Fair enough.
But then the author proceeds to dismantle karma and reincarnation
as "morally indefensible and downright repugnant" in themselves,
as well as empirically false.

The author finds the notion that what happens to a person is the
result of prior lives, or karmic reasons, morally indefensible. For
him it is as if one would blame the victim for being a victim. You
suffer because you deserve it. You must have done something hor-
rible in a previous life. And if you lead a good life it means that you
are rewarded for previously good deeds. For the author this is absurd. It justifies all sorts of injustices and legitimizes all sorts of
unjust institutions such as the caste system in India and presumably
slavery itself.

The moral foundation of karma, according to him, is no more
sound than the social Darwinism of the early part of this century.
"The emptiness of the Karmic theory can be seen most clearly if
we compare it to another pseudoscientific theory that on analysis
turns out to be completely empty. I am thinking of social Darwinism
as advocated . . . by the American sociologist William Graham Sum-
ner." The latter preached that only the fit should survive and that

social classes owe each other nothing. Those who are at the bottom of the society in fact deserve to be there either because of karma, according to the Eastern notion, or because they are not fit to survive, according to the social Darwinists.

I thought it interesting that the author would dismiss the law of karma as a "pseudoscientific" theory. Belief in karma preceded the invention of the scientific method by several thousand years, and the sages who presented their insights to the world never argued the validity of that insight on the basis of scientific thinking, which has come into existence only during the last two to three hundred years.

Historically, beliefs about karma did become popular among ruling classes, which employed and distorted them to legitimize their domination and injustices. But to dismiss karma and reincarnation as morally absurd on the basis of such social and historical abuses is like blaming Jesus for the Inquisition. The law of karma, according to esoteric teachings, is nothing more than the law of cause and effect. And this notion is found not only in the teachings of the great oriental mystics but also within Judeo-Christian civilization. In the words of Saint Paul: "Brethren, be not deceived. God is not mocked, for whatsoever a man soweth that shall he also reap." Obviously that could not work only in a short lifetime. Had it meant that the statement would not make any logical sense. Of course this karmic law can and does work in the short term. But it is only when the notion of repeated lives is inferred that Jesus' reprimand of Peter "if you live by the sword you shall die by the sword" would make any sense. After all, many murderers and tyrants do die peacefully in old age.

The author's moral objection to karma is the notion that the world is ultimately just. "The vacuousness, as far as moral prescriptions are concerned," the author writes, "follows from the Karmic doctrine that the world is just. A Karmic believer's commitment to this proposition is unqualified. . . . He maintains that the world *is* just regardless of what in fact we do. No matter what happens, whether we help the underdog or not, whether our efforts at making lives less full of suffering and sorrow succeed or not, the ultimate outcome will be just, in the sense that every human being will be getting exactly—no more and no less than—what he deserves." It is more rational therefore, according to the author, to accept that morally the world is absurd (how else can we explain atrocities in history such as the Holocaust?) and act to ameliorate this absurdity.

The problem, I think, with this type of reasoning is twofold. First, it is based on the assumption that the workings and details of karma ought to be understood and be accessible to ordinary logic, in order for karma to claim a basis in reality. The Skeptical Inquirers assume that that which cannot be understood by ordinary scientific logic cannot be true. Perhaps it is for this reason that intellectual arguments on such topics cannot persuade anyone. That there are certain truths that an individual has to apprehend not only with one's logic but also with one's being in its totality is an unacceptable idea to many.

Second, the Skeptical Inquirers consider absurd the notion that when one suffers it is necessarily the product of some past sin. Presumably no innocent person could then be caused to suffer wrongly. If that were the case, then we would conclude that the many martyrs in history, including Jesus Himself as well as Paul and Peter, deserved their punishment. I believe to a large extent this problem is based on a false interpretation of the law of karma. According to the esoteric teachings, rather than the popular versions that the Skeptical Inquirers keep referring to, there are no such things as rewards and punishments externally imposed. According to the theory of elementals, for example, whatever energies we project outward, in terms of thoughts, feelings, and actions, ultimately return to us, not as punishments but as part of the physics of elementals and the mechanism through which human beings acquire experiences for their spiritual evolution. It is for this reason that all the great teachers have advocated the golden rule—that is, the "Do unto others as you would have them do unto you"—for in reality according to these teachings whatever we do we ultimately do to ourselves.

Now the Skeptical Inquirers invoke morality as one of the arguments to refute karma and reincarnation. But there is a certain fundamental contradiction in doing so. On what moral grounds do they themselves stand when the logical consequence of their antispiritual and totally materialistic posture is not morality but the annihilation of every value? In fact their moral arguments are based, without their realizing it of course, on the very moral principles that they are trying to refute. After all, where do their humanistic values, passions, and concerns come from if not from the teachings of such great masters of humanity, such as Buddha, Krishna, Pythagoras, Socrates, Plato, and so on? It was these very sages who taught of the workings of the law of cause and effect and the evolution of the soul through a series of lives, not as theories but as facts of life, accessible as knowledge to anyone who is a serious researcher of the truth.

The author goes on to raise questions on "Karmic Administration Problems," such as who keeps score of all the details that makes possible the presumed workings of karma. Is there some kind of cosmic computer that serves as a clearinghouse so that one gets exactly what one deserves? This suggestion was made in a mocking tone, so as to expose the absurdity of karma. My immediate reaction to that idea was to note on the margin of the book, "I will tell you if you tell me who was behind the Big Bang that set our universe into motion!"

Paul Edwards as well as other writers in the volume thundered against the fad of past-life regression as "the grand illusion." What is happening in these experiences, they claim, has nothing to do with past lives but is "cryptoamnesia"—events and experiences in our lives register in our subconscious, then, by hypnotic means, the individual "regresses" into past experiences of *this* life, which come to the surface in the form of "memories of past lives." This is precisely what Erevna teaches on this form of experimentation. "When people try through artificial means to remember past incarnations," Kostas told me once, "in reality what they are entering into most often is their subconscious." It is said, according to Erevna, that only very advanced souls can actually remember past lives. Memory is awakened at a point when such memories will not create a disturbance in the present personality. That is why it is unwise to prematurely awaken the past. Oblivion is a form of divine mercy allowing the personality to focus on the present incarnation without the intrusion of memories of past status, problems, and tragedies. Oblivion in this case is needed for one's spiritual evolution.

By focusing on questionable cases the Skeptical Inquirers conclude that past-life remembrance is a "grand illusion" and the idea of the continuity of human consciousness beyond the material body is a mirage. Similarly, the "objective" Skeptical Inquirers would focus on cases of reincarnation which could easily be proven false, and arrive at similar dismissive conclusions. I have noticed that scientific researchers in the pursuit of evidence against either reincarnation or nonmedical healing commonly build their arguments on the dismantling of cases that the more serious Researchers for the Truth would themselves dismiss.

In the voluminous collection of *Not Necessarily the New Age* I found no discussion of one of the most spectacular cases on nonmedical healing, one which could provide perhaps indirect support of the type of healing that the Skeptical Inquirers consider "impossible." As I was turning one page after another I saw no reference to the case of the Brazilian villager Arigo, whose incredible healings have been well documented and also videotaped by medical researchers, astounded by the healing phenomena he caused.

John G. Fuller's account of *Arigo*[7] is a breathtaking document of probably the most spectacular case of nonmedical healing of this century. In Brazil the name Arigo is even more famous and generates deeper emotions than that of Pelé, the legendary soccer champion. Yet it is hardly known by North Americans and Westerners in general. It was after I had written on such matters myself that this work came to my attention—my friend Demetrios, an acupuncturist from New Bedford, mailed it to me after reading my books.

The case is so diligently documented—with verification by medical doctors, photographs, newspaper clippings, names of persons healed, dates of the healing episodes—and written by John G. Fuller, a respectable American researcher and writer, that there cannot remain the slightest suspicion that the story is a hoax. Naturally a Skeptical Inquirer would prefer not to mention such a case and would focus on easier targets.

Arigo was a humble man with a third-grade education from the village of Congonhas do Campo. A deeply religious man, he began one night to experience full-scale hallucinations after a period during which he suffered from excruciating headaches. A fat, bald-headed doctor who identified himself as Dr. Adolpho Fritz appeared in front of him during his hallucination. He told Arigo that he had died during the First World War and that his work on earth had never been completed. He further reported to Arigo that he and a group of other spirits who were also doctors had been observing him for a long time and, realizing his generosity and goodness of heart, had chosen him as a vehicle to carry on their work on earth. The experience for Arigo was so real and disturbing to him that he ran into the streets naked. Medical doctors found no problem with him and he eagerly sought the help of both the local priest and several psychiatrists. The latter found no problem with Arigo, either. But Dr. Fritz continued to make his appearance and persisted in trying to make Arigo accept the role of becoming a vehicle of these discarnate doctors. If Arigo was to find any peace, he would have to begin healing the sick and troubled people who needed his services.

When Arigo finally succumbed to the pressure his headaches disappeared. He eventually became a legend as he got to the point where he healed, on the average, without exaggeration, three hundred people a day. People came to him with all sorts of maladies, journeying from all over Brazil and other Latin American countries. It's equally remarkable that Arigo, under the strict instructions of Dr. Fritz, never accepted any money for his services.

Arigo's fame attracted the attention of the medical community and of Dr. Henry Puharich, a medical doctor from New York. Puharich traveled to Congonhas and, with his colleagues, videotaped some of Arigo's extraordinary feats. He would enter into a state of semitrance and then, speaking with a German accent, would not only give complicated diagnosis and prescriptions that worked, but carried out on the spot difficult surgical operations using nothing more than a knife from his kitchen. He conducted these operations without any anesthesia or prior sterilization of the knife.

Here is how John Fuller describes the first episode in which Dr. Puharich witnessed Arigo's medical interventions:

> Suddenly and without ceremony, he [Arigo] roughly took the first man in line—an elderly, well-dressed gentleman in an impeccable gray sharkskin suit, firmly grasped his shoulders, and held him against the wall, directly under the sign THINK OF JESUS. Puharich, standing next to the man, was startled by the action, wondered what to expect next. Then, without a word, Arigo picked up a four-inch stainless steel paring knife . . . and literally plunged it into the man's left eye, under the lid and deep up into the eye socket.
>
> In spite of his years of medical practice and experience, Puharich was shocked and stunned. He was even more so

when Arigo began violently scraping the knife between the ocular globe and the inside of the lid, pressing up into the sinus area with uninhibited force. The man was wide awake, fully conscious, and showed no fear whatever. He did not move or flinch. A woman in the background screamed. Another fainted. Then Arigo levered the eye so that it extruded from the socket. The patient, still utterly calm, seemed bothered by only one thing: a fly that had landed on his cheek. At the moment his eye was literally tilted out of its socket, he calmly brushed the fly away from his cheek.

As he made these motions, Arigo hardly looked at his subject, and at one point turned away to address an assistant while his hand continued to scrape and plunge without letup. In another moment, he turned away from the patient completely, letting the knife dangle half out of the eye.

Then he turned abruptly to Puharich and asked him to place his finger on the eyelid, so that he could feel the point of the knife under the skin. By this time, Puharich was almost in a state of shock, but he did so, clearly feeling the point of the knife through the skin. Quickly, Puharich asked one of the interpreters to ask the patient what he felt. The patient spoke calmly and without excitement, merely stating that although he was well aware of the knife, he felt no pain or discomfort.

Arigo, still speaking in a harsh German accent, told them that he often used this technique as either a diagnostic tool or for eye operations. To Puharich, this violated every medical technique he had known in his twenty years of experience since studying medicine at Northwestern. For Henry Belk [a companion of Dr. Puharich] who had studied psychology at Duke, the procedure was simply inconceivable. He felt limp and slightly nauseated.

Within a few moments, Arigo withdrew the paring knife

from the eye, bringing out with it a smear of pus on the point. He noted it with satisfaction, then unceremoniously wiped the knife on his sport shirt and dismissed the patient. "You will be well, my friend," he said. Then he called the next patient. The entire "examination" had taken less than a minute.[8]

Arigo always claimed that it was not he who was carrying out the healings but Dr. Fritz, and claimed that he remembered nothing of what he was doing during the healing sessions. Furthermore his German accent faded away once the day's healing episodes were over.

Arigo's fame soared after he healed a Brazilian senator by the name of Lucio Bittencourt, who never stopped talking about his miraculous surgical experience. The press picked it up and Arigo became a foremost topic of conversation in Brazil. Inadvertently this generated a reaction by the Brazilian Medical Association and the Catholic Church. The result was that Arigo ended up in jail for practicing medicine without a license. It was interesting to note, however, that none of the thousands of people that Arigo treated was ever harmed in spite of the efforts of his accusers to find such cases during the court proceedings.

The popular reaction was so intense that in seven months Arigo was pardoned by the then president Juscelino Kubitschek, who himself was a beneficiary of Arigo's healing powers. Arigo was then allowed to practice his exotic healings with the supervision of Brazilian doctors.

Arigo was such an extraordinary phenomenon that a team of American and Brazilian doctors headed by Dr. Puharich monitored and systematically studied him. To the delight of Arigo a hospital was in the process of being built in his own town in order to facilitate both his work and the doctors who were observing him. But it was not to be. Arigo died on January 11, 1971, in an auto accident at the age of forty-nine, and the project was canceled.


Coincidentally, I had learned firsthand about Arigo from two witnesses that met with me after reading my books, Professor Jacques Brack and Henry Belk, both from North Carolina and both longtime investigators into paranormal phenomena and friends of Dr. Puharich. Henry Belk, who was mentioned in John Fuller's book, accompanied Puharich in Brazil. He told me how shaken he was when he witnessed Arigo carry out surgery exactly the way Fuller described it. And Jacques Brack described to me in great detail his own investigation in Brazil into the Arigo phenomenon, and how he and a woman minister of the Spiritualist Church had "sensed" Arigo's moment of death as it took place twelve miles from where they stood.

The problem for the American and Brazilian doctors who observed Arigo was not the fact of his unbelievable healing abilities. These they witnessed and meticulously documented. The difficulty they faced was in how to explain it. Their training in Western medicine was of no use. What they observed could not be explained through conventional modes of thought. The physicians were at a loss as to how to cope with that extraordinary challenge.

Luis Rodriguez, a Brazilian intellectual thoroughly versed in Western thinking and psychiatry, and a reputed researcher of paranormal and spiritual phenomena, wrote a letter to the American team volunteering an explanation. For Rodriguez the real explanation is the explanation given by Arigo himself, that Dr. Fritz was in fact a discarnate spirit. Here are some extracts from the long eloquent letter of this respected Brazilian:

    . . . This close collaboration between Arigo and his discarnate friends cannot be understood and cannot possibly be repeated by others unless these basic hard facts of life are taken into account:

1. That man is an incarnate soul.
2. That this soul was *not* created at the time of birth.
3. That it has had many other lives on earth and that others will consequently follow.
4. That contact between the incarnate and discarnate persons has been taking place since man appeared on earth for the first time.
5. That the psychic faculty known as mediumship is the method devised by nature to establish this necessary and enlightening contact.
6. That primitive peoples all over the world are well acquainted with these simple facts of life.

What I have learned is that it behooves us to improve the nature of this contact by enhancing its reliability, and separating it from the superstitions involved in religious creeds, doctrines, or dogmas, from rites and rituals. Likewise, not to waste time with obdurate skepticism that retards progress by postulating pseudo-scientific explanations that explain nothing.[9]

Frustration with scientific dogmatism is a perennial problem that serious researchers who study paranormal phenomena experience once their research comes under fire from the Skeptical Inquirers. Cases like that of Arigo would normally be dismissed a priori on the assumption that what is reported cannot be true, and must be the result of human error or charlatanism. An objective and serious look at the evidence is never undertaken. The British philosopher-writer Colin Wilson, who was himself originally a skeptic, is right on the mark, I believe, when he laments the predicament of modern scientists who confront the issue of paranormal phenomena:

. . . Sceptical scientists living in London or New York have already concluded that the paranormal does not exist because it *cannot* exist. Almost without exception they would not take the trouble to go and see a psychic surgeon even if one lived round the corner: they tell you wearily that they know nothing will happen, or that if it does it will be trickery. All they *are* prepared to do is to consider the evidence at second hand, preferably in some easily digestible form, for they all lack patience, and then think up objections. And the result of their deliberations is then accepted by the rest of the scientific community as the unbiased conclusions of hard-headed scientists. In fact it is little more than a regurgitation of the opinions they have been expressing for years, opinions which are change-proof because the scientists have no intention whatever of studying the evidence.

Then Wilson proceeds to express his own position on the subject. "I could only endorse," he said, "the irritable comment made by the American researcher Professor James Hyslop, who remarked, 'I regard the existence of discarnate spirits as scientifically proved and I no longer refer to the sceptic as having any right to speak on the subject. Any man who does not accept the existence of discarnate spirits and the proof of it is either ignorant or a moral coward. I give him short shrift, and do not propose to argue with him on the supposition that he knows nothing about the subject.' "[10]

I flipped the pages of *Not Necessarily the New Age* to further absorb its critical wisdom. Over and over I noticed the same complaints by the various writers against the New Age—a perceived disrespect for science and rationality, unconcern with factual information, utter subjectivity, irrationalism, et cetera, et cetera.

Ted Schultz's article is typical.[11] Schultz, a biologist, considers as the main "recurrent" themes of the New Age: (1) Materialistic science and rationalism in general are the source for most of the evil in the world. (2) Objective truth is an illusion. (3) All knowledge originates from a spiritual plane "higher" or more important than the material world. (4) We are each "personally responsible" for the conditions of our lives. The author calls the last point "Shirley MacLaineism."

As far as the first complaint goes, that materialistic science is responsible for most of the evil in the world, there is a certain truth to the charge. If, for example, we manage to destroy the earth either through a nuclear holocaust or through an ecological catastrophe, then materialistic science certainly *would* share the primary blame for making that possible. After all, it is only through the cooperation of materialist scientists that either "smart" bombs or big dumb bombs can be built. And it is through the expertise and cheerful cooperation of scientists that deadly pollutants are created. What greater evil is there than what some ecologists call "ecocide," the destruction of our planet through either bombs or poisons.

At the same time, we desperately need science to help resolve the problems that it helped bring about. And it's also true that many New Agers do not perceive similar dangers in their own uncritical fascination with psychic powers and occultism. According to the perennial wisdom such powers may also be employed for evil purposes, consciously or unconsciously. It is for this reason that sages throughout history have warned against the frivolous indulgence in using these powers, often denouncing them as "demonic." The great universal traditions, from Patanjali to the early fathers of the Church to the present, have admonished their adherents about the importance of cultivating the spiritual part of the self. Overcome ego, purify yourself from egotistical self-indulgences, and then psychic powers will naturally unfold within you. According to Erevna, if you pursue the development of such knowledge and powers prematurely, through "technical means," then you run the risk of degenerating into an evil magician, harmful to others and to yourself. Therefore knowledge of and cultivation of psychic abilities, what the parapsychologists call "psi," must follow the spiritual awakening of the self.

The same admonition could perhaps apply to materialistic science. The problem is not with science itself. For after all, materialistic science deals with knowledge of how the gross material world operates, in itself a very worthy enterprise. The problem is that many scientists are in reality black "magicians" expressing varying degrees of good and evil. They have attained knowledge of the secrets of the gross material world and acquired awesome powers through "technical means" without first purifying their subconscious from egotistical desires. It is as foolish to advocate the abolition of scientific knowledge as it is to abolish knowledge about psychic abilities. But what one can insist upon is that the pursuit of and acquisition of power resulting from knowledge of either the psychic realms or the gross material level must parallel the spiritual development and awakening of the individual scientist.

"Objective truth is an illusion. . . ." This point is hammered over and over by Skeptical Inquirers as representing the universal beliefs of New Agers. Alan M. MacRobert in his article "New Age Hokum"[12] writes with a sense of resigned despair: "The real significance of the paranormal boom is that so many of us take it so uncritically. It is as if the question 'Is this so?' has become irrelevant—and has been replaced by the attitude, 'If it feels good, it must be right for me.' This is a very fundamental shift. That an objective reality exists outside our internal viewpoints, and that this objective reality is worth studying, is a relatively new idea in the history of the world. It did not gain a firm foothold until as late as the Renaissance, and though it rapidly led to the sciences that have transformed the world, perhaps this idea is more alien to human nature than we might think."

I doubt that serious thinkers and explorers of the so-called New Age movement would argue that objective reality does not exist. I can't imagine, for example, such thinkers as Ken Wilber, Colin Wilson, Marilyn Ferguson, Huston Smith, Barbara Brennan, Charles Tart, Matthew Fox, and Jean Houston coming up with such nonsense. By focusing on the statements of pop channelers, astrologers, and street-corner crystal peddlers the Skeptical Inquirers draw the absurd "scientific" generalization that in New Age thinking "there is neither morality nor reality. Everything is in accordance to your preferences and your subjective imagination." If anything, such thinking is the direct product of the utter relativism characteristic of an age that has lost its traditional transcendental moorings. And of course, with a host of scholars, philosophers, theologians, and anthropologists to choose from, the Skeptical Inquirers focus, for this "issue," almost exclusively on the writings of a Hollywood actress whom they have defined as an easy prey. Skeptical Inquirers as a rule would shy away from more difficult targets, such as Barbara Brennan, for example, mentioned above. As a former NASA scientist committed to objectively verifiable knowledge, she is at the same time an internationally recognized healer who has done an extraordinary job in bridging the gap between science and the healing arts that are at the core of New Age.[13]

From the point of view of all the great esoteric traditions—New Age and Old Age—the apprehension of "objective reality" is, in fact, the goal. The confusion of the Skeptical Inquirers lies with the premise that subjective experience cannot be "objective." It is taken as a basically unexamined axiom that one is the exact opposite of the other. Experiential knowledge is unverifiable with the instruments of science. Therefore, the reasoning of the materialist goes, it cannot be real. But even the most scientific, empirical knowledge has a subjective component to it. The scientists must "subjectively" agree that what they observe is true. There cannot be any scientific "objective truth" without the subjective agreement of scientific observers. And the scientists' collective agreements of what constitutes scientific truth has proven to be quite relative over time. What is scientifically true today may not be so tomorrow. And what may be considered "impossible" today may be accepted fact tomorrow.

Ever since Thomas Kuhn published his controversial opus *The Structure of Scientific Revolutions*[14] in the early sixties we have become quite conscious of the relativity of scientific truth itself. And this is precisely what the Skeptical Inquirers cannot tolerate—that scientific truth is not necessarily "objective" truth, valid for all time. And it is for this reason that serious philosophers and mystics would consider the truths of the perennial philosophy to be of a superior quality, since that type of knowledge *is* "timeless" and indeed valid for all time, and accessible to any serious student of esoteric practice. It is for this reason that philosophers like Huston Smith are emphatic about keeping the perennial philosophy independent of science, since the latter is bound by the vagaries of time and change.

In *Eye to Eye*[15] Ken Wilber identifies, with the precision of a logician, the three ways through which we, as human beings, can apprehend the world. Drawing on the work of philosophers and mystics Wilber shows that we obtain knowledge of the world through (a) the eye of the five senses, (b) the eye of reason, and (c) the eye of contemplation. These are three different domains through which knowledge can be apprehended. The eye of the senses is the means through which we perceive the external world of space, time, and objects. Empirical science is a historical invention, a method that has sharpened our capacity to observe and apprehend external objects. And those who have mastered this method have a privileged access to knowledge which they can share with one another. For example, two or more trained parasitologists can, through laboratory experiments, reach a scientific consensus that a particular virus is negatively affecting a certain type of potato. When the overwhelming majority of similarly trained parasitologists reach the same conclusion, then a parasitological scientific fact is established.

A similar procedure must be followed to establish a certain truth through the eye of the mind. Logic in philosophy and mathematics are examples. To be able to apprehend a certain truth in philosophy or logic or mathematics you must undergo long analogous training in these fields. In other words you must train the eye of the mind so that it may be able to see certain truths that someone who is not trained in such fields will not be able to perceive.

Similarly the eye of contemplation requires an analogous and arduous form of training before it can open up the "third eye" and see certain truths and realities that cannot be seen with the other two eyes. It is through this "third eye" of contemplation that we can comprehend the Divine realms within, something that neither the eye of the senses (science) nor the eye of the mind (philosophy/mathematics) can help us do. At the same time the eye of contemplation cannot tell us of any scientific truths that can be discovered in the laboratory of science.

Each domain, Wilber claims, is a legitimate domain of knowledge and a "category error" emerges when one perspective illegitimately invades the territory of another. For example, a pure rationalist like Descartes excluded all other forms of knowledge (empirical scientific and contemplative) and categorically asserted that there is only rational truth.

By the same token all the great religions committed "category error" by assuming that through the opening of the eye of contemplation it was possible to grasp the truth of the other two domains. Therefore, Justinian, the Byzantine emperor at Constantinople, shut down the schools of philosophy in Athens because he reasoned that philosophy was unnecessary and dangerous since the truth had already been revealed through Jesus Christ.

In a similar way the eye of the senses, i.e., modern empirical science, has come to dominate the other two eyes and attempted to reduce their insights to its own empirical measurements. The scientific method has become *scientism*, a dogmatic ideology—namely the belief that the only valid truth around is scientific truth. With the impressive successes of science the eye of the mind (philosophy) has become positivism, the philosophical position postulating that the only valid truth is "objective," external truth obtained through the experimental method. The eye of contemplation that can reveal the truth of "inner," higher spiritual space becomes debased by an imperial science and an emasculated philosophy that tries to conform to the expectations of experimental science.

Wilber points out how the eye of contemplation is sharpened with training analogous to that of the eye of the senses and the eye of the mind. That we can have what Rudolf Steiner described as a science of the spiritual worlds. All the serious students of mysticism have pointed out that spiritual knowledge, like all other forms of valid cognitive knowledge, "is experimental, repeatable, and publicly verifiable." This is so, says Wilber, because like all other valid modes of knowledge, it consists of three processes: a formula on what one must do to get certain results, the cognitive apprehension resulting after one follows the directions, and communal validation. The latter means that you must check your results, your experiences, with others who have taken up that particular practice.

"If you want to know about the actually transcendent realms themselves," wrote Wilber in *A Sociable God,*[16] "then take up a contemplative-meditative practice . . . and find out for yourself . . . at which point the all-inclusive community of transcendence may disclose itself in your case and be tested in the fire of the like-spirited." It is the same sober advice that Frits Staal, another serious student of mysticism, offers.[17] That the only viable way to explore the truths of the eye of contemplation is by taking up a contemplative practice yourself under the tutelage of an experienced teacher. It has been the way of all the esoteric traditions of all the great religions.

The Skeptical Inquirers, I thought, as Wilber's ideas flashed through my mind, are the imperial guards of the eye of the senses, barking in alarm as the eye of contemplation is attempting, in these declining decades of the sensate phase of Western culture, to make a comeback. It is making a comeback in the midst of a civilization that since the triumphant decades of the scientific revolution has decisively forced the contemplative mode underground.

When I heard noise at the door I put down the Skeptical Inquirers. My brother-in-law's two boisterous puppies, affectionately known as "the fat girls," sprang into action as Emily, her brother, and the rest of our two families returned from their sojourn to downtown London.

# 7

# FILTER OF
# AWARENESS

THE FIRST THING I DID UPON ARRIVING IN CYPRUS WAS CONTACT Kostas in Limassol. The week we arrived on the island he was involved with the bureaucratic legalities of setting up a new business related to the management of a gasoline station. We made arrangements to spend time together as soon as he was freed of his business problems. In the meantime I took the opportunity to enjoy a week's adventure at Akamas along with Emily and our two children.

Our friend Yianis, an associate of Kostas and a member of his circles, invited us to spend a few days at the mobile home he kept parked on a beach at the northwesternmost part of the island. To get there we had to drive through Paphos, the mythical birthplace of Aphrodite and the place where the Apostle Paul, tied to a pole by the local ruler, was allegedly given thirty-nine lashes for preaching Christianity and trying to convert the pagans.

The beach was six miles west of the picturesque town of Polis, right at the beginning of the Akámas peninsula, a yet unspoiled corner of Cyprus not far from the Turkish-occupied part of the island. Because of its remoteness relatively few tourists ventured there. The absence of luxury hotels and tourist accommodations was an irresistible attraction for Emily and myself, who longed for the

Cyprus of our youth. There were still open fields, and a significant number of local people made their living as farmers, shepherds, fishermen, and small-town traders, not as waiters, busboys, and developers. We knew, sadly, that we were witnessing and enjoying the last vestiges of a world that was rapidly disappearing under the bulldozers of economic "progress," and greed.

I spent my morning with Emily swimming across the long bay. Constantine and Vasia were snorkeling with their friends and playing with a small inflatable raft. After ninety minutes in the water we walked up to the trailer, which was parked next to a small family-run and -owned restaurant-café. The heat of the day was modified by a pleasant wind blowing from the southwest toward the sea creating a deceptive calmness near the edges of the seashore. Reading a book under the tent that we set up, and periodically resting my eyes on the blue horizon where sky and sea meet, was my idea of bliss on the gross material level.

I plowed into *Quantum Healing*,[1] the groundbreaking work of the Indian-born endocrinologist Deepak Chopra who, after years as an established medical doctor in New England, discovered the wisdom of Indian Ayurvedic medicine which he tried to introduce to the West. In this book he explored the frontiers of mind/body medicine, the type of work that the Skeptical Inquirers would not bother even to read, yet would have no hesitation in dismissing as "pseudoscience." *Quantum Healing* is based on the premise that the mind is not confined in, nor explained by, the body.

In the chapter I was reading, Chopra discussed the life and world of the *rishis* and *sadhus* (holy men) of India, whose life is exclusively dedicated to inner exploration and silence. Chopra investigated the spiritual traditions of India and their contemporary relevance in offering light on some seemingly inexplicable phenomena in medical practice. He mentioned how as a child his knowledge of these holy men came from the stories that one of his uncles, who traveled all over India selling sports equipment, used to tell.

"Let me read you this," I said to Emily who sat next to me absorbed in her own reading. "It is a short vignette." Emily interrupted her reading, watched the horizon through her sunglasses and listened.

" 'Bara Uncle was hugely affable and gregarious. He spun fabulous tales about the wonders he met on his way. The most vivid happened in Calcutta. Bara Uncle was pushing his way through the crowds when he almost stumbled over an old sadhu sitting near the curb. Absentmindedly, my uncle reached into his pocket, found two annas (about two cents), and put them in the sadhu's bowl. The sadhu shot him a glance and said, "Make a wish for anything you want."

" 'Taken aback, my uncle blurted, "I want some *burfi*." Burfi is an Indian candy, like fudge, that is usually made from almonds or coconut. Very calmly the sadhu reached his right hand into the air, materialized two pieces of fresh burfi, and gave them to Bara Uncle. Astounded, he stood transfixed for a few seconds, just enough time for the sadhu to rise and melt like a shadow into the crowd. My uncle never saw him again. In a way, he got a fair exchange, since his two annas would have bought him two pieces of burfi from a sweetmeat vendor on the street. But every time he told the story, my uncle would shake his head and mourn, "I am still thinking of all the things I could have wished for." ' "

I turned toward Emily and abruptly asked her: "Suppose you faced such a situation—what wish would you have made? Don't think. Just answer quickly, quickly," I said with a teasing tone in my voice as I tried to rush her toward an answer.

"Immortality," she shot back.

"Oh no!" I reacted as if she lost the chance of her life. "You really blew it, my dear. You really did."

"And why, may I ask, did I blow it?"

"Because you have asked for something that you already have," I replied with a self-assured tone in my voice. "Wouldn't you say that it is not prudent to ask for something that you already have?"

"What would you have asked for?"

I pretended as if I had not thought about it before and after a few moments I said triumphantly, "Enlightenment, of course. That is what I don't have."

In fact I was almost certain that had I been asked the same question and been forced to answer instantly without prior reflection, I would have probably given an identical answer to Emily. Instinctively we all crave immortality because we cannot imagine the world existing without us. But from the point of view of esoteric teachings it is taken for granted that we are immortal beings. We simply don't know that. What we lack is knowledge, the knowledge of our own inner, immortal Self. Because of our ignorance we are afraid of our death and, as Ernest Becker[2] tells us, we are all into denial, the denial of the reality of our own mortality. In fact whatever we do in life is an effort to cope with that recognition, the certainty of our death.

We crave immortality, whether we are believers or nonbelievers. And we always try to find pseudo-solutions to our predicament. The underlying motivation of our pursuit of careers, profits, power, success, or heroic social visions is our attempt to deny our mortality. We want to forget that our life's clock is ticking inexorably toward our end. And most of us consciously or unconsciously consume our energies to attain immortality through substitutes.

But there are possible difficulties in recognizing the inherent limitation of all "immortality projects." If people took their death seriously, the sociologist Peter Berger[3] warned, most of the activities that people engage in would come to a standstill. Few would care to produce. Just think of the Tibetans who perhaps more than any other people have taken their death seriously. Prior to the Chinese invasion of Tibet a huge proportion of the male population of that country, some estimates said one-third, were monks spending their time meditating and exploring inner realities.

"Jesus!" I yelled and jumped off my seat as if I had been bitten by a scorpion. We were so absorbed with thoughts on immortality that we hadn't noticed that Vasia with her friend Ultredt were drifting in the small rubber boat. The wind blowing out from the land was pushing them toward the open sea. The pair of toy oars they held were of no use since they were unable to coordinate their rowing.

I tried not to panic, and ran frantically down to the beach. There were no speedboats nearby and I knew from experience that when the wind blows from the land it is easy to lose an inflatable object. Fortunately I was still wearing my swimsuit and I had with me a pair of flippers. I knew that without them I had no chance. They had already drifted far enough to deeply worry me about my endurance. I put on the flippers and swam as fast as I could, hoping to reach them before losing my strength. That was the only wish I could make at the time. All notions of immortality and enlightenment vanished as I gathered all my energies to reach the rubber boat in time and rescue the two eleven-year-old girls. With the help of my adrenaline and Jesus prayers I reached the rubber boat just at the point when my strength was beginning to fade. I grabbed the side of the boat without saying a word. I had no extra strength to unleash a boiling desire to yell and scream at the two girls who were giggling happily. Using the flippers as propellers I slowly pushed them back to shore. **Children should not be left unattended when playing with this product** I read next to my nose as I was pushing.

I fell on the pebbles exhausted and thanked God for not having to search for them near the Turkish coast, forty miles away. I have seen enough inflatable objects, from balls to rubber mattresses, disappear on the horizon during similar weather conditions, to give me a real scare.

"Getting to them was as miraculous as the Indian holy man materializing *burfi*," I whispered to Emily who, like the two girls, thought that the entire episode was more comic than potentially catastrophic. That made me even more furious, but I was too exhausted to react. Instead of bursting in anger I closed my eyes and tried to catch my breath and transcend my fury.

I breathed deeply for a few minutes, visualizing white light penetrating every particle and every cell. I tried to see and feel this luminous energy penetrating my entire body. With every inhalation I visualized my aura becoming brighter and brighter. Ten minutes of this exercise and all the physical and psychic turmoil was gone. I then pondered the kind of lesson my daughter and her friend were offering me with their mischief.

Soon after sunset Yianis arrived from Nicosia with three other friends, new practitioners of the esoteric arts. Yianis himself, prior to his involvement with Erevna, had belonged for a while to an Indian cult. They were strict vegetarian ascetics, routinely washing both hands and feet with cold water every morning. Yianis claimed they were highly educated and sophisticated. So deeply was he into meditative practice with that group that one day, he claimed, he found himself levitating. "I was sitting in bed meditating," he said, "when I began levitating and the bed sheets came up with me as I suspended myself a couple of feet high."

One time, a couple of bearded pink-robed initiates came to the island, each carrying with him a skull and a dagger. What finally alienated him was when he heard that the two yogis entered a cemetery at night and sat over freshly dug graves meditating and breathing deeply, presumably to absorb the etheric energy of the newly deceased. Two Greek policemen, suspecting they were grave thieves, stalked them, as certain bizarre phenomena began to occur: The cypress trees in the cemetery started bending. Crosses were pulled out of the graves and, along with stones, were tossed around the cemetery. The hapless policemen were petrified. As the monks calmly walked out of the cemetery the officers approached. Shaken, and with trembling voice, they requested that the monks never repeat whatever they had been doing. They did not arrest them.

Yianis told us this story as we were building a campfire on the remote and quiet pebble beach, an extraordinary luxury on an island suffering from overdevelopment. Just imagining the hilarious scene with the poor policemen brought laughter to all of us.

"After I heard about that episode," Yianis said with a chuckle, "I quit."

The laughter continued when Emily told them of my misadventure with the rubber boat and the conversation that preceded it. Sitting around the campfire on the tiny pebble stones we went on until the early hours of the morning discussing the perennial questions of human existence.

"The Indians," I said, as I stirred the burning wood with a long stick, "have developed an elaborate and most impressive psychology to account for the nature and variety of human desires. They have answered with great sophistication the question of what human beings really crave."

"Tell us about it," Lenia, a teacher in a local high school, urged as she passed around crackers and cheese.

"I recognized this," I said, "after being exposed to several Hindu masters, including the work of Paramahansa Yogananda. But the most thorough and eloquent presentation of this topic by a Western philosopher," I went on to add, "I found in Huston Smith's *The Religions of Man*,[4] a book hailed as a classic." I had Smith's discussion on the subject freshly in mind, as I had assigned it as a text in my sociology of religion course.

"The Hindus say that whatever you desire you shall have," I said.

"Isn't that marvelous!" Yianis quipped.

"This is similar to what Erevna teaches," Emily pointed out.

"Precisely. The elementals of desire that we project outward eventually must be fulfilled. If you desire pleasure, pleasure you shall have. If you desire wealth, wealth you shall have. If you desire power, power you shall have. Sooner or later. Within eternity all desires must be fulfilled. Your desires may not be fulfilled in this life. They may be fulfilled in the next life or in the life after that or in some distant future incarnation. In the end all your desires will become actualized. But is that what you really want? Because, according to this cosmology, it is your desires that bring you back into this world of suffering and tragedy. If you are poor in this life, for example, and you craved for wealth you may get it eventually, but this will not necessarily bring you happiness and fulfillment. Success that you craved for may in fact bring you misery, as is so well documented in the biographies of the famous and the powerful. Whatever your desires, they will bring you back to this earth so you may have them fulfilled, be satiated by them, and eventually transcend them."

"What about noble desires, such as being altruistic, being of service to others?" Lenia asked.

"All desires bring us down to earth, noble or selfish. In fact the bodhisattva tradition within Buddhism is based on this principle— that the most advanced on the spiritual path will always return until the last person on earth attains God realization. So, the desire to help others will also bring you down to this dimension, in the same way that the desire to get wealthy, or successful or whatever will cause your birth in this world. Desire, period, is the magnet that pulls us down to the three dimensions."

"That is not very promising," Yianis said with a sigh. "I'd rather stay on the other side. That is what I desire."

"That is one desire," I quipped, "that will have to wait until all your other desires and those of everyone else's on this planet get fulfilled and transcended. According to the mystical teachings, as I understand them, no one really attains total liberation alone. We are all in the same cosmic boat and totally interdependent on each other. That is why the great mystics have been coming down time and again to help those of us who live at a lower stage of spiritual evolution. So you see, at the deepest levels of our being we are all one." I stopped for a few seconds and stretched on the pebbles to rest my back. Then at the encouragement of the others I proceeded to outline the evolution of desire according to the Indians, as I understood it from my reading.

"According to the essence of Indian religion, human beings begin their journey as incarnated souls, by desiring physical pleasure. But the pursuit of pleasure is inherently precarious and of short duration, leaving the individual soul to wish for something more durable. What comes next on the ladder of desire is worldly success. It appears to the ego to be of longer duration. However, worldly success of wealth, fame, or power has its own inherent limitations not much different from pleasure. They are precarious too since others also compete for them. One has power because others don't. One has wealth because others are deprived of it. And one is famous because the majority of people are not. It is a tough zero-sum situation.

"The desire for worldly success as the central goal in life," I went on, "can never be satiated. The Indians would say that to try to extinguish the drive for wealth with money is as effective as trying to extinguish a fire by pouring oil over it. The sociologist Émile Durkheim, without any knowledge of Indian religion, was right on the mark when he proposed that human desires left on their own are unlimited and infinitely insatiable. Therefore, he concluded, people need to be restrained by powerful moral rules."

"Of course," Yianis pointed out, "success is also ephemeral."

"That is what the Hindus claim," I said. "Whatever one achieves it cannot last."

"So pleasure and success are bad according to the Hindus?" one of Yianis's friends concluded.

"No, on the contrary. They consider them as necessary toys for young souls. But as one matures from one life to the next, one overcomes the fascination of this Path of Desire and searches for something loftier. The next stage in the evolution of the soul, according to this tradition," I went on, "is what the Hindus call the Path of Renunciation. It always comes after the Path of Desire."

"That's a pretty negative way of putting it," Lenia said.

"This is a misinterpretation. It is said that the true meaning of this doctrine is analogous to the athlete in training who avoids indulgences that would interfere with his or her goal. The Path of Renunciation comes when the individual reaches the point of saturation with pleasure and success and recognizes the inherent triviality of all these things in light of human mortality and the flux of time.

"This is the beginning of authentic religion. It paves the way to the religion of duty, the third great objective of life according to the Hindu worldview. The human soul—that is, after overcoming the fascination of pleasure and success—genuinely devotes himself or herself in the service of society."

"You mean by becoming patriotic?" Yianis interjected.

"It includes patriotism and all forms of social and communal activism. But in the end even this activity has its own tragic limitations and cannot fully satisfy the human quest. The individual will sooner or later recognize that society is finite, that it will not live forever and that it obstinately resists perfection. This point is more poignant today with the discoveries of modern science. Now we know, for example, that our planet and the solar system have a specified life span. In fact, if the 'Big Bang' scientists are correct, the entire known universe will eventually collapse on itself.

"Sooner or later human beings will question whether that is all there is to life," I went on to say. "So if neither pleasure nor success nor duty to community can fully satisfy us, then what next? What are, in fact, our real and deepest wants and desires?

"When I asked Emily this morning to make one single wish she replied, 'Immortality.' This is precisely what the Hindu religion identifies as being the first real desire. We want to *be*. We cannot imagine the world existing without us. Hamlet's question must be answered affirmatively here, To Be. Yet this is not enough."

"I don't get it," Lenia said, and there was laughter.

"We want to be, but we want to be in full consciousness," I said. "We cannot possibly long to be an immortal vegetable."

"So then," Lenia concluded, "the Indians believe that what human beings really crave for is immortality and consciousness."

"Not quite. The Devil is immortal and fully conscious," I said and chuckled. "Beingness and consciousness are not sufficient states in themselves. It is an intolerable notion to live forever and in full consciousness in hell."

"So then," Yianis concluded, "we want beingness, consciousness, and joy."

"Exactly. We want bliss, unlimited infinite bliss.

"What we really want according to esoteric Hinduism," I went on, "are these three things: infinite beingness, infinite awareness, and infinite bliss."

I stirred the burning pieces of wood to generate more flame. "Most importantly," I added, "is that all three, infinite beingness, infinite consciousness, and infinite bliss, are within reach of every human being. We can have what we deeply crave for. In fact, deep down we are already there but we don't know it. Therefore, the ultimate aim of life is enlightenment, the realization that we are in fact Divine beings having all the attributes of Divinity."

"How is this different from what Erevna teaches?" Yianis asked.

"Frankly I don't see that much difference. To my knowledge all esoteric traditions teach essentially the same lessons. The difference may be cultural in terms of where the emphasis is put in expressing identical truths."

"Yet I know people," Yianis pointed out, "who are on the Path of Desire and have no existential problems. They don't seem to be bored by it."

"Maybe not in this life. According to Hinduism it is possible for people to spend an entire life exclusively focused on pleasure and on their deathbed they may feel that they have lived a full and meaningful life. I have heard people tell me, 'I have lived a full life. I am ready to die anytime.' And by 'full life' they mean pleasure—i.e., sex, travel, good food, good friends, song, dance, et cetera. And if they are educated they would often call themselves 'Epicureans,' to provide a philosophical framework to their lifestyle. I suppose someone like Kazantzakis's Zorba would be such an example. But as the soul matures pleasure would lose its central appeal. It would be the equivalent of placing a university graduate in a class of elementary school children. He or she will be bored to death and will long for something more fulfilling. But for the child the elementary school will be exciting and challenging. For the Hindu esoteric tradition, pleasure, if it becomes the exclusive focus of life, is for elementary school children."

We continued our discussions until very late at night as we baked chestnuts over the fire and listened to the soothing sounds of the ripples splashing on the pebbles.

The following day in the early afternoon I had to drive to Paphos to meet Bob Newman, a physician from Australia who had written several letters to me and called a few times expressing his great wish to visit Cyprus and meet with the people of Erevna. From our conversation over the phone I realized that Bob was a serious student of esoteric wisdom. He claimed that for some time he had been living in an inner psychic world identical to that which I described in my books. He wished to meet Kostas and get some advice from him. We planned to meet at a hotel in Kato Paphos, near the "Tombs of the Kings," and then drive together to Limassol to meet Kostas.

I have always been fascinated to meet people who claim that the world I describe in my books explains their own reality. It has become such a pattern for me that by now I am convinced that there are two types of cultures, the exoteric and the esoteric. Exoteric culture is the culture that most people are conscious of. This is the culture also of science and the one studied by my own discipline, sociology. Esoteric culture, on the other hand, is the culture of the mystics and practitioners of the contemplative arts. It is the culture of inner space that the great majority of humanity, particularly Western humanity, is unconscious of. Perhaps another way of identifying the two cultures is to call the exoteric the conscious part of culture and the esoteric the subconscious, or invisible part of culture, accessible only to a few shamans, saints, and mystics in every society.

Bob was a vigorous, pleasant man with a round face and a broad smile hidden behind a well-groomed beard. We sat on the veranda of the hotel facing the sea (always the sea!) and chatted for a while. He told me how he had been applying the material in my books to carry out healings while working as a conventional physician. He told me of extraordinary healing phenomena that were taking place in front of his eyes as a result of this practice and how his life had been totally transformed.

"You may be interested to know that I was not always like this. In fact, until 1985 my life's philosophy was very self-centered and materialistic. I was a follower of Ayn Rand's 'objectivism' for twenty-one years," he said with a grin. "My attitude toward life had been nonaltruistic, nonreverential, nonsubmissive. I believed in total selfishness on philosophical grounds and that one should trade things of equivalent value."

"It sounds to me you were a true follower of Adam Smith," I quipped. "But what caused you to change so drastically?"

"Everything changed on August 19, 1985, when I received a call from my sister to say that my parents, who had just migrated to Israel and lived in an apartment in Jerusalem, had been found dead. Apparently it was a murder-suicide."

"Oh my God," I muttered as Bob sighed deeply and continued.

"That evening, before I received the tragic news, I was overtaken by a desire to write my theories about life based on Ayn Rand's philosophy. I rushed to my word processor as if I had a project to complete and a deadline to meet and kept writing with frantic obsession. It was eleven-thirty on August 19, 1985, when I turned off the computer. At eleven-fifty that very night I received the tragic news from my sister.

"My theories on life, that I had just written down, did not help me one iota to cope with life during this period of acute bereavement. I eventually abandoned them as useless. I started visiting the synagogue, and a spiritual awakening began to take place within me. I got involved with Rudolf Steiner groups and started a serious meditation practice. I reached the point when I had out-of-body experiences at will and met intelligences and guides that live in higher vibrations of existence. And this transformation in me took place just after the tragedy with my parents. The coincidence of where I stopped with my writing is significant to me. It revealed to me that I had been absorbed and engrossed with the development of the lower self up until August 19, 1985." We remained silent for a few seconds as I pondered Bob's sad but meaningful tale.

"Have you had any external confirmation that the experiences with guides and out-of-the-body travel were authentic experiences and not the creation of your own imagination?" I asked.

"Yes. Let me tell you of one of my early experiences that did just that," Bob said without hesitation. "After the tragedy I started going to the synagogue, as I said. I used to go every night to say *Kaddish*. There I met a man named Bill Stein. I met him every night and we used to say *Kaddish* together. Sometimes it was difficult for him to say *Kaddish* because he was so anguished for his beloved son Jon, who had died in an auto accident just after he had been qualified as a doctor.

"Bill was often frustrated by my newly acquired peace of mind and often remarked that as doctors were so busy, how could I find time to sit and pray in the synagogue. His son, he said, worked around the clock and couldn't even find a single minute to do anything else."

"Well, what did you tell him?"

"I replied that I had to make the time. One night he invited me to his beautiful house for a drink. He seemed to be obsessed with extraterrestrial beings and was looking for confirmation from the Torah for their early existence. He was deeply sad because he was very close to his son, whom he loved with tremendous emotion. He could not understand why he was granted the ability to love with such intensity and then the object of his love was taken away from him. I told him that I would try and 'speak' to some of my friends and find out what I could. I did not tell him that I would be doing the research myself.

"I went into my meditation," Bob went on to say, "and asked Xanox to protect me."

"Xanox who?"

"My spirit guide," Bob replied.

"Oh, I see." By now I had become accustomed to psychics telling me of their ongoing liaisons with spirit guides, so his matter-of-fact reply did not bring about an incredulous look on my face as it would have in former times.

"I asked," Bob continued, "whether I could help and be permitted to find Bill's son. I asked protection to try and make some kind of contact or try and receive some kind of message in order to alleviate Bill's agony. I asked my spirit guide to take me where I needed to be taken.

"During my meditation, and when I invoked Xanox's help, I began to receive a picture of the place of the accident, and Jon lying on some rocky outcrop in a lifeless position. I was then aware of an unpleasant feeling in my muscles, as though I wanted to stretch or run. It was a feeling of muscular irritability or physical anticipation that reached such a pitch that I came out of the meditation because I found it so unpleasant. I was aware upon emerging that my neck had been lying at an acute angle. I stood up, felt light-headed and went back again into the meditation, since it seemed unfinished. When I had retired to bed I again was conscious of these unpleasant muscular sensations.

"The following morning," Bob went on to say, "I visited Tina, a friend of mine who is also a medium. I told her of my experience. This is how she interpreted it for me. She said I had been placed close to the physical shell of my friend's son in order to know where he was and that he needed help to transport him into the world of the spirit. The pain was due to my close proximity and the fact that I was a novice and did not treat the situation at arm's length.

"Actually," Bob said, "I had experienced the pain, the soul experience that he had after his fall. Tina advised that I should meditate again and go back to the spot and explain to him that he had already passed over and that he could move his etheric form, etc. And that once I had him moving I could leave him to go on to the friendly spirits who were waiting for him.

"This explanation intrigued me greatly," Bob continued. "I asked Tina what made her assume that I was capable of or was in a position to do such advanced spiritual work. She replied that the capacity is present in all of us. It just needs to be tapped. You see at that time I was quite naive. I was vulnerable and unprotected and therefore open to strange etheric, elemental forces of which I knew nothing."

"So did you go into meditation to find Jon?" I asked.

"Yes. I was very excited. That was going to be my most ambitious adventure yet. I said a prayer to God and thereafter asked Xanox to protect me and take me back to the spot where I had been made aware of the physical form of Jon. I did what Tina had advised me to do and from within myself I greeted Jon and introduced myself as Bob Newman. I told him that his physical shell was lifeless and that since he was now in the beautiful world of spirit there were no fallibilities, only perfection. I encouraged him to feel that he was able to move and that he should realize that there was no pain or anything broken within his spiritual being, which was a mirror image of his previously known physical self. His neck was straightened and he stood up. There were no words of communication from him of which I was aware but he seemed to be receptive to my thoughts.

"After having done that I asked my spirit guide to take his hand and escort him to those spiritual ancestors that were waiting to receive him. I felt a little vulnerable standing there all alone and felt I should ask my guide not to be long and come back to me as soon as the handover had been completed. This he did. I then tried to see to whom Jon was handed over. I was unable to do so. I asked for a sign or a name that would mean something to Bill and myself so that what I had experienced was fact and not imagination."

Bob stopped for a few seconds and mentioned that by now he learned that one should, as a rule, never ask such questions. He said he acted in ignorance but with the correct intentions. When I asked Bob whether he got any answer, he said yes.

"Whether the name 'Mordecai' came to me during the actual meditation or my sleep, I am not sure. But when I woke up that morning I knew that I had to ask Bill about that name.

"A few days later in the synagogue I asked Bill whether there was anybody in his family tree called Mordecai. He did not know of anyone, so we went to his house for a scotch and asked his eighty-five-year-old mother. After a spirited discussion in Rumanian, his mother said . . . 'Aaaah, Mordecai!' Mordecai was confirmed to be a prominent figure in the family! He was Jon's great-great-grandfather who had been the religious leader in their congregation. This information and confirmation of my meditation made me feel very humble and I thanked God for having given me the privilege, with the help of Xanox, to enter into the world of spirit and to be instrumental in assisting Jon to take the step into the next world. This event has been the greatest sign to me to date. I have never asked for proof since that episode."

"I think we should be heading for Limassol," I said to Bob after thanking him for sharing with me his extraordinary experience. "Kostas will be waiting for us. I am sure you will have a lot of things that the two of you will want to talk about."

Inspired by the beauty of the scenery as we drove from Paphos to Limassol Bob began reciting poetry that he composed after the tragedy of his parents had resulted in what he considered as the beginning of his own spiritual awakening. He hoped, he told me, to have it published one day.

"Tell me about Kostas," Bob said a few minutes after I brought to his attention the fact that the pebble beach we had just passed, on our right, was the legendary birthplace of Aphrodite.

"Well, what do you want to know about him?" I asked.

"Anything. After all, that is why I came to Cyprus."

I went on to briefly describe my more than ten-year association with Kostas, much of which I'd already written about in my books. "Two things impress me about him," I said.

"First, he is a philosopher of metaphysics with an impressive and unique insight into the nature of reality. You see, he is not just a healer. That really has always impressed me, particularly when you consider that he has no formal training either in religion or philosophy. And most importantly, he never reads any books. The only books he read, he assured me once, were the engineering texts assigned by his professors while a university student in England. To me this is a phenomenon in itself that needs to be explained."

"What does he say about it himself?" Bob asked.

"The knowledge he teaches, he says, comes from within himself, from his inner self. He claims it is inside every human being and ultimately accessible to everyone."

"Yes, I can relate to that." Bob nodded with understanding. "But what was the second thing that impressed you about Kostas?"

"His integrity," I said, focusing on the road.

"To tell you the truth," Bob said after a few moments of silence and hesitation, "the major reason that brought me to Cyprus is to find out why so many gurus and reputed masters turn out to be so lacking in ethical integrity. I am glad you are so reassuring about Kostas."

I pointed out to Bob that this issue has puzzled me a great deal. I had assumed, like most people usually do, that someone who demonstrates not only psychic power and healing abilities but also great wisdom must be a bona fide saint in terms of his or her everyday behavior. But in recent times we have learned about so many venerated masters that turned out to be the exact opposite of what was formerly thought of them by their followers. "In fact, this problem," I said, "has grown to epidemic proportions."

"Actually, you may be interested to know, Kyriaco," Bob went on, "that I belonged to such a group. We had a teacher who was very powerful as a healer and truly profound as a teacher of wisdom. But then we discovered that he had serious flaws which he cleverly hid from our view for a very long time . . ." Bob hesitated for a moment before revealing what the secret was. "He liked young boys . . . We had a pedophile for a guru and we thought of him as a living saint."

"Well," I said and shook my head. "You are neither the first nor the last to be fooled by the charismatic aura of false messiahs."

"You see, what was terrible," Bob said, "was that he lured teenage boys, presumably to spiritually guide them, and then through all sorts of psychological manipulations would persuade them to allow him to perform fellatio on them or convince them to sodomize him. And while these acts were performed he reassured these kids that what they were engaged in was a form of sacred healing ritual for their enlightenment!"

"This is what Swami Muktananda[5] was accused of doing," I said, keeping my eyes on the road. "But he was a connoisseur of teenage girls, not boys."

"He even convinced one fifteen-year-old," Bob continued, "that he needed his semen for his health, making the boy feel that it was his duty to save his master. In fact, one of them told me, after the scandal broke, that as he was sodomizing him the guru reassured him that what they were engaged in was a sacred love communion. Figure that out." As Bob was talking I could see after a quick glance dismay appearing on his face mixed with a nervous chuckle.

"What happened to these boys?" I asked.

"Some needed long-term psychotherapy.

"This man," Bob continued, "had a cunning capacity to cover up his weaknesses and fool even mature people. He presented himself as a paragon of selflessness and goodness and made people believe that whatever rumors were circulating about him were simply vicious falsehoods deliberately spread by his enemies."

"And you say this man had great ability to disseminate wisdom."

"Yes. This is the paradox. Not only was he a great teacher of esoteric wisdom but he carried out healings in front of our eyes. And he repeatedly demonstrated his clairvoyant abilities. That is why he fooled us all."

"I wondered about such paradoxes myself and I am sure Kostas will have a lot to tell us about it. Just before I came to Cyprus I met with my friend Demetrios, an acupuncturist from New Bedford and an experienced healer himself. Over coffee at the Café Paradise near Harvard Square, in Cambridge, he explained to me that healing can take place in two ways. First, someone can become so saintly and purified that the Holy Spirit simply works miracles through him or her. This is the way of the saints in the Eastern Orthodox tradition, for example.

"The second way, Demetrios explained to me, is through technical means. You can learn how to heal. But it is necessary that at the time of healing your motives must be pure—that is, you must care about the other, otherwise healing will not work. So, he said, you may live a life which is not saintly at all, but through various learned methods you may be able to heal, just like any skilled doctor whose personal life may be in shambles.

"You see," I went on, "things are not black and white, as we have assumed. Emerging out of a materialist civilization, we are not well equipped to make these finer distinctions. With such experiences, however, we will hopefully develop the appropriate sensitivities and learn how to discriminate between the spiritually authentic and the spiritually inauthentic. In any event, even inauthentic gurus can often do some good. Wasn't it the prophet Elias who said that the Lord does not anoint everyone but that He acts through everyone?"

We were approaching Limassol. We had just passed the British bases and the ancient sanctuary of Apollo. On our right the sea was beginning to change colors as the sun touched the horizon. At the tourist pavilion built on a cliff overlooking Kourion beach we stopped for a while to let our senses absorb the magic of the moment.

"You were lucky to eventually extricate yourself from the spell of your master without harm," I said as we sat on the veranda of the pavilion enjoying the fresh breeze coming from the sea and watching the sun submerge itself. "I have known others who were not so lucky. A woman I met still wails for her lost youth spent at the feet of a corrupt guru who at one point almost cost her her life. I have read somewhere of a Tibetan proverb that got imprinted in my mind. It goes like this: 'A guru is like a fire. If you get too close you get burned. If you stay too far away, you don't get enough heat. A sensible moderation is recommended.' "[6]

"Fortunately for me," Bob said, "I practiced this proverb without knowing about it. For me it was a gradual, painful realization of what was going on. You see, the problem was not only the sexual exploitation of young boys. To cover up his weakness he had to resort to all sorts of lies and manipulations. I was beginning to notice that what he was preaching was the exact opposite of what he was doing. When I began to emotionally disentangle myself from his influence I started also to notice other patterns in his behavior that before I could not see. I began to observe how he was manipulating people in other ways."

"Such as?"

"Money and status. People were enchanted with the healings that were taking place in front of their eyes and were awed with the great wisdom that he was disseminating. Once under his spell, when people offered their love and trust to him, some shameful things began to take place." Bob stopped for a few seconds.

"Like what, for example?" I asked.

"I noticed some very subtle and some not so very subtle ways of extracting money from people. Also using devotees to spread his philosophy, which I eventually saw as primarily ego projection. I noticed that often these concerns for money and fame became so central that they overshadowed all other interests, such as healing and focusing on spiritual issues. Being a powerful psychic it was all too easy to exploit those around him. And the saddest thing of all was to see what happened once the people being manipulated had nothing else useful to give. Then they were often cruelly dropped and black-listed and other followers were strongly advised to steer clear of them. And so the splitting up of peoples and loyalties continued as well as the circulation of people who fell in and out of his favor."

"It sounds to me like a very narcissistic personality," I said, "but typical of similar other cases that have come to my attention."

"And another thing," Bob said. "I noticed that the way he manipulated people followed a certain pattern. First flattery. Second, getting at one's weaknesses and using them to advantage."

"Well," I said, as we got back into the car for the last leg of our trip, "all these must have been lessons of tremendous importance."

"Certainly. It is a warning that we need to keep our eyes open when in the company of gurus with extraordinary psychic abilities."

"Let us see what Kostas has to say about all this," I said as I parked the car next to his house. It was seven in the evening. Kostas had just come out of the shower after a tiring day's work. Setting up his gas station required his full attention and long hours both from him and his wife. Ever since he became a refugee from Famagusta in 1974, after the Turkish army took over the coastal city, Kostas had faced extraordinary obstacles in whatever economic projects he had undertaken. Coming from a wealthy family that lost everything during the Turkish invasion intensified his sense of "relative deprivation." Both he and his wife invested great hopes in their new adventure. Yet there were still difficulties and legal complications that absorbed a great deal of his time, time away from healing and Erevna work.

Kostas was adamant about not making healing his full-time occupation. "One way to avoid possible corruption both of healing and the Research for the Truth is to practice them during one's spare time," he had often said. He stuck by this principle even at a time when more and more people, both in Cyprus and overseas, were seeking him out.

There was an immediate affinity between Bob and Kostas. They hit it off well, and conversation flowed easily. For the next twenty minutes we sat in the living room, had tea and talked about Bob's interest in coming to Cyprus. When Bob told Kostas about the problems with his former guru, Kostas sighed and shook his head.

"This is an issue that I have faced repeatedly," he said. "People come and tell me all sorts of horror stories about the way they had been abused by their spiritual teachers. We can talk about it tomorrow, if you wish. Tonight I have to give a lesson which starts in about half an hour," Kostas said, and quickly looked at his watch. "Would you like to come?"

"Oh yes," Bob said. "But I don't know any Greek."

"Don't worry. It so happens that tonight the lesson will be given to a group of overseas visitors like yourself. It will be in English. You see, you came at an auspicious time," Kostas said with a grin.

"What's the topic going to be, Kosta?" I asked.

"I don't know yet," he quipped. "I'll find out when I get there."

Kostas told me many times that he hardly prepared for his weekly talks on metaphysical issues. Much of what was said during these meetings emerged spontaneously, particularly during the question-and-answer period.

The audience was made up of Germans, a few Britons, several Swiss, and two Americans. There were also four Greek Cypriots. Among them was Maroulla, the secretary of Erevna, a teacher herself and Kostas' "right hand." Altogether there were about twenty-five people in the room, a small apartment rented by the organization. Large enough to fit forty people its walls were bare of any decorations or anything one might expect to find at a spiritual center, except a huge painting of "The Tree of Life" [similar to the Cabalistic tree of life] that Kostas used for instructional purposes. Its Spartan ambiance and decorum was in marked contrast to the Greek Orthodox churches with their icons and candles and other religious artifacts. The setting, in fact, was a reflection of Erevna's approach to reality—nonritualistic, nondenominational, and essentially rational-philosophical with meditation practices as the experiential component. I had come to realize that Erevna was what the Hindu sages would call "jnana Yoga," the wisdom path to Spirit. As an academic I found it a suitable method. The Socratic approach of exploring metaphysical questions appealed to me. It was partly for this reason that I had focused on this material for over a decade.

Bob and I sat in the first row next to Maroulla as Kostas began the lesson. It turned out that the topic was the relativity of the meaning of good and evil. Kostas claimed that conceptions of the good as collectively conceived at a given time often become conceptions of evil in a future time, when human awareness has evolved to higher stages.

"For example," Kostas said, "the spiritual methods employed in past epochs to explore reality were, by definition, the product of the level of awareness of that period. It is logical to assume that, don't you think?" I was not exactly certain what Kostas was insinuating but I reserved my questions for later.

"Likewise," he went on to say, "what we consider as good and right today, from the vantage point of the future, when our filter of awareness will have reached greater levels of development, may become totally unacceptable. The good of the present becomes the evil of tomorrow. That is, the filter of human awareness through which we apprehend Reality will increasingly become purer and purer, offering us a progressively clearer vision.

"At the end," Kostas continued, "the only thing that will remain will be the *Agathon*—that is, the Good in itself beyond all human meanings or definitions. At Theosis the Self will fully and directly express the absolute Love of God. So both good and evil as humanly perceived will eventually be transcended because the individual at the highest stage of self-realization or Theosis will not be expressing a self through the limitations of humanly constructed meanings and conceptions, through the limitations imposed by human awareness.

"We as Researchers of the Truth must struggle to know reality, but we should never forget that all we can know is the relative reality. We constantly ascend and come closer to reality and we reach one step higher each time on the scale of *relative truth*. Therefore, we should never expect to find the Truth while working and researching. As we have said many times, no one knows what truth is before one becomes the Truth.

"We must always keep in mind," Kostas went on after a pause, "that we live within the worlds of balance and not of harmony." He briefly explained that the worlds of harmony exist where human awareness has not intervened. God created the universes in harmony. But human awareness acts upon this harmony and transforms it into universes of equilibrium, of balance.

"Can you please explain to us what you mean by balance?" a woman asked in a heavy German accent.

"The worlds of balance mean the worlds of good and evil. Within these worlds there is as much good as there is evil. There is as much dark as there is white. Never assume that within these worlds the dark is weaker than the white.

"For example," Kostas continued, and turned toward Bob, "whatever psychic power can be manifested through the white can equally be manifested through the dark. It is the law of balance at work. It is for this reason that so many people are fooled by powerful psychics and mystics who express more of the dark than the white. It is for this reason that I am personally wary of using ancient methods of spiritual practice that were employed by mystics who, from the vantage point of today, must be considered as more dark than white. Of course, there may be some of these practices that can still be relevant today. On the whole, however, this is not the case, since human awareness has progressed to higher levels. Therefore, different approaches more appropriate to the present stage of collective awareness, must be employed."

I wanted to ask Kostas many questions on this point but I reserved it for later during more private encounters. I noticed that the international visitors were eager to ask questions of their own.

"There are people today," Kostas continued, "who assume or even teach that to gain psychic powers you can employ all sorts of technical methods, and they would say there are no other ways. For us this approach is totally unacceptable. For us the proper method for the acquisition of power is through the psychonoetic development of the individual—that is, the growth of awareness. Psychic abilities will simply be byproducts of this process and must not be pursued directly. Those who will acquire psychic abilities that are not the product of their spiritual or psychonoetical development inadvertently will use them for evil purposes without them even realizing it."

"I am distressed with the notion that good and evil are of equal power," an English Jungian therapist commented. "If that is the case, what is the point in struggling to make the world a better place?"

"When I said that good and evil will always exist in a state of equilibrium and balance within creation I mean within the totality of creation, not within an individual planet like our own. Of course we must struggle to make the world better. But let us not have any illusions that we can create a perfect world anywhere within creation, within the worlds of polarity, of balance and of separateness. Perfection is only within the Autarky of the Absolute and the only perfect human being that has ever walked on our planet has been the 'Only Begotten Son.' No one else.

"Let me put it this way," Kostas went on to say. "Suppose the good destroyed and defeated all the elementals of evil within the totality of creation. Evil is permanently and irrevocably defeated forever. In such a hypothetical case human entities would not have been offered the opportunities to acquire crucial experiences at the lower stages of awareness through the process of several lives or incarnations. The law of karma would have been canceled out and birth into the lower worlds of polarity and balance would have been pointless.

"Yes, evil is ultimately transcended," Kostas went on after a few moments of silence. "But this transcendence takes place internally, within individual human consciousness. This is the real meaning of the second coming of Christ. It is not an episode that will appear in some historical time and place as popularly understood. It is an individual, psychological state that will emerge inadvertently at a certain point in the evolutionary ascent of every individual soul. It is the resurrection, if you will, within each and every human being of his or her Christ consciousness. It is the opening of what oriental mystics would call the heart chakra, a prelude to the ultimate and radical transcendence and liberation from the worlds of good and evil, of polarity and suffering.

"You see," Kostas went on, "in the past I assumed that good ultimately triumphs over evil. But upon further research and contemplation I learned that this is not the case, not within the lower worlds of creation, anyway. The humanly constructed meanings of good and evil are always evenly balanced through the law of karma, and are continuously being transformed to higher and higher levels of understanding until they are both replaced with the *Agathon* [the Good, unmediated by any humanly constructed meanings]. Contemplate on these issues and draw your own conclusions."

For the next half hour there were more questions from the audience related to various metaphysical issues. After Kostas guided us through several meditation exercises he informed the visitors that he would be able to continue the lesson and further discussion the night after next.

Bob felt privileged that Kostas was to take the following day off and spend time with us, along with the two Americans, at Plataniskia, a village by the coast about forty-five minutes west of Limassol. Maroulla invited us to her home there to go swimming and spend the next day in a free-floating conversation about spiritual questions. We were looking forward to a real symposium, figuratively and literally speaking.

"Tomorrow," Kostas said to Bob before we dispersed, "we can talk in some detail on the issue that you raised at the beginning of the evening." Kostas referred to the apparent paradox of mystics who are capable of disseminating great wisdom and who cause extraordinary healings but at the same time are seriously flawed in their daily conduct. We were led to understand that the discussion that had just ended was in some way an introduction to the issues that we were to explore the next day, within a more leisurely context.

It was eleven o'clock at night when I reached my in-laws' apartment on the fourth floor of the building complex next to the city's municipal park. I was alone. My in-laws were spending the summer at a mountain resort, and Emily had remained at Akámas with Constantine and Vasia for a few extra days. Having no interest in sleep I did what I rarely do, I lit a pipe. I then sat on the balcony facing south toward the sea, which was only a hundred meters away. Being on the fourth floor I had an open view of the area. On my right there was the zoological park with its tall pines, eucalyptus, and palm trees and its two roaring lions. In front of me below there was a large orange grove owned by an old aristocratic family who, thanks to their wealth, had kept most of the area free of apartment buildings. At the far edge of the orchard was the main road, running parallel to the sea.

I puffed the aromatic smoke and watched the starry sky and the boats anchored in the distance outside the harbor, waiting their turn to load and unload their cargoes. In spite of rampant development it was still possible to watch the stars in Limassol. It was still possible to gaze at the Milky Way and doing so raise the unavoidable question that humans have been raising since the beginning of human consciousness, the "Who Am I?" I can't imagine anyone watching the stars without that question popping into his or her mind. How sad, I thought, that most people today live in crowded cities that pollute the night sky with artificial light and smog, and are cut off from the experience of fixing their eyes on the Milky Way and reflecting on their place in the universe.

Kostas' ideas of good and evil, balance and harmony, revolved in my mind. The notion that good and evil exist in equilibrium within the totality of creation, in order to offer human beings experiences and opportunities for spiritual growth and awakening, seemed both insightful and unnerving. It certainly offers some answers as to why evil is so ubiquitous even under the most utopian conditions and why its presence leads people, like Ivan in *The Brothers Karamazov*, to reject the notion of a loving God altogether. "How could God be real and allow this . . . ?"

But Kostas claimed that the dynamic juxtaposition of good and evil plays a most crucial cosmic purpose. Perhaps this is what Saint Augustine had in mind when he taught that higher things are better than lower things but that together they are better than higher things alone.

One of the problems, I thought, of "New Age spirituality" is the gross underestimation of the power of evil and the assumption that all metaphysical phenomena are, by definition, spiritual and good. Consequently, people in the West, craving spiritual experiences and having no traditional guidelines, have become easy prey to unscrupulous gurus, yogis, and masters who liberally demonstrate wisdom, psychic powers, and healing phenomena. Perhaps now, as we move toward Sorokin's "ideational" pole where spirituality is making such a tumultuous comeback, no other warning is more important to keep in mind, I thought, than Saint John the Evangelist's admonition in his first letter: "Beloved, do not believe every spirit, but test the spirits to see whether they are of God; for many false prophets have gone out into the world."

Thinking about Saint John and the question of good and evil put me in a religious mood. I put my pipe away, stood up, turned toward the east and spread my arms up toward the Milky Way. For an instant I contemplated the original, primordial explosion that took place only 15 billion years ago and created everything—the stars, the planets, my body. I shuddered. I always do when the implications of that event hits me. I murmured an invocation of the Holy

Spirit that is routinely recited in the Greek liturgy: "O Heavenly King, Comforter, the Spirit of Truth, Who art ever present, and fillest all things, the Treasure of all Blessings and Giver of Life, come and dwell within us, and cleanse us from every blemish and save our souls, O Blessed One."

# 8

## FALSE
## PROPHETS

PLATANISKIA LIES WEST OF THE BRITISH BASES AT AKROTIRI, ON a dry, sun-baked elevation overlooking the sea, twenty minutes from the shoreline. The hills and valleys all around this peasant village, as far as the eye can see, are covered with vineyards and some wheat fields, olive and carob trees popping up here and there. It is in the middle of the wine-producing area of Cyprus, and in times past the peasants, during harvest, would load their bamboo baskets of grapes on the backs of their donkeys and mules and travel east in long caravans to the wineries of Limassol.

Before the tragic events of recent times Plataniskia was a mixed village consisting of Greek and Turkish Cypriots carrying on their traditional ways in amicable neighborliness. Church and mosque co-existed and villagers attended one another's weddings, baptisms, and circumcision ceremonies. The British, who controlled the island un-til 1960, provided the umbrella under which both ethnic groups felt relatively secure. But the establishment of independence in 1960, when the British were forced to leave after a four-year guerrilla war waged by Greek Cypriot nationalists, opened the way to mutual ethnic mistrust and suspicion. When mainland Turkish troops in-vaded the northern part of the island in 1974, the last nail was driven into the coffin of Greek-Turkish coexistence at Plataniskia and on the rest of Cyprus. The Turkish inhabitants fled to the British bases nearby and from there were moved to the northern, occupied part of the island.

Emily and I lived through those shattering days when, on leave from the University of Maine, I worked for a year at the Cyprus Social Research Centre conducting field research in a village not far from Nicosia, the capital. The village was later overrun by Turkish troops, and the Greek inhabitants fled south.

Those experiences marked both of us for life. It was a rude realization of the fragility of the world in which we find ourselves. For Emily the invasion was particularly painful as she lost her home in Famagusta, the once prosperous tourist center of the island, now an abandoned "ghost town" controlled by Turkish troops and monitored by UN observers. Her parents became refugees after the invading tanks rolled into town. Like every other Famagustian refugee they have lived with the tormenting yearning for an eventual settlement of the Cyprus problem and the hope that they can someday return home. It was that bitter experience that turned Emily into a peace activist.

Maroulla, like Emily and Kostas, was herself a refugee from Famagusta. Having lost her own home she was allotted on a temporary basis one of the abandoned Turkish houses in the village of Plataniskia. She could use it as her home and take care of it until the ethnic problem was solved and the rightful occupants returned. But Maroulla, being a professional physiotherapist rather than a farmer, took up residence in Limassol, and used the village house as a weekend retreat for herself and her daughter.

Following her directions, I drove with Bob to Plataniskia on Saturday morning. Driving through its narrow streets the village appeared to us quite small. It seemed as if no more than a couple of hundred souls lived there. Many houses looked abandoned, and had it not been for the two parked cars on the dirt road outside of

Maroulla's house, and the old tractor in an adjacent field, the scene could have popped out of a bygone century. Goats were roaming in the surrounding fields and a tall donkey tied to a carob tree complained intermittently.

It was nine-thirty when we reached her retreat, a well-kept simple traditional house with a huge fig tree shading the front yard. Built at the edge of the village in the middle of an open field it offered a privileged, which is to say spectacular, view of the area. The combination of colors—the green vineyards, the golden harvested wheat fields and the dark blue of the sea in the distance below—provided a landscape that would have stirred the aesthetic passions of any artist. I could see why Maroulla chose to spend her weekends in that setting of isolated pastoral tranquillity.

Kostas was already there along with the American couple, Anthony and his wife, Helena. All four of them were sitting under the fig tree sipping Turkish coffee and eating pastries that Maroulla baked the night before. "We have been waiting for you to go to the sea and have a swim first before we start serious discussions," she said lightheartedly as she introduced the two Americans to Bob. I knew Anthony and Helena through Erevna, and we had become friends. Anthony was a computer engineer with a keenly rational, methodical mind, and a veteran of spiritual groups and holistic associations. Helena was a therapist using dance and Jungian principles in her practice. Both had become teachers of Erevna and headed a circle in the New York area. I always enjoyed their lively company, and was a happy beneficiary of their knowledge of esoteric matters, spiritual wisdom, and refined taste of things.

We drove down to the sea to a spot unknown to tourists, a secret place known only to Maroulla and a few others. Finding an isolated beach, something we took for granted as we were growing up on Cyprus, was nowadays a luxury. Everything had changed with the arrival of the jet plane and the developers with their morbid love affair with cement.

"It has been a long time since I had such a break," Kostas said as he stretched on the sand and baked his back in the sun for a few minutes. We swam for an hour and by eleven-thirty were back in Plataniskia. After washing the salt from our bodies with water from Maroulla's well we were ready for serious discussions under the fig tree. Soon after we finished our quick lunch I opened the conversation.

"Last night," I said, "we started exploring a very important issue that Bob brought to the forefront of our awareness by his coming here. I mean the apparent and disturbing paradox of venerated gurus that are sources of great wisdom and yet seriously flawed in their everyday behavior, particularly when it comes to sex, money, and power. There are so many examples of teachers of spiritual wisdom who have contributed a great deal to the awakening of spiritual consciousness while in their actions they themselves have not lived up to what they have taught their disciples. Take for example the case of Bhagwan Shree Rajneesh, whose books have captivated the imagination of so many intelligent people. Yet the society he founded was plagued with scandal upon scandal, which eventually led to his expulsion from the United States." I then went on, mentioning a number of other famous names.

"I can also add Baba Muktananda to this list," Helena interjected.

"Right," I said. "In fact I have here an article that was sent to me recently by a friend in reference to the alleged abuses this guru inflicted on innocent devotees. Here is a man who was referred to as the 'guru of gurus' who taught his disciples a long list of shoulds and should-nots. These involved such instructions as 'Do not turn the ashram into a land of pleasure and license.' 'Conduct yourself according to the sanctity of the place,' and 'First practice yourself what you want to teach others.'

"According to his accusers the great guru was sexually molesting young girls and was obsessed with money."

"That is exactly what happened in our case," Bob added.

"Here is what Stan Trout, a former close associate and devotee, had to say," I went on and read some extracts from his published letter.[1]

" 'There is no doubt in my mind that he [Muktananda] was an extraordinarily enlightened, learned, and articulate man who possessed a singular power, a dynamic personal radiance and charisma that drew people to him and inspired them to lay their lives at his feet. Surely such a power is divine; yet there is no way to justify the way in which he used this power. . . . He staged a deliberate campaign of deceit to convince gentle souls that he had transcended the limitations of mankind, that through realizing the eternal Self, he had attained holy perfection. He planted and nourished false, impossible dreams in the hearts of innocent, faithful souls and sacrificed them to his sport. With malicious glee, he cunningly stole from hundreds of trusting souls their hearts and wills, their self-trust, their very sanity, their very lives. . . . He ended as a feeble-minded sadistic tyrant, luring devout little girls to his bed every night with promises of grace and self-realization.

" 'Muktananda's claim of perfection,' " I went on reading as everybody listened, " 'was based on the notion that a person who has become enlightened has thereby also become perfect and absolutely free of human weakness. This is nonsense; it is a myth perpetrated by dishonest men who wish to receive the reverence and adoration due to God alone. There is no absolute assurance that enlightenment necessitates the moral virtue of a person. There is no guarantee against the weakness of anger, lust, and greed in the human soul. The enlightened are on an equal footing with the ignorant in the struggle against their own evil—the only difference being that the enlightened person knows the truth, and has no excuse for betraying it.' "

I noticed Kostas nodding and Bob pointed out that what I had read represented almost a replica of the situation with his own former guru, the difference being the latter's weakness for young boys.

"My dear Kyriaco," Kostas said, "this is what we have been try-ing to convey to people all along. Wisdom, knowledge, and enlight-enment do not necessarily presuppose the highest spiritual state of awareness. This is what people refuse to understand."

"Such people," Anthony pointed out, "are so charismatic that they can convince people of their pure motives in an absolute way. As you read that, Kyriaco, it reminded me of Matthew's Gospel that 'For false Christs and false prophets will arise and show great signs and wonders, so as to lead astray, if possible, even the elect.' "

"Let me read you a few more of Muktananda's admonitions to his devotees," I said, and pulled from my "scandal file" a photocopy of an extract from a book published by the SYDA foundation he set up before his death in 1983.[2] " 'Give up pride and egoism. Humility leads to perfection, while conceit is self-deception.' Then a few par-agraphs down he tells his followers: 'There is no deity superior to the Guru, no gain better than the Guru's grace, no *japa* more re-warding than the remembrance of the Guru, no state higher than meditation on the Guru—therefore become a true child of the Guru.' "

Kostas shook his head in dismay. "These people are most dan-gerous," he said, "because they convince their followers that their wisdom and their demonstrated psychic abilities are the product of their spiritual purity, that they have somehow attained God realization."

"It seems to me," Maroulla interjected, "that such characters, given their knowledge about esoteric matters, must know the con-sequences of their actions. However, their enchantment with their ego is much stronger than the knowledge of certain self-punishment through karma that will follow as a result of their actions."

"Precisely," Kostas replied. "They know that they will suffer eventually, that they will pay as a result of their actions. Yet they do it because their awareness is stranded inside the cocoon of their enchantment. The magnetism of this enchantment is a greater force in them than their awareness which vibrates at low spiritual levels. Again, wisdom does not necessarily mean purity. Such persons can express knowledge and wisdom because they have developed their noetical body. They may express this kind of knowledge without themselves being well-integrated, balanced personalities.

"You see," Kostas continued, "wisdom and knowledge are inside us, inside every human being, inside our subconscious, inside every particle of our material and nonmaterial existence. Consequently it is possible through various means, technical means or whatever, to coordinate ourselves with that part of our subconscious and succeed in opening the floodgates of that wisdom. And wisdom could come forward independently of our psychonoetical development. These methods have been known to human beings through the centuries and they have been passed on from one generation to the next. For this reason we will see throughout history unbalanced personalities expressing great esoteric knowledge and wisdom and exemplifying extraordinary psychic gifts."

"In fact," I said, "Colin Wilson[3] in his historical study of many notable occultists has drawn similar conclusions. His investigations showed that some of them were not only strangely gifted but highly promiscuous, while often weak in body and integrity."

"What is really happening," Kostas said, "is that many of these people, through various methods, began working on the psycho-noetic centers, what we call sacred discs and the Hindus call chakras. But instead of working on those centers that lead to the upliftment of their awareness and spirituality they stimulated centers of power."

"Can you be more specific about this?" Helena asked.

"The other day I received a phone call from a woman who got into trouble because she started certain exercises on the *Kundalini* center, the one at the base of the spine. Now, that was very dangerous. The *Kundalini*, or what we call the sacred serpent or sacred fire, will be awakened only naturally with the spiritual growth of the individual. The energy that will be unleashed will then move upward as it should and energize the higher chakras. When that begins to take place the present personality becomes spiritually purified."

"It is the way of the saints," I interjected.

"Right. But if you awaken this sacred fire prematurely through technical methods, then you may end up an unbalanced personality who cannot master the energy that has been liberated. This is what apparently happened to this woman. The present personality is taken over by unmanageable sexual urges. I would bet this is what must have happened also with people like Muktananda and Bob's former teacher.

"It is possible," Kostas went on, "that either in the present or previous incarnations these individuals have focused on these centers and instead of the energy moving upward, as it should under normal conditions, it moved downward toward the lower centers of the genitals and the anus with the disastrous results that we know. You see, with proper spiritual practice, where the focus is the upliftment of awareness, that is the upliftment of the way one thinks and feels, the *Kundalini* energy gradually unfolds and moves upward. As it does so it energizes and purifies the higher chakras, it purifies the present personality. This is the baptism of fire that we have been talking about. It is what John the Baptist meant when he said, 'I baptize you in water but He who comes after me will baptize you in fire.' It is what the Apostles underwent during Pentecost.

"It is inconceivable," Kostas continued, "that a person who presumably has reached high levels of spirituality is at the mercy of his or her instinctual urges. These people, who preach that they have gone beyond their lower urges and yet express themselves inappropriately in this manner, are to me most problematic, to say the least."

"Yet people like that," I pointed out, "may express great wisdom and perform miraculous healings and . . ."

"Yes, yes. This happens. These are abilities that one can develop through technical means, as we said. But we must keep in mind that these abilities and wisdom are independent of how these people will actually behave within time and space. And let me tell you, the road for such so-called masters is much longer than that of ordinary people who live in ignorance. They themselves have made it longer."

"When we say that such individuals can have wisdom and knowledge of reality, we mean of course, knowledge up to a certain point," I clarified.

"Yes, up to a certain point," Kostas repeated. "You can't ascend to the highest realms under such conditions. But knowledge of relative realities can be attained by anyone regardless of spiritual development since it is possible for one to coordinate himself or herself with the subconscious mind through various technical methods. And these methods, as we said, have been known to people through the centuries and have been used by mystics of low awareness or psychonoetic development."

"The question that comes to my mind," Bob said, "is whether a person under the guidance of a flawed guru can make spiritual progress."

"It has been suggested," I volunteered, "that it is possible to progress spiritually under such a guru in the same way that a placebo can cause you to feel better.[4] But I am not sure whether this is the most appropriate metaphor. My friend Michael Lewis suggested that a flawed guru is more like an imperfect medicine with bad side effects." When I said that there was a burst of laughter.

"The question," I went on to say, "is how far a person can grow under the guidance or misguidance of a master who does not himself or herself live the Truth."

"Of course," I added, as an afterthought, "all of us are masters and students to one another since we all have the Divine in us and we all offer lessons to each other through karma. From this point of view we are all gurus."

"I have a parallel question to what you have just raised," Maroulla said. "Is it possible that such flawed masters may have at the same time benefited humanity by bringing forward this knowledge? I mean is it possible for that knowledge to be more useful for individuals at a higher psychonoetic development than for those who tapped into it themselves?"

"Oh, absolutely," Kostas responded. "The knowledge itself is blessed from high up. It is the knowledge that is part of each one of us, and is Divine in its origin. It is God's knowledge."

"We need to separate the message from the messenger," I added.

"Correct. There is no problem when people who are exposed to this knowledge are not subjected to the guru's exploitation. Knowledge in itself is useful and as long as you get only the knowledge, then you will be benefited. Why not? The problems come when the offering of that knowledge to you by the master or guru has as its price your entanglement in his or her deeper, pathological motives."

"This is true in any field of knowledge, whether it is science, theater, music, or spiritual wisdom," Anthony remarked.

"That is precisely the case, my dear Anthony," Kostas responded. "We must overcome our uncritical enchantment with gurus and masters and see them as ordinary human beings like ourselves. Stay away from anyone who goes around claiming to be a master and expecting to be adored like a god."

"A great scientist or a great artist that has made a major contribution in his or her field may not necessarily be the kind of a person with whom you would want to get entangled on a personal level.

"All masters," Kostas went on, "will be credited on the basis of their level of awareness—that is, the level of their psychonoetic development and the degree to which they can live up to the greatness of the wisdom, not the fact that they channeled the wisdom itself. Do you follow what I am saying?" Kostas looked around and stretched on the reclining chair he was sitting on. With our body language we showed that we did follow what he was trying to convey.

"Another thing that we must perhaps keep in mind," I said after a while, "is to be compassionate to gurus who have shown serious weaknesses and flaws in their behavior. That is, we must avoid the tendency to demonize them. In our disappointment and anger it is easy to do that. Yet they have made throughout history major contributions in the collective advancement of human consciousness. Perhaps this is part of the Divine Plan also that is beyond our rational comprehension."

Kostas responded that compassion should be the guiding principle for all human beings, including flawed masters. "However," he said, "we also have a responsibility to protect the innocent from being abused by such persons."

"Why," Bob asked, "does God allow His wisdom to be channeled not only by saintly personalities but also by personalities that are so scandalously flawed?"

Kostas smiled and shook his head. "His wisdom? But my dear, His Life is inside each one of us, regardless of our spiritual level. This is what we said earlier. Had it not been so, that is, possible that flawed personalities can acquire knowledge and wisdom, there wouldn't be any polarity within creation to offer us experiences for spiritual development."

"Let us take a concrete example," I said. "I have in mind Socrates and what we know about him. He was responsible for injecting great wisdom in Western civilization presented through the dialogues of Plato. From what you are saying there is no way of knowing the level of Socrates' spiritual development. Is there a possibility that this man of such great wisdom and knowledge was not also morally and spiritually advanced?"

"Yes, it is possible that Socrates may not have been a balanced personality. However, I don't believe that to be the case. But on principle it is possible. If you take the teachings alone you cannot know."

"But he did drink the hemlock after all," Anthony pointed out with a tone of humor in his voice.

"In reality we have no right to judge a personality even if we had all the information about that person. Only God has the right to judge."

"But if you are a God-conscious individual that has come into what the fathers of the Church would call 'an erotic relationship with God,' you cannot be an unbalanced personality," I pointed out.

"Precisely. In other words, you cannot be a purified individual and be unbalanced in your expression at the same time, by definition."

"I have become aware lately," I went on, "of the incredible spiritual literature that was produced by the early fathers of the Church. Between the years A.D. 400 and A.D. 900 some of the Greek fathers produced some very profound mystical writings which I am beginning to familiarize myself with. I cannot imagine that any of these individuals could have been at the same time unbalanced personalities."

"Why? . . ." Kostas reacted, and he gave me a strange look bordering on irony.

"I don't know." I shrugged, taken aback by his response. "You tell me."

"How can you judge the personality of authors by just reading what they wrote? How can you know the motives behind what they put down on paper?"

"So on the basis of books or what mystics have left behind on paper about their thoughts and their experiences you can never know with certainty the quality of their character. This is what you are saying. Right?"

"Right. Strictly speaking and as a matter of principle, no, you cannot," Kostas emphasized.

"So how is a simple human being like myself able to distinguish

one case from another, the truly advanced master who both dissem-
inates wisdom and lives up to it, and the other who does only the
first?" I asked.

Kostas thought for a few seconds. "You shall know them," he
said, "neither by what they say nor by what they do."

"I am not sure I understand what you mean," Bob interjected.

"The only way to understand such a person is to enter within
the context of his or her motives. You will get a better understanding of their motives and character when among other things you
observe their overall behavior within society. See how that individual reacts when provoked. Then you may get a better picture of that
individual's character. For example, when a master at one moment
is like a river of great knowledge and wisdom and the next moment
begins to use foul language against people, gets agitated and upset
toward those that don't pander to his or her narcissism, a disciple
should be extremely cautious. Otherwise you can easily be fooled
because gurus who are capable of such feats are also great actors
that can deceive not only the gullible but also those who have experience with these matters."

"I have an epistemological problem now," I said with a certain
agitation in my voice. "I cannot know the quality of people in their
everyday life that I read and admire."

"That's right. You can't."

"How can I know whether Saint Paul, or Peter or John or the
other Apostles and evangelists, were well-integrated, balanced
personalities?"

"My dear Kyriaco, what you should do is to absorb the wisdom
that they left behind. This is what matters. This is what I have been
saying all these years.

"Now of course," Kostas went on, "you mentioned specific personalities, which is not fair . . ."

"Just a minute now, why not?"

"You have mentioned saintly personalities that have reached great heights of spiritual attainment. Otherwise they would not have been the disciples of the Most Beloved One."

"This is what I want to know. What are the criteria that you can use to distinguish a saintly personality?"

"You cannot distinguish, based strictly on what they wrote, that is."

"I suppose," I concluded, "that when you have a personal relationship to a master you must keep your individual judgment, integrity, and values intact. One should never abdicate control of one's life."

"Absolutely true," Kostas stressed.

We took a break from our discussion as Maroulla and Anthony brought us a delicious and refreshing red watermelon, one of the summer delights in Cyprus, a major producer and exporter of the fruit. We needed time too in order to digest what we had just talked about. After we had quenched our thirst with it we resumed our discussion.

"According to the teaching of Erevna . . ." Maroulla started saying.

"Just a minute, Maroulla, dear," Kostas interrupted her, "Erevna does not have any teaching."

"What is this, now?" Maroulla said with a chuckle and the rest of us shared her puzzlement.

"Erevna is *involved* with the Teaching."

"What's the difference?"

"There is a big difference. If you call it the teaching of Erevna, then you appropriate it as your own, as if the wisdom of God is the property of this or that group or organization." Kostas paused and then proceeded with emphasis. "Erevna is preoccupied with the Teaching and tries to convey it to others."

"But whose Teaching is that?" Maroulla asked again.

"No one's. This Teaching springs from the Universal Subconscious. It is the outpouring of wisdom, which everyone has access to. It is not owned by anybody in particular. It is neither the monopoly nor the property of any guru, or any mystical group."

"Or any particular culture, religion, or civilization," I added.

"Right."

"But it is always filtered through particular cultures, religions, civilizations, and therefore always colored and distorted," I said further.

"Exactly," Kostas agreed. "And the more we clear up this filter of our awareness the more we will be able to apprehend this relative Wisdom."

"So what Erevna does is clear these filters," Maroulla said, and being true to her lighthearted, humorous nature she continued to chuckle.

"Yes. It is simply an approach to the Truth. It is just a method. We are not interested in just channeling the Truth. What we are interested in is to assimilate it, make it part and parcel of our expression within time and space. As I said many times, while developing our knowledge we must also develop, parallel to that, our awareness, meaning the purity of our thoughts and feelings."

"So Erevna is not interested in channeling?" Bob asked.

"No, of course not. Had this been our aim it would have been very easy," Kostas responded.

"So you consider channeling, which is very popular today, an unorthodox way of approaching the Truth?" Bob asked further.

"Of course. We are not interested in that ourselves. We are not interested in becoming mediums. Our aim is to coordinate our awareness with our subconscious in such a way so that whatever comes out as knowledge will be part and parcel of our own expression in terms of our thoughts, feelings, and actions.

"Channeling by itself is nothing more than just reading a script without having any clue as to what the script is all about," Kostas continued. "You see people who enter into trances and channel material or languages that they don't even know. What they channel does not represent their level of psychonoetical development. This is not our approach."

"Isn't it possible," I asked, "that a purified personality may be used by higher intelligences to express a particular aspect of the Teaching?"

"Of course it is possible," Kostas replied.

"The Koran is one example that comes to mind," I said. "Mohammed was in a state of trance when he dictated the Koran to his relatives who were writing it down. He himself was illiterate, yet the Koran is high-quality poetry. It is said that Mohammed was also a very compassionate person."

"The *Course in Miracles*[5] would be another example," Helena interjected.

"Also the Seth material of Jane Roberts,"[6] Bob added.

"However, it is quite clear to me," I said, "that channeling has been going on throughout human history affecting it in very direct and indirect ways." I then mentioned the name of Jon Klimo[7] and others who have masterfully shown beyond any doubt the continuous impact of channeling on culture and civilization.

"I am not discounting the importance of these revelations," Kostas clarified. "They do contribute to the awakening of humanity, to the truth of higher realities. It is simply not our approach, that's all. You see, our efforts and emphasis are toward the attunement of our lower self, what we call our present personality, with our inner reality, the Spirit within. What is important to us is the degree to which we can express our real Self through the upliftment of our awareness."

Kostas went on again to point out that what he means by "awareness" is the way one feels, thinks, and acts. "Awareness, therefore, is something distinguishable from knowledge or wisdom. Someone may express great wisdom through channeling or other means and his or her awareness may not necessarily be at par with that wisdom. The aim of Erevna as taught by Kostas is not only to tap into our inner sources of wisdom but simultaneously to uplift the level of our awareness so that it is true to that wisdom."

By three o'clock the heat was beginning to interfere with our concentration and philosophical discussions and we decided to follow the local custom and take a siesta for a couple of hours to rejuvenate ourselves. By five o'clock the heat would have receded as the late afternoon breezes came up from the seashore.

When we reassembled again under the fig tree Anthony came up with a list of questions that he wished Kostas to answer.

"Last night I wanted to ask some questions on what you had presented but I didn't get the chance," Anthony said.

"Well, here we are now. I am listening."

"You talked about balance and harmony and the *Agathon* as distinct from the humanly conceived good. You said that meanings exist within the worlds of balance only, and not within Beingness Itself."

"Right," Kostas nodded.

"Therefore, should we assume that whenever we contemplate or reflect on something, in whatever direction, we are creating a disequilibrium, or a disturbance of the balance?"

"To be more precise," Kostas replied, "there is never a state of disequilibrium. The worlds of balance will always remain such. We may use the word disequilibrium as a manner of speaking. Balance is automatic. The human individual is gradually liberated from the influence of meanings. One does not strengthen a particular meaning versus another, because meanings are always in a state of balance and equilibrium. What is happening is that within time and space —that is, through human experience on a given planet—the meanings of good and evil continuously fade away but they are always in a continuous state of balance and equilibrium. They will remain so until that point when the level of awareness of the individual will be led where only the *Agathon* is expressed—that is, the All Goodness of the inner Self beyond all human meanings."

"Can such a person live among other human beings who themselves carry on an existence within lower levels of meanings of good and evil?"

"Of course. For those persons who have reached the *Agathon*, their expression within time and space does not pass through any filter of awareness. They directly manifest their true nature, their Divine Self.

"Such individuals," Kostas continued, "will look at their fellow human beings, entrapped as they are within the world of meanings and ignorance, with total compassion. That is why they will never discriminate between 'good' and 'bad' people. Rather they will embrace both in the same way, that is, with unconditional love, which is the nature of the inner Self. God, as the Christ Logos, is 'the light that lighteth every human being that descends upon the earth.' "

"Can you please elaborate further on what you mean by harmony as distinct from balance?" Helena asked. "It is still somewhat unclear to me."

"It is difficult if not impossible to talk about the nature of harmony because it is a state beyond humanly constructed meanings. It is a state of the characteristics of the Autarky of the Absolute. Balance is the world of existence through the workings of the law of karma. Balance is maintained at the various levels of the expression of human ignorance.

"Of course," Kostas went on, "we are inside harmony but we are not aware of it. We had harmony. We have it at this very moment, but we do not express it. We must go through the worlds of balance and equilibrium and eventually become liberated from our ignorance and reestablish harmony."

"Aren't the worlds of existence also within harmony?" Helena asked.

"But of course. The worlds of existence are within harmony but they are altered by the intervention of the ignorance of human beings. Everything is inside harmony and Autarky since everything is inside God. There is no natural world of polarity, of opposites. It is the intervention of human awareness that generates polarity and opposition within these worlds. Now get this point: If and when human beings are liberated and disentangled from the meaning of opposites, of polarity, then the material worlds, and by that I mean not only the gross material but also the psychic and the noetical, will no longer be worlds of polarity, of the dual opposites.

"To repeat, it is not the nature of the world that we find ourselves in that generates polarity, the meanings of good and evil, and so on, but the nature of our awareness. It is human awareness that transforms the harmony of the world, which is its nature, into a world of balance through the workings of karma. If my awareness gets transmuted to the highest states, beyond the humanly constructed meanings, then I can walk on this earth and do what I must do and yet I will not be living within a world of opposites but of harmony. And the least of my concerns would be the various roles that I will be playing within society."

"Oh," I exclaimed, "I have just read during our siesta a beautiful quotation on this very topic by the religious scholar Shankaracharya. Would you like me to read it for you?" I brought out a work edited by Stanislav Grof. In one of the articles the author quoted the Indian sage.[8]

" 'Sometimes a fool,' " I read, " 'sometimes a sage, sometimes possessed of regal splendor; sometimes wandering, sometimes as motionless as a python, sometimes wearing a benignant expression; sometimes honored, sometimes insulted, sometimes unknown— thus lives the man of realization, ever happy with supreme bliss. Just as an actor is always a man, whether he puts on the costume of his role or lays it aside, so is the perfect knower of the Imperishable always the Imperishable, and nothing else.' "

"So basically," Maroulla interjected after I passed on the book to her and she flipped through its pages, "the worlds of polarity, of opposites, do not exist except within human awareness."

"Completely," Kostas replied with enthusiasm in his voice. "This world that we find ourselves in now is the grandest dream that humanity is experiencing. It is the only dream. There will be others, smaller ones within the psychonoetic dimensions, but in comparison to the dream that humans undergo now, they will be insignificant."

"Therefore," Helena added, "as long as humans are inside this dream they will be creating and living in a world of balance and equilibrium."

"That's it."

"Now suppose that all human beings on this planet," Anthony said, "have collectively reached the highest stage of the development of their awareness, will the world of balance on the planet continue to be?"

"No, it will not," Kostas replied.

"So what is going to happen? Will the world of balance and equilibrium become transmuted into a world of harmony?"

"As I said, the planet is already within harmony. But the planet is under the impact of the disharmony caused by the elementals that humanity constantly creates. A disharmony is created within harmony as a result of the abuse of the power that humans are endowed with. Do not underestimate the power that human beings constantly project outward. This is the underlying cause of even natural disasters that human beings erroneously attribute to God, calling them acts of God or scourges of God. Such disasters are due to the elementals that we ourselves have created and return back to us in the form of so-called acts of God, such as hurricanes, earthquakes, et cetera."

When Kostas said that, I thought of the concerns of ecologists and others about the warming of the earth, the greenhouse effect and the depletion of the ozone layer. If natural calamities begin to surge—devastating hurricanes, the raising of the oceans, the submersion of entire cities under water—their cause will not be "acts of God" but the "elementals" of industrialism that we have been furiously producing, individually and collectively, during the last three hundred years. But Kostas was saying something deeper. All disasters that are inflicted on the human race since the beginning of human awareness, causing the destruction of communities, bodily harm, and loss of life, are ultimately caused not by God but by the flaws and ignorance of humanity. It is the law of karma at work within the context of the world of balance and of opposites.

"I have some further questions, Kosta, that I would like to raise with you," Anthony said after we drifted for a few minutes to less "serious" conversation. "I have learned that you are rather critical of the widespread practice of mantra yoga."

"You mean the repetition of words?"

"Yes. It is an old method practiced by mystics to enter into transpersonal states of awareness, sometimes called cosmic consciousness. Why do you have reservations about this method?"

Kostas remained pensive for a few seconds. "I can only speak on the basis of my own personal research into this matter," Kostas went on to say. "By repeating words, or mantras, over prolonged periods of time, you may enter into certain conditions that you will not be able to master.

"You see, during sleep you enter into such states momentarily. But through this practice you try to prolong your stay in that condition. You experience a certain peace and tranquillity that presumably is not subjected to any influences. Most people don't understand, however, that the present personality under those states is subjected to various subconscious influences. It is so because at that moment the subconscious is wide open. People don't realize this until it is too late. Of course you will ask, do all practitioners of this method reach that state? Fortunately not. Divine mercy does not allow that. And I ask, what are the benefits of this practice? The answer, as far as I am concerned, none."

"Why?" Anthony asked.

"Because with this practice you don't work on your awareness. You simply enter into a tranquil state without anything preoccupying your present personality. That is what you think," he said with emphasis.

"Real spiritual value," Kostas continued, "comes when you enter into these higher psychonoetic states and you are master of these states. Spiritual growth, which in reality is the upliftment of awareness, does not come about by employing methods that are like tranquilizers that get you there without being your true expression as awareness. It is really not that different from the condition that one can get into with drugs, or through hypnosis. Our aim is to work on our awareness by continuously mastering the states that we find ourselves in. This is what Research for the Truth is all about, according to my understanding. Otherwise, what do you gain? You just open the gates of your house, i.e., your subconscious. People don't realize that this house is surrounded by the most savage beasts of the planet."

"You mean the elementals," Bob noted.

"Yes," Kostas said. "And when these beasts smell food nothing will stop them from entering."

Kostas then described several clinical cases of individuals who fell victim to some kind of negative psychic energy due to such practices. One fellow wrote that while in deep meditation, after an entire day's mantra yoga practice in a London apartment, workers outside his window began drilling the asphalt with a jackhammer. The shock he experienced from the sudden demoniacal noise was severe and he felt something entering him. That nonphysical "thing," he wrote, remained inside tormenting him for years. He was desperately seeking help. Another man, who earned a living as a reliable government official, lost his job because after taking up this type of practice he started behaving in bizarre ways unbecoming to a bureaucrat. These and other cases convinced Kostas to have grave reservations about such methods of spiritual practice, which have become so popular today.

I pointed out that it may not be fair to dismiss a practice that has benefited so many millions of people around the world just because some individuals have gotten into psychic trouble from overdose and without proper guidance. Some people who are already prone to mental problems, I said further, should stay away from such practices. A conventional form of psychotherapy may be more appropriate than mystical practices for transcendence. I also pointed out that research has shown that some types of meditation, such as repeating a word for periods of no more than twenty minutes twice a day, is beneficial to health. I then mentioned the work of Dr. Herbert Benson[9] of the Harvard medical school, who invented the "relaxation response," i.e., mantra yoga as a technique of deep relaxation, and that of Dr. Dean Ornish[10] who incorporated such a practice into the treatment of cardiac patients with great success.

Kostas responded that his position was based on his observations of the many people who sought his help after using mantras for prolonged periods of time with the aim of opening up their subconscious to psychic states and influences that they were not in a position to master. He was not referring to methods, he said, for calming down the nervous system for medical reasons.

"Kyriacos had mentioned to us earlier, Kosta," Helena said, "that you do not recommend the practice of past-life regression either, fashionable as it is today among many New Agers."

"Definitely I am against it for similar reasons that I mentioned in reference to mantras." When Helena asked what exactly he found to be so objectionable, Kostas went on to elaborate. He said that the veil of oblivion, namely the reality of not remembering past lives, plays a very important role in allowing the individual to focus on the present life, because it is the present life that is of importance for the spiritual development of the self. Digging into the past may bring forth memories that, as elementals of past incarnations, can plague the present personality.

"When you consider," Kostas said, "that our awareness moves constantly forward to higher and higher stages, then attuning yourself with a past incarnation means that you will come in contact with a part of you that was at a lower stage of development. You may come in contact with an incarnation when the meaning of good and evil were different, that is, at a lower stage, than the meaning of good and evil of the present. This can be very disturbing to the life of today. We should avoid stirring up that ocean we call the subconscious mind. We should recognize that what we are now is the result of past lives and the choices we made in terms of feelings, thoughts, and actions within the context of those lives. If we stir the waters, other situations could arise and appear on the surface and then the present personality will suffer the consequences. Never assume that in a past incarnation you were in a higher stage of awareness than the stage you are now. Forget the past, forget the future, and focus on the present moment because it is the present moment that matters."

"Kosta, don't you think that sometimes past-life regression may be therapeutic? There is important work done on this subject by responsible psychotherapists," I said, and mentioned such names as that of Brian Weiss[11] and Roger J. Woolger.[12]

"That is a different story, Kyriaco. Yes, of course. Sometimes it may be helpful to do past-life regression in order to help an individual resolve certain problems in the current life. But this is a very serious work and has to be done by someone highly knowledgeable and responsible. My objection to past-life regression is in regard to treating it like a sport, a matter of curiosity."

Kostas then repeated what he said many times: that the veil of oblivion, that keeps memories of past lives from rushing forward into the present, will be lifted in a natural way with the spiritual development of the present personality so that when the memories begin to manifest themselves they will have no effect on the present.

"You see," he said, "in reality the subconscious does not have any boundaries. The very moment you begin to submerge yourself in this ocean you must make certain that you wear the analogous diving suit. That means you have mastery over your subconscious, you have mastery over the memories that you will uncover. They must not come to the surface and become your current expression as a present personality. The memories of past lives must not become like a board that will come up and float on the surface of the ocean. These are the dangers when trying to go back to episodes of past incarnations."

"I have a suggestion," Maroulla said with excitement in her voice. "It is already six-thirty and the sun will disappear soon. You can't imagine how beautiful it is to go swimming at this hour."

There was consensus that Maroulla's suggestion was brilliant. We got into two cars and in less than twenty minutes we reached the coast, put on our swimsuits and splashed once more into the sea. Facing the setting sun all six of us swam slowly, absorbing the golden rays on our faces. The discussions continued as we swam parallel to the beach for the next hour.

"I have a few more questions about what you said last night on the relativity of good and evil in regard to the practices of mystics of previous epochs, Kosta," I said as we kept ourselves afloat, facing in the direction of the setting sun. "Based on what you said, mystics of the past would be viewed, from the vantage point of the present state of the general development of human awareness, as servants of not so benign forces."

"Right. But you have to keep in mind that mystics of the past did contribute to the growth of human awareness. If those mystics, however, were to live today and express themselves from the vantage point of their awareness of that earlier epoch, then the general average level of human awareness attained by humanity today would consider those mystics as servants of the darker forces than of the light. Yet in their time they were popularly viewed as being servants of light, the light as far as humanity on the whole could gaze at, at that time. Light and darkness are relative terms. We say that someone serves the light and somebody else serves the dark. In reality we are all servants of the light from the height that each one of us finds himself or herself. In God's name I cannot accept that there is Darkness, in Reality. There are only dark interpretations based on human awareness. Or, if you will, there are elementals created by human awareness that keep humanity stranded in ignorance. Darkness is ignorance that keeps us away from gnosis or knowledge and wisdom."

"But we have discussed earlier that you can have wisdom and not be self-realized."

"I mean wisdom and knowledge that you have assimilated in your current expression. That your present personality is at par with the wisdom that springs from within your inner self."

"I think there is a possible difficulty here," I said, as we continued to keep ourselves afloat with slow movements. "Who defines what the level of awareness is that you can use as a yardstick to compare and authenticate. How can you determine, for example, whether a certain mystical practice belongs to a lower stage of development of human awareness?"

"The closer you are to the *Agathon* the higher your stage of awareness," Kostas replied.

"But who can determine that?" Helena interjected.

"Who can tell," I added, "that a particular practice or the behavior of a particular mystic will fall under the category of the acceptable and normal, based on the current stage of awareness, and what would come under the category of the unacceptable or pathological?"

"Let me say this first. No master, regardless of his or her level of awareness, will in reality manifest the inner self in its totality, no master in this dimension, that is. So your question is how can we know that what we express today is much higher than what we were expressing yesterday? The answer is simple. The standard of comparison must be the *Agathon*, the All Love of God. How close are we to that?"

"Okay, so this is the yardstick," I said.

"Of course it is. Look, some masters of past epochs used to preside over rituals of human sacrifice. Are these acceptable from the vantage point of today's awareness?"

"Can you call those mystics?" Bob asked, making an extra effort to keep his head above water since his swimming skills were not very good.

"In the past? Oh yes!" Kostas replied. "Human beings used to consider them mystics and masters."

"But were they mystics as we understand the word mystic today?" Maroulla, a born swimmer, asked.

"From the vantage point of today's awareness, no, they were not. But for human beings of those days they were considered masters, and people used to kneel before them."

"And they did have psychic powers," I added.

"Of course they did. A lot of them demonstrated awesome psychic powers. Yet these very mystics, without fear or remorse, would take the life of someone and think nothing of it. They had great powers all right, regardless of their level of awareness. That is why, as I said before, we should not be so enamored by mystics today who exemplify these types of power and liberally employ them. You can summon all kinds of powerful elementals and accomplish spectacular feats that can mesmerize your devotees. But are these permissible today? Not in my book."

"Yet the demonstration of such feats," I pointed out, "although unacceptable from the point of view of serious spiritual work, may be helping humanity to overcome its obsession with the dominant materialist superstition that only this world exists. Perhaps these manifestations of power can have the effect of attracting the attention of mainstream science to investigate these phenomena."

"Perhaps so, but for us as Researchers of Truth such practices are not acceptable. And those who engage in them for egotistical reasons rather than for healing will be debited analogously by karma, regardless of what the unintended and indirect positive effects may ultimately have been on collective human awareness," Kostas said, and splashing his head into the water turned on his back and vigorously swam for five minutes.

The sun had disappeared half an hour earlier. We sat on the beach for a few more minutes and covered our bodies with towels. The sand was still warm and the temperature ideal. I have never found anything more soothing to the senses than sitting on the beaches of Cyprus during sunsets. I never lose an opportunity whenever I am on the island to be by the seashore during these moments of the day, a habit formed very early in my life.

We listened to the ripples of the waves and contemplated the horizon disappearing in the distance as we continued our conversation for a while longer.

"I still have a problem, Kosta," I said, and chuckled. "I don't mean to play the devil's advocate, but mystics of the past were not all on the same level."

"Alas if that were the case," Kostas quipped.

"There were mystics that even in deep antiquity must have been able to enter inside the *Agathon*, inside the All Love of the Absolute beyond any humanly constructed meanings, and come from that state and tell us about it. Otherwise, those of us at lower stages wouldn't have a clue that there is the *Agathon*."

"Absolutely. But keep in mind that the *Agathon* is inside you."

"We have to differentiate the mystics of the past from someone like the Buddha, for example . . ."

"But Kyriaco," Kostas interrupted, "we are not talking about those exceptions like the Buddha or the disciples of the Most Beloved or some of the other great teachers of humanity. We are talking about the mystics of the past that most human beings considered as mystics and the practices that they were engaged in during their times. Yet we must remember that even the greatest of mystics when conveying to their contemporaries their experiences always employed linguistic expressions appropriate to the times they lived and the level of society's awareness."

"Therefore," I added, "linguistically expressed knowledge and wisdom will always be relative."

"Exactly. It cannot be otherwise. Look, take the teachings even of Jesus Christ. He has offered one Teaching using the language of His time. How many interpretations of the Gospels have come up, how many dogmas, heresies, and so on? Yet the underlying Teaching is one, but always approached from different angles based on one's level of awareness. We claim that what we teach here ourselves is also consistent with the Gospels and take at face value what Christ said, that the kingdom of heaven is *endos emon* [within ourselves]. So we research within ourselves, and when others talk about the resurrection of bodies and the Second Coming of Christ we speak of the Second Coming as a psychospiritual state, i.e., opening up to Christ consciousness."

"From your vantage point then, or the vantage point of Erevna," Helena said, "any mystical practice that leads to Christ consciousness is authentic religion, whether it be called Mahayana Buddhism, Sufism, Vedanta, or Christianity."

"Whatever mystical practice leads to the unfoldment of Love, the Christ Logos within us is authentic, by definition," Kostas stated.

We went on discussing these issues for another twenty minutes. Then at the suggestion of Maroulla again we decided to put on our clothes and drive two miles to a nearby fishing village to have supper of traditional Cypriot fish *meze*.

I met with Kostas and the group at Plataniskia a few more times, usually in the evenings, further exploring issues related to the Erevna. Kostas was always ready and willing to meet with the various visitors that sought him out, but particularly with people like Anthony and Helena who headed Erevna circles in New York. Bob asked for the okay to begin a circle in Australia, and Maroulla promised to mail the transcribed lessons as given by Kostas in his usual spontaneous way.

After these visitors left I had further opportunities to meet with Kostas through the summer, often at his gas station where, in between customers, we would engage in endless philosophical discussions. He never failed to astonish me with his penetrating insights into esoteric knowledge, even if on occasion we would disagree on some particular detail. "My real work is not this," he reassured me one day while engrossed in a pile of legal documents. He had just returned from a two-day business trip to London to sort out his affairs with Shell Oil Company management. He did not have to explain to me the meaning of his words since I knew that Kostas' conception of his mission in this life was not to pump gasoline but to be a healer and to disseminate esoteric wisdom through Erevna. Yet Kostas, a devoted husband and father of two, had to work in the ordinary way to make his living. His wife, too, who as it happened was a cousin of Emily's, was particularly emphatic in not wanting her husband to turn into a revered and distant full-time guru. Already their lives have been affected by the endless influx of visitors not only from Cyprus but from all over the world seeking healing and spiritual wisdom. In spite of all the international attention there was this dignified, I would say heroic, stubbornness on the part of Kostas, who was determined not to fall into the trap of guru worship.

# 9

## TRANSITIONS

THE SUMMER OF 1990 WAS COMING TO AN END WHEN WE SPENT A few days with Stephanos and his wife, Erato, at Platres, a mountain village-resort where they found refuge from the August heat. They have been very close friends of Emily and me for many a year and their company has always been one of the attractions of our visits to Cyprus. Both of them were for a number of years teachers of "Practical Philosophy," an esoteric school that had its headquarters in London. From there it disseminated the teachings of a "self-realized" Indian *Shankaracharya*—a title like "Bishop." Stephanos was essentially the local "pillar" of that school, not only managing it and teaching this particular brand of oriental mystical philosophy and practice, but also training people how to meditate along lines similar to Maharishi Mahesh Yogi's Transcendental Meditation.

While carrying on my "participant observation" research within the context of Erevna I had also maintained ongoing contact with Stephanos who, for me, served as an anthropological "informant" and advisor on what was going on with other spiritual groups in Cyprus and overseas. Most important, Stephanos was a trusted confidante. I had the privilege of enjoying his seasoned wisdom, which was based on several decades of experiential participation in various spiritual traditions during his twenty-year stay in London and prior to his return to his native Cyprus.

I felt that what I learned from Stephanos complemented what I learned from Kostas. Since they were not acquainted with one another I brought them together on several social occasions during which time they exchanged views on matters related to spirituality. My thought was that Kostas and Stephanos could become a formidable duo if they ever decided to join their spiritual work. They respected each other and recognized that they followed parallel but different paths. It did not prevent, however, some of Kostas' students from attending Stephanos' discussion groups, and vice versa.

Stephanos' spiritual odyssey began in London after an accident that almost cost him his life. Until that episode, which kept him in a hospital bed for two whole years, he said he'd literally lived the life of the Prodigal Son, pursuing pleasure and chasing after money in every possible way. As he put it, "Had you met me then you wouldn't have wanted to have anything to do with me."

What was most interesting about Stephanos was his "road to Damascus" transformation, his metanoia, during and after the accident. He remembered, he told me, that as he was being rushed to the hospital a brilliant white light covered his body. He felt no pain. The light stayed with him for three days and gave him a sense of reassurance that in the end he would be all right. It was the beginning of his spiritual awakening. During his long hospitalization he began reflecting on his "sinful" and meaningless life. When he was finally released from the hospital and was able to walk again Stephanos was a radically transformed person. He totally left behind his former self and entered the road of spiritual renewal. "At that point," he told me, "I believed that God had offered me that experience as a lesson for my own awakening."

His search for meaning and enlightenment led him to various spiritual groups, from Sufi orders to Zen to Practical Philosophy. But his spirit continued to be restless. In spite of his popularity as a teacher and meditation guide he was still searching for something deeper, as he had said to me many times.

The last few years, however, Stephanos, to everybody's amazement, began undergoing another radical transformation in his spiritual development, a transformation that also had an impact on my own life and work. He began familiarizing himself with the Eastern Orthodox spiritual tradition. At a certain point he reached the conclusion that the mystical path of Eastern Christianity as practiced within the monastic orders and as manifested in the writings of the fathers of the Church, both ancient and contemporary, was a powerful road to the Divine. This reorientation in his mind from Eastern mysticism to Eastern Orthodox spirituality eventually led him, and his wife, to the dramatic decision to resign from their posts as teachers of Practical Philosophy and redirect all their energies to the devotional path of Eastern Orthodoxy. His meeting in Essex, England, with Father Sophrony, a ninety-six-year-old Russian Orthodox monk considered to be "a living master and saint," sealed Stephanos' spiritual baptism into the Eastern Orthodox path.

"What are you finding in Orthodoxy," I asked him once, "that you didn't find in these other traditions?" I assumed that the reason why he finally chose to follow the Eastern Orthodox way was because it was part of his own cultural tradition. Yet the primary reason, Stephanos assured me, was because he discovered in the Orthodox path a more decisive and effective way for overcoming egoism and narcissism. And that way, he said, is the way of humility.

Usually the people who are more likely to influence us in our lives are people that either we consider our peers or who we look up to. For example, if a Harvard professor of psychiatry engages in research about UFO abductees and seriously considers the tales of such people I will be more inclined to take notice and read his or her work than articles on UFOs written in popular magazines found at the checkout stands in grocery stores. In my own personal experience I was introduced to Transcendental Meditation and practiced it for several years only after a colleague and friend of mine, a TM teacher himself, persuaded me of the efficacy of the practice. Similarly, in the case of Stephanos I took notice of his turn toward Eastern Orthodox spirituality because he not only was and still is a close friend, but because I looked up to him.

Through our many contacts and discussions Stephanos introduced me to the rich spiritual and poetical literature left behind by the practitioners of this tradition in the form of confessions, aphorisms, and other descriptions of their spiritual lives and prescriptions for the attainment of humility and sainthood. "This literature," Stephanos told me once, to my astonishment, "is by far more meaningful and profound to me than the Vedas and Upanishads." With such statements he triggered my determination to find out more about this mystical tradition lying right in the very heart of Western culture, yet almost totally ignored.

As I began my exploration into Orthodox spirituality I tried to see possible connections with Erevna. In my own consciousness I had begun to look at Erevna as a form of jnana yoga within the Western spiritual tradition, and Eastern Orthodox spirituality as the devotional path to God, what the Indians would call bhakti yoga. I wanted to find out what there was about Orthodox spirituality that could be relevant to a modern individual who is not a monk and who is not necessarily a Greek Orthodox. Is there anything or any practice within that tradition that could be "exportable" and relevant to anyone within the West? Or is it a tradition strictly for Greek Orthodox and only Greek Orthodox? Keeping in mind Kostas' reservations about "past practices" that may not be appropriate for today's level of awareness I wanted to explore for myself the extent to which some of the Eastern Orthodox practices might be useful to Erevna work itself.

During our stay with Stephanos and Erato we all visited a couple of monasteries and some of the remote chapels that are so plentiful on Cyprus. It was an opportunity for Emily and me to become acquainted experientially and intellectually with Eastern Orthodox spirituality. Stephanos introduced us to some of the prayer meditations of the mystical part of this tradition and we practiced them together. He also engaged us in long theological discussions based on his understanding of the writings and teachings of some contemporary spiritual masters like Russian Orthodox Father Sophrony[1] also a former disciple of oriental mysticism, who'd had such a decisive impact on Stephanos. In addition he brought us in contact with an elderly local monk whom Stephanos considered a "self-realized holy man" gifted not only with total humility but also with clairvoyant sight. When I met him it was as if I had in front of me Father Zossima in Dostoevsky's *The Brothers Karamazov*. With such exposures my appetite grew to learn more about Eastern Orthodox mysticism as practiced in monastic orders.

"I want you to take this along," Erato said to us as we were preparing to leave Platres and return to the United States. "It is a little gift from me and Stephanos." Emily opened the flat rectangular package. "The Icon of Saint Mamas!" she exclaimed, and embraced Erato.

It was one of Emily's favorite icons, the rare image of a young saint riding on a lion and holding a lamb with his left arm. The icon that Erato gave us was similar to a wall painting at the chapel of Asinou that we had visited the day before. It is a small church built by the Byzantines during the twelfth century in the midst of a pine forest at the northern foothills of the Troodos mountains. We had visited Asinou several times in the past to absorb the beauty of the surrounding hills and admire the priceless religious paintings that cover the entire inside of the small church.

Emily always marveled at that image of Saint Mamas riding the lion. He is a celebrated saint on Cyprus, where he is credited with innumerable miracles. Over forty-five churches were built in his honor and a village was named after him. Yet, he was not a Cypriot, but an early Christian martyr from the nearby coast of Asia Minor, who was thrown to a pack of hungry lions by the Romans. When the beasts miraculously refused to devour him the soldiers were ordered to torture and kill him with their swords.

There are many legends about the saint and his relationship to wild beasts. One has him milking lions and making cheese out of the milk for the poor. Another has him employing lions to guard his flock of sheep. Yet another, invented by local Cypriots during the Ottoman years, turned Saint Mamas into a rebel against taxation. According to this lore, when Saint Mamas heard of the intention of the Turkish *pasha* (governor) in Nicosia to raise taxes against the peasants he mounted a lion and rode into town. When the *pasha* heard the roaring lion and saw the saint mounted on it he became so terrified that he ordered the abolition of the new tax that was to have been levied on the already overburdened peasants. Saint Mamas became a patron of the oppressed, a saint that the Cypriots could readily identify with.

Emily liked the icon not only for its unusual artistry but primarily for its multiple meanings. "To me," she said, "it symbolizes the harmony that can prevail between human beings and nature. Perhaps Saint Mamas is a forerunner to deep ecology." We reflected a few moments on what Emily had said as we focused our eyes on the icon.

"I can think of a couple other possible meanings," I said as I took it in my hands to examine it more closely. "Someone suggested that the lion symbolizes power and risk, the risk that one must assume when embarking consciously on the spiritual path. But I see an additional meaning. The saint symbolizes the Soul that must ride with the lion, the ego, to gain experience of the lower worlds. It is the ego, the 'lion,' that eventually must be mastered by the Soul and transcended."

Erato said that we failed to see another most important meaning. "You forgot," she chuckled, "that Emily is a Leo!"

# 10

## PILGRIMS AND
## SCHOLARS

IN THE LATE MORNING OF MARCH 24, 1991, I DROVE WITH MY
friend Demos from his house in Wayne, New Jersey, where I'd
spent the evening, to Astoria, New York. We set off to visit some
Greek coffee shops, restaurants, and grocery stores and spend the
day discussing personal matters and Greek and Cypriot politics. I
was to fly to Athens the following day. Astoria, with a heavy concentration of ethnic Greeks, is the place to learn the latest news
about Greece and Cyprus.

Demos, a fellow Greek Cypriot and a colleague in political science, has been a most compatible companion to engage in conversation on political and other mundane issues totally unrelated to the
spiritual questions that have preoccupied me during the past decade
or so. He has been neutral to such esoteric concerns and we rarely
talked about them. What had fed our friendship for over twenty
years was our mutual passion about the fate of Cyprus and our formidable encounter with America. When Turkey invaded the island
in July of 1974 Demos, his wife, Maria, and several others went on
a hunger strike outside the United Nations and slept on the pavement for several days. Emily and I found them there upon our ar-

*214*

rival in New York from Cyprus where we had experienced firsthand those shattering events.

My fondness for Demos had been cemented by his unmatched humor, particularly when we indulged in gossip about Greek, Cypriot, and American politicians, such as the various presidents of recent times. "Who knows, Demos," I said to him, laughing after he cracked a hilarious joke about Ronald Reagan, "perhaps we were cousins or brothers in some previous life." He gave me a side look and reminded me that with all due respect to our friendship such matters were not his cup of tea and that they made him rather "nevrous," as he would jokingly put it.

We finished our Turkish coffee in a Greek *cafeneion* and after I secured my Olympic Airways ticket from a local tour operator and Demos bought Cypriot beer and some Greek groceries that one finds only in Astoria, we walked for a while. The sounds of bouzouki music were heard everywhere we turned. Many faces, which betrayed recent immigrant status, engaged in animated Greek conversations. I felt I was already in Greece, right there in New York City.

As we casually strolled along, my eye caught a small book shop at a street corner selling a variety of Greek Orthodox paraphernalia, from crosses and icons of the Holy Virgin to books written by the early fathers of the Church, as well as pamphlets written by contemporary "hell and damnation" Greek theologians. I entered the book shop to do some browsing for a few minutes. Demos followed me.

I had vowed to explore Orthodoxy, and the aim of my upcoming trip to Greece was to visit Mount Athos, "the Holy Mountain," where over two thousand hermits and monks lived. I presumed that the book shop would have some material on the subject.

The shopkeeper approached us with a broad smile, a large golden tooth revealing itself under his meticulously trimmed thin mustache. He was a short, baldheaded man in his fifties with a black tie and a suit of British cashmere. He must have arrived from Greece only recently, I thought, since his mannerisms, his dress, and overall composure were of the typical shopkeeper in downtown Athens.

"Sir," I said, "do you by any chance happen to carry any books related to Agion Oros [Holy Mountain]?"

"Yes, of course," he replied, as a bearded man who was absorbed in reading a book turned toward us upon hearing "Agion Oros." "But may I ask why you are interested in the Holy Mountain?"

Imagine, I mused to myself, entering a book shop on Fifth Avenue and having the manager inquiring on the reasons why you were interested in buying a particular book. The beauty of America is its diversity.

"I will be there in a few days to celebrate Easter and do some studies," I said. "I have been told that a lot of interesting things go on up there. I am curious to find out."

The man's face lit up and he excitedly informed us that he had been to Agion Oros several times himself. "I wish I could join you," he said with a sigh. "They will be celebrating *Kyrion Pascha* [Major Easter] this year."

"That's one of the reasons why I am going there now," I replied and looked at the shelves to see if there were any relevant books.

It was my friend Antonis, a Cypriot businessman, who had urged me to join him for Easter on Mount Athos, since this year, according to the old calendar that the Athonite monks use, Easter coincided with the Annunciation, on April 7, 1991. This was of great symbolic significance for the monks. Such convergence occurs only once in a century. Most importantly for me, the *Kyrion Pascha* coincided with my sabbatical leave from the University of Maine. Unencumbered by routine academic duties I was in a position to heed Antonis's urge that in my explorations of esoteric matters, it was of utmost importance that I familiarize myself with the "living heart of Christianity." He had visited Mount Athos himself and returned to Cyprus completely transformed and enchanted.

The Greek shopkeeper was more interested in talking about the Agion Oros than selling books, and it was clear that his work was of secondary importance to his religious commitments. The bearded man sitting there joined the discussion—he himself was preparing for the priesthood.

"I was told," I said to him, "that many unusual phenomena take place up there. Do you know if this is true?"

The man waved his hand indicating that in fact "miracles" and extraordinary occurrences is what the Holy Mountain is all about. "You must meet Father Vasilios," he said with emphasis, almost in the form of an order.

"Who is he?" I asked.

"The Lion of Mount Athos," the man replied, and his eyes beamed.

"I thought Mount Athos had only wolves," I quipped. "But lions?"

"Oh, my friend, he is a living saint, a legend. The miracles he performs are out of this world. Nobody knows how old he is. Some say he is ninety-five, but he looks no more than sixty."

I had first heard of Father Vasilios from the pastor of the Greek Orthodox Church in Bangor, Maine, who spoke about him with similar reverence. But I was warned that meeting him was very difficult because he lived by himself in the middle of rugged mountains, three hours on foot away from the nearest monastery.

"Father Vasilios can take a look at you and tell you everything about yourself, everything that goes on in your heart. He can literally see through your soul as if you were an open book. And he lives with just a little dried bread and water each day. He is the master of masters there," the man said.

The talkative shopkeeper went on to say that there are many holy fathers on Mount Athos who demonstrate such abilities, but they refrain from talking about them.

"Miracles are happening up there all the time," the man said. He hesitated for a moment and then went on. "In fact I was present when an extraordinary event took place. Several years ago I spent Easter in one of the monasteries. During the liturgy on Easter Sunday one of the holy fathers, while burning incense in the sanctum over the skulls of monks considered to be saints, saluted them with the *Christos Anesti, Adelphoi* [Christ is Risen, Brothers]. And believe it or not, we heard the skulls respond with the *Alithos Anesti O Kyrios* [Truly the Lord is Risen]."

The shopkeeper insisted that what he heard, others heard also, and that what they heard was not some kind of hallucination or trick by other monks to bewitch gullible pilgrims. I noticed that Demos could hardly betray a smile dripping with skeptical irony upon hearing this story. But he said nothing, and the shopkeeper, excited as he was, hardly noticed.

"But why don't they allow women to visit Mount Athos?" Demos, who could no longer control himself, asked provocatively. "Why this anachronism in this day and age?" His question put the two pious men on the defensive and both began explaining why since the tenth century no woman has ever been allowed to set foot on Mount Athos. Presumably this rule was established in order to allow the monks to engage in their spiritual practices without the presence of worldly temptation. Once that rule was set up in the tenth century, it became a rigid tradition, and as such became impossible to change. Religious institutions are not noted for their flexibility and readiness to adapt to new situations.

"Women," the younger man with the newly grown beard said, "are by nature inferior to men."

I felt my eyes widening and my mouth half opening upon hearing that. Being accustomed to the American academic scene, the utterance of such a statement was not only scandalous but deeply painful. Both Demos and I were crudely reminded of the cultural milieu of which we had been products.

"Now why is this so?" I asked as I tried to hide my incredulity.

"Because, my friend," the older man replied, "it was woman who sinned first by listening to the snake and deceiving her husband."

The younger man signaled us to stop the discussion as a woman entered the shop. After she bought some church incense and stepped outside, the older man continued. "Of course on spiritual grounds both men and women are equal. They have an equal chance to reach heaven. God loves them the same way as He loves men. They are inferior to men only socially and intellectually." Then he went on to quote several Apostles and saints to provide legitimacy to what he had just said. The discussion brought to my mind the medieval debate among theologians on whether women had souls.

Neither Demos nor myself was in the mood for an argument which would have been pointless anyway. We simply listened to the painful utterances of the two men who I believed represented a considerable portion of male opinion within contemporary Greek culture.

I bought a book about Mount Athos, and the shopkeeper, an otherwise sympathetic-looking man, probably a loving father and devoted husband, wished me a "worthy pilgrimage."

"I am surely glad our wives are not with us," Demos, shaking his head, murmured with relief as we left the book shop. "I can't understand why nice people like them carry in their heads such notions."

For a few seconds a certain sad feeling overtook me as I pondered the road that Greek society had to traverse before it could become part of the "modern age." Not that the latter is utopia, but at least on such issues as human rights, equality of the sexes, ecumenicity, and tolerance for diversity, by comparison, the "modern age" had made notable advances. For Greece, I thought, such a cultural transformation was long overdue and imperative, if the country was to avert another catastrophic war with Turkey.

"I hope you haven't changed your mind about going to Mount Athos," Demos said teasingly as we crossed the George Washington

Bridge on the way back to his house. "But tell me, why do you really want to visit Mount Athos? I thought you were critical of the Church."

I laughed at his puzzlement. "There are many reasons why I want to go there," I said, and briefly explained to Demos my association with Stephanos and how he had influenced me in taking a serious look at Eastern Orthodoxy. "But it was Antonis, another friend and a former secular skeptic like yourself, who triggered my interest in Athos," I went on to say. "I know you don't believe in such things, but he brought to my attention that so-called paranormal phenomena that we have associated with shamans, psychics, healers, and clairvoyants are routine matters and shared secrets on the Holy Mountain."

Demos gave me a side look with eyebrows slightly raised but I persisted. "Antonis told me that during the recent severe political crisis that brought Greece and Turkey to the brink of war some of the holy fathers were allegedly working around the clock to prevent the tragedy. It would have been catastrophic not only for Greece and Turkey but also for Cyprus—the Turks would have surely taken over the entire island. The Papandreou government in Greece, if you remember, ordered its fleet to sink a Turkish boat that provocatively searched for oil in disputed Greek waters. According to Antonis, who had established close ties with several Athonite monks, the more spiritual and 'advanced' of the fathers were presumably engaging in out-of-body travel and worked to change the minds of Turkish and Greek officials to prevent a war. They were reputedly right on the decks of the Greek and Turkish ships with their psychonoetic bodies trying to calm the sailors and the captains of those ships."

"The war was averted at the last moment," Demos said wryly, "when President Ozal of Turkey who, as you remember, was recuperating from an operation in London, showed enough sense—as in the case of Nikita Khrushchev during the Cuban missile crisis—to telephone his government and order the Turkish boat out of Greek waters. Why the need to resort to such fantastic and exotic explanations?"

"But, Demo, I am not arguing necessarily for the ontological validity of these stories. I am simply intrigued because the official Church has traditionally been suspicious of lay practitioners of such spiritual arts. More often than not the Church hierarchy has viewed such practices as likely manifestations of Luciferian energies.

"It is partly these stories that made up my mind to pay a visit and learn more about the Agion Oros," I went on to say. "It would be of utmost significance, I think, if in fact such experiences, whether true or fictitious, that have been associated with Tibetan monasteries and Hindu yogis could as well be detected right in the very heart of the Christian tradition."

"Why would you be interested in that?" Demos asked again.

"I will tell you," I said. "For the last hundred years, scores of Western intellectuals, disillusioned with mainstream Christianity, have turned toward the East, to Hinduism and Buddhism, in search of what they thought was lacking within the Christian tradition, that is, a method of ecstasy."

"A method of ecstasy?" Demos murmured.

"By that I mean a way to stand outside of ordinary reality and explore realms of existence beyond the reach of the rational mind." I went on to tell Demos of an episode that Jacob Needleman narrates in the opening pages of his celebrated work *Lost Christianity*[1] in regard to the hunger he perceived among people who wished to remain within Christianity but were attracted to the contemplative experiential traditions of the Orient because they were unable to find something analogous within their own traditions. Needleman recounted his meeting with a Catholic bishop who had studied Zen meditation and worked closely with well-known humanistic psychologists to introduce contemplative methods into the life of his diocese.

" 'He was constantly scanning my face,' " Needleman wrote, " 'for some sign of approval, and this eventually made me so ill at ease that I blurted out in a half-joking way, "Well, I've always imagined that you leaders of the Church have a secret monastery someplace, where you go to refresh your inner lives under the direction of a wise spiritual guide." . . . I was quite startled by his reaction. He leaned toward me over the top of his huge desk and, without any pretense or sense of position asked simply: "Where? Where is it?" ' "

"And you think you will find such contemplative traditions on Mount Athos?" Demos asked, assuming, like most secular Greeks, that Mount Athos was primarily important for cultural reasons, a Byzantine preserve so to speak.

"From what I have read and heard so far," I said, "I am pretty convinced that there is something very important up there that may be of value to contemporary Christianity and in fact to the world. In spite of the medieval context, which is completely at odds with modern society and contemporary values and beliefs, I want to go there with an open mind, as much as that is possible."

"So then," Demos asked as he got off Route 80 on the way to Paterson, "you are not going to explore Mount Athos as a sociologist."

"Not in the conventional meaning of that term. For example, I am not particularly concerned with the sociological reasons why individual monks end up on Mount Athos, although that question in itself must be of central interest to the sociologist of religion. Or to focus on the social organization of monastic life. These kinds of studies have been done repeatedly. I don't think I will have anything new to offer. No, my aim is to explore the degree to which an experiential spiritual tradition does exist today, within organized Christianity, and whether individuals who embark on such a spiritual adventure reach states of consciousness that in the parlance of transpersonal psychology would be considered either as forms of altered states of consciousness, self-realized awareness, or God consciousness."

I had to briefly explain to Demos these terms because he was not familiar with such vocabulary and he was not the least interested, in spite of the open invitation, to attend any of the workshops I had given in the New York area.

"I have heard rumors," Demos said with a certain hesitation in his voice, "that there are ascetics up there that in fact are not so ascetic. A few days ago there was an article in *Ethnikos Kyrikas* [a Greek paper published in New York] reporting that several cases of AIDS had appeared among the monks there. I think I have saved it for you. Have you heard about such rumors?"

"Look, Demo," I said, "one can find what one looks for. I would not be surprised if reports like that have a basis in reality. But what does it mean? Not all clergymen or monks are necessarily saints beyond all human frailties. Often isolated cases are overblown in the mass media for obvious reasons. Because in our cultural imagination we have been socialized to believe that whoever goes to the Holy Mountain is somehow a holy man we get scandalized when cases like that come to our attention. Then there is disillusionment and cynicism. This is what happened to Nikos Kazantzakis on his brief visit to the Holy Mountain followed by his debunking piece in *Report to Greco*.[2] But on the basis of what I have read so far, I am almost convinced that very important things take place on Mount Athos that can be of great value to contemporary civilization. I am personally interested in meeting saints or self-realized beings, or individuals who after many years and decades of spiritual practice have attained wisdom and have reached a stage high up on the ladder to Theosis. As I said, one could find what one looks for."

I stopped as Demos pulled into his driveway, but our discussion continued in the late evening while we drank herbal tea and ate Cypriot sweets that Maria, his wife, a computer expert, had baked that afternoon. After Demos described to her in every tortuous de-

tail our encounter with the Orthodox bookseller, we resumed discussing the reasons for my upcoming trip to the mountain of monks
and hermits.

"There is another more historical and sociological reason that is
attracting me to the Agion Oros," I said after Maria sat with us
sharing her views on the subject.

"That will certainly be closer to my interests," Demos quipped.

"I am not sure whether you know about Ken Wilber."

"Never heard of him."

"He is a leading transpersonal psychologist. He claimed[3] that
Eastern religions cannot serve as large-scale models for Western
transformation toward higher modes of consciousness. He argued
that the contact with Eastern religions that has influenced so many
western intellectuals has played only a catalytic, provocative role—
that is, to awaken the West to the possibility of alternative modes
of knowing, other than the rationalistic-scientific worldview that has
taken over the West during the last three hundred years. Which,
by the way, you so totally espouse," I added with a chuckle.

Both Demos and Maria laughed. "But why don't you talk a language that I can understand?" Demos pleaded.

"Ken Wilber's point is that if the West is to reach higher levels
of awareness en masse, it will have to be done from within its own
symbolic universe—that is, from within the symbolism that springs
from the Judeo-Christian-Hellenic tradition, and not from that of
Tibet, Zen, or through the various yogas of the Hindus."

"If I understand what you are driving at," Maria said, "you suggest that such practices and ways may be found on Mount Athos, a
place that no woman is allowed to set foot?"

"I appreciate the implications of what you are saying. But what
I suspect is that the Holy Mountain, in spite of its medieval value
system and norms, may have preserved for us an experiential spiritual tradition that was lost to the West. Once that tradition is freed

from its medieval social and cultural context it may in fact contribute to that massive transformation that Wilber is talking about."

I was not certain whether my friends understood me. So I tried to shift my argument using a language more compatible with mainstream social science. "Look," I said, "the West, as the German sociologist Max Weber argued at the turn of this century, has become 'disenchanted' whereas the East, meaning Asia, remains an 'enchanted garden.'[4] Western civilization became rationalized very early in its development, opening the way to the scientific and industrial revolutions. A cerebral, logico-experimental, scientific approach to confronting reality took center stage displacing all other modes of knowing. The Western Church tried to resist these developments. But it did so by opposing science and rationality by rational means—intellectual scholastic arguments on the rightness of its position. From the very beginning the Church's position was doomed, for it chose to fight its battles on the turf of rationality and science.

"The Protestant Reformation, which was a radical rebellion within Christianity, further undermined the position of the Church, therefore accelerating the process of 'rationalization.' In fact, according to Weber, it paved the way to capitalism since there was a 'cultural affinity' between capitalism and Protestantism.[5]

"Protestantism denounced 'otherwordly asceticism,' shut down the monasteries and urged its devotees to focus their attention on and practice a 'worldly asceticism,' that is, glorifying God in this world through hard work and the denial of bodily pleasures. The contemplative, experiential tradition, so much a part of the early Church, was finally eliminated from the Protestant cultures that were to play the leading, pivotal role in setting up the capitalist, industrial, and intellectual agenda of contemporary Western civilization."

"I am beginning to feel dizzy with all this theorizing," Demos said jokingly, a grin on his face. "But I am still waiting to see what you are driving at."

"In a minute, in a minute," I said, and continued. "The Western Church was at the very center of this social, political, and intellectual turmoil, trying desperately and unsuccessfully to maintain its centrality in the face of a secularizing cultural environment. Eventually the Church was pushed from the center of Western culture and society to its periphery. The secular state filled the void.

"The Eastern part of Christianity, on the other hand," I went on to say, "remained cut off and outside of this epochal turmoil. Consequently it retained the qualities of the 'enchanted garden.' An encyclopedic scholar like Max Weber failed to see that. For European scholars, like Weber, the history of Christianity meant the history of the Catholic and Protestant churches. And basically this is true to this day. The Eastern Orthodox Church has remained outside the field of their scholarly vision."

"That is because of the fall of Byzantium in 1453," Demos pointed out.

"Precisely. The Greek world was under the Ottoman Empire for the next four hundred years and was therefore completely cut off from the West. The battles of Orthodoxy were not waged against science and rationality but against Ottoman Turkey and Islam. The central concern was to preserve the Christian tradition, carried over intact from earlier centuries, in the midst of an alien dominating culture. Mount Athos, it seems, played an important role in preserving the experiential, esoteric part of that tradition."

"So, you are saying," Maria interjected, "that the backwardness of Greece, as a result of the Ottoman occupation, had the effect of preserving the early Christian tradition, lost to the West."

"Exactly." I nodded. "The Eastern Church preserved the more mystical side of Christianity. And it was not only Greece that preserved this tradition—when I say Greece, in this case, I mean

Mount Athos. But thanks to their own social backwardness, societies like Bulgaria, Rumania, Serbia, and particularly Russia also played a decisive role. These Orthodox societies were also cut off from the intellectual and political currents and conflicts that were raging in the Western Catholic and Protestant societies.

"Sometimes I wonder," I said, "what will happen now that the Berlin Wall has come down and the Iron Curtain has been lifted. I felt a sense of awe when I saw on television Boris Yeltsin attending mass and Alexei, the Orthodox Patriarch of Russia, giving a speech in the Kremlin, of all places. He explained the fall of Communism as the unavoidable outcome of its antispiritual, materialist dogmas. What will happen now, as over two hundred million people that have traditionally been considered Orthodox, begin to practice that form of Christianity after so many decades of Communist oppression?" I stopped for a few moments, then with some trepidation I proceeded.

"Do you know what I was told? This will not mean much to you, Demo. But Edgar Cayce, 'the sleeping prophet of Virginia Beach,' as he was called, prophesied in the 1930s, during the Stalinist purges and terror, that Christianity will be rescued by the Russians. That was a preposterous statement to make, particularly at a time when churches were being destroyed and priests were summarily executed. In fact, more Christians were killed for their beliefs during Stalin's regime than during the time of Nero. So you can see why not very many people took Cayce's prophecy seriously, in spite of his proven capacity to diagnose illnesses while in trance and to predict other events that did come true. I am not saying that what he said was objective truth. But it is an interesting coincidence that the experimental mystical tradition that was lost to Christianity may return back to the West via Russia.

"Perhaps," I went on, "Malcolm Muggeridge, the late British satirist, a deeply religious man, knew something when he said that one of the wonders of the twentieth century has been the incapacity of the Communist system in Russia to destroy the Orthodox Church."

"Are you sure," Demos said, "that you are not imposing your own wishful thinking upon historical events that have no other significance except that they are part of a historical drift?"

We laughed with Demos' penetrating debunking observation. "I cannot guarantee you," I said, "that what I am saying has any basis in truth. These are the tentative hypotheses, if you like, that I have arrived at, by being both a student of historical sociology and transpersonal theory."

"Does history have a purpose?" Maria wondered.

"This is the question that all social philosophers try to answer. Most of the secular historians and sociologists try to find a meaning in the very processes of history itself, whether it be the inevitable 'triumph' of rationality and secularism or the attainment of 'full Communism' à la Marx. I believe that if history is to be meaningful its meaning must originate outside of itself—in other words, outside of time and space. Any meaning that is derived exclusively from within history is itself in the final analysis but another socially constructed illusion, unavoidably leading to nihilism and despair. Isn't that what happened to Friedrich Nietzsche who went mad after his conclusion that 'God is dead'?" I stopped for a few moments. Then Maria protested my evaluation of Orthodoxy.

"I can't imagine how you can say that Eastern Orthodoxy could have any impact on the West. It seems to me that the Eastern Church is a backward institution overfocused on ritual that no one understands and controlled by illiterate priests."

"If you mean the 'exoteric' Church, you are probably quite right. But my interest is on the 'esoteric' teachings of the Church."

"Esoteric, exoteric, what is that?" Demos asked, a puzzled grimace on his face.

"The esoteric part of the Church is the body of teachings and practices that aim at contacting the Christ Logos within and discovering inner worlds. It is the experiential path to union with God, the 'kingdom of heaven,' which is within us.

"It seems to me that the official, 'exoteric' part of Eastern Orthodoxy is also cut off from this esoteric core of the teaching and to that extent it does not differ much from the Western churches. I think it is very crucial today to bring to the surface of our awareness this inner, esoteric core of Christianity. That is why the Holy Mountain may be so important. It preserved the esoteric practices of Christianity."

"I hope you will have a worthy pilgrimage," Demos said with a touch of friendly irony as he quoted the Orthodox shopkeeper. "Who knows, maybe next time I'll come with you." It was late when we went to bed. I had a long day and a long flight to Athens ahead of me.


Before I slept I reread Antonis's letter, which instructed me on what I should carry with me on our journey to the Agion Oros. "Make sure to carry your passport with you," he wrote. "They will not let you in unless you have a passport. Since you are a Greek Orthodox you will not need a visa. But you will need a passport. Bring along a backpack, shaving gear, a towel, pajamas, a gym suit, walking shoes, and blue jeans. Nothing else. Except also bring a soap, a couple of pairs of underwear, a couple of socks, a plastic cup to drink water at night, and a sweater because it is *cold* there. Oh, I forgot to tell you that you should also bring a couple of boxes of baby wetties. Call me as soon as you arrive in Athens. Love, Antonis."

I was ready. I understood that we were to walk over considerable distances since there were no means of transportation on Mount Athos. Roads were in reality foot paths linking one monastery to another. Blue jeans and sneakers were the appropriate attire for such an adventure. But baby wetties? I just couldn't figure that out. However, I trusted his advice and did as he instructed me in his letter.

The first impulse that overwhelms you when you arrive in Athens is not to visit the Parthenon and the magnificent museums and archaeological sites. The immediate urge is to get out of town as quickly as possible. That was precisely how I felt as I faced the congested traffic, breathed the most polluted air in any west European city, elbowed my way through throngs of nervous pedestrians, and stoically listened to taxi drivers and motorists zestfully curse one another on the flimsiest of provocation. One can only weep at the predicament of the city that once "gave light to the world." Now an extremely polluted megalopolis, Athens is crowded with almost half of Greece's ten million inhabitants, choked with ugly cement buildings and suffocated under the ubiquitous *nefos*, the thick smog that hangs constantly like a Damoclean sword over the Athenians. "Where are you, poor old Pericles, to look at your Athens?" laments a popular bouzouki singer.

Yet I had a memorable, pleasurable time in Athens. Waiting for Antonis to arrive, I stayed three days with my cousin Loukis, who with his Athenian wife made certain that, in that short period of time, my perceptions of his adopted city softened considerably.

I paid homage to its ancient monuments and the Parthenon, visited just about all the major museums, and at the tavernas below the Acropolis satiated whatever feeble Dionysian streaks remained in my character. Alas, I also hopelessly caught myself indulging in another old passion that, in spite of my many years among rational Anglo-Saxon Protestants, lurked only slightly below the surface of my consciousness: Greek politics. Loukis played a key role in the brief revival of my Greek political passion as he brooded over the condition of the country after decades of political upheaval and gross mismanagement. The latest front-page news was an ultimatum from the Council of Europe: unless Greece made painful adjustments and changes, such as trimming its hopelessly gigantic and parasitic government bureaucracy, the country would be expelled from the European Economic Community. Greek *philotimo* (sense of honor) was wounded, not for the first time.

"We come first in so many things," my cousin said as we sipped a glass of *retsina* (resinated white wine) at an outdoor taverna near Constitution Square, under the shadow of the Acropolis. "Greeks," he said as he quoted published statistics, "come first in per capita cigarette consumption in the world. Greece comes first as the poorest country in the European community, poorer than Portugal. First in inflation. First in auto accidents. First in air pollution. First in the most chaotic government among all the other western European countries. And," Loukis continued, "we come first in entertainment and in hostility toward work. In short, cousin," Loukis sighed with a sense of bitter humor, "this is a hopeless country."

"Cousin, you are exaggerating," I said, trying to make him feel less despondent. "Just think. Greece is the only Balkan country that has no problem of cultural identity and ethnic conflicts. It is the only Balkan country that is part of the European Economic Community. It is the only Balkan country that is part of the Western alliance. Its seashores and islands are the least polluted of all the developed countries of the Mediterranean, particularly in comparison to Spain and Italy. Do you want me to go on? Not to mention its breathtaking beauty and the epicurean lifestyle you carry on here, like drinking retsina and eating as we do tonight under the Acropolis."

There was a grin on Loukis's face. "I guess," he said, "it is how you want to look at your glass, whether you want to see it half full or half empty."

On Holy Wednesday I was ready to head for the Agion Oros. Antonis flew that day from Cyprus and with his bearded friend Akis, an architect who lived in Athens, we drove north toward Salonica. What a great relief to be out of Athens, and what a delight to experience the Greek countryside. The Greeks, perhaps unwittingly, have sacrificed Athens so that, for the time being at least, they spare the rest of Greece from "progress" and "development."

It was the first time I traveled north, and the experience of passing through legendary and historical sites was both fascinating and demystifying. "This is Thebes?" I pointed with disappointment, looking at an undistinguished small town on the foothills of a mountain. In the recesses of my subconscious Thebes meant "Oedipus Tyrannous" searching for the slayer of his father, not knowing that it was none other than himself.

"Just imagine," I said to my fellow travelers as we passed by Thermopylae, "had Xerxes won those Persian wars there would probably not have been any Western civilization, at least as we have known it. No Christianity, no Enlightenment, no industrial revolution."

"No Byzantium and no Mount Athos either," Antonis added.

After seven hours of virtually nonstop driving we reached Salonica, the northern city of Greece, and headed east, to the third, easternmost promontory of the Khalkidhikí peninsula. We turned south, and by six o'clock in the afternoon and after more than nine hours of driving, arrived at the small resort town of Ouranópolis (Heavenly City), the last stop before embarking on a ferry boat that would take us deep into the Athonite peninsula. The Holy Mountain is inaccessible by land—only by boat can one reach the monasteries. At Ouranópolis we checked into a modest hotel overlooking the harbor and spent the evening talking about Mount Athos, the Greek Orthodox Church, and the circumstances that brought us all there.

I was surprised to realize how devout Antonis had become. When I first met him in Cyprus, he was a worldly, rational skeptic. Religion and spirituality were the last things that occupied his mind. At that time his real love was philosophy, and for someone whose British university training had been in civil engineering, his knowledge of the subject was impressive. But now, he told me, as we watched the boats at the small harbor, he grew tired of philosophy and "intellectualisms." For him the Holy Mountain was the answer to his search. He said to me, half seriously, that had it not been for the love of his wife and two teenage children he would have perhaps considered "withdrawing from the world" to spend the rest of his life in contemplation on Mount Athos. "The business world I find myself in is like a jungle. On the Holy Mountain there is real peace and serenity," he said, "and the aura of some monks that I met is just brilliant."

Ever since his visit to the Holy Mountain, Antonis has attended church every Sunday, lit candles, kissed icons, and prayed, just like the humble village folks in Cyprus and Greece. "I have never felt better," Antonis said. "My life has changed drastically ever since I visited Mount Athos. Coming back to the world required quite an adjustment for me. But I am in regular communication with my Athonite friends. That keeps my mind in proper perspective."

At nine-forty-five the following morning we boarded the only boat for Daphni, the port of disembarkation for all visitors who had as their destination any of the more than twenty major monasteries situated all over the Athonite peninsula. There were no women on the boat, only men—pilgrims and a few bearded monks dressed in their all-black cassocks. Under the law enacted in 1045 during the reign of the Byzantine emperor Constantine IX Monomachus, the Athonite peninsula, an area of 389 square kilometers with a length of 57 kilometers and about 10 kilometers wide, was declared *avaton*, meaning only men could live in or visit the monasteries.

One of the key vows of the monk is chastity for life. The monk loses forever the right to marry, even in the event that he returns to society. In addition, he denies himself the freedom to satisfy his sexual urges in any form. Realizing the difficulty of such a commitment, the monastic community on Athos had come to the help of its members by totally banning women from setting foot on the Athonite promontory. Presumably this draconian measure would allow the monks to carry on their religious work without distractions.

Even today the monks, rigidly adhering to tradition, refuse to change the ancient morbid prohibition. Several years ago Melina Mercouri, the famous Greek actress, then minister of culture, offered the monasteries substantial economic assistance with the stipulation that she be allowed to deliver the check personally. The monks refused.

It became clear to me while cruising next to the magnificent Athonite coast, passing monastery after monastery, that I was stepping back in time, back into the Byzantine era. Constantinople, the capital of the empire, fell to the Ottoman Turks in 1453 but on Mount Athos the flag of Byzantium, golden in color with a black double-headed eagle, was flying proudly from the top of every bell tower.

We reached Daphni at about midday. After we had our passports checked we were issued an official document, a *diamoniterion*, with the seal of the governor of the Agion Oros, granting us permission to stay for a maximum of seven nights at the monasteries of our choosing, as guests. The token fee was the equivalent in drachmas of fifteen dollars.

When the abbot of the Monastery[6] that was our destination learned that Antonis was coming he sent their only automobile at the Monastery—a Land Rover, the gift of a wealthy pilgrim—to pick us up. I felt a little embarrassed since everybody else, about a hundred people, had to walk for an average of three hours before they could reach the nearest monastery. According to a travel guide one has to calculate his time so as not to arrive after sunset at any of the monasteries. At sunset the doors close and everybody goes to church for evening vespers and prayer. If you are late, the guidebook indicated, you will have to sleep outside in the company of wolves.

Waiting for the Land Rover to arrive we sat around an outdoor table at the only coffee shop, chatting and watching the Aegean and the crowd of pilgrims, monks, and a few customs officials.

In one of those strange coincidences I recognized among the crowd an old acquaintance, a Cypriot named Petros, teacher of Greek history and philology. He was shocked to find me on Mount Athos since he assumed that being an American sociologist I was a bona fide agnostic, or worse, an atheist. My profession does have a reputation for being grounded in a thoroughly secular interpretation of the world. And in the minds of outsiders, sociology is, quite often, confused with socialism.

Petros, a good-natured, sympathetic man who reminded me of the shopkeeper in Astoria, knew that I was not a zealot of Greek nationalism and I was therefore suspect in his eyes. He, on the other hand, was devoutly Greek and deeply Orthodox. With his horn-rimmed glasses and short, thick mustache he stood out—he was the only one wearing a three-piece suit, black tie, and polished shoes. With his right hand he carried a large and apparently heavy conventional suitcase. It was clear that walking to the nearest monastery would be a real golgotha for poor Petros. It was his first visit to Mount Athos and he was not well instructed on the vicissitudes of transportation and the need for casual attire, appropriate shoes, and backpacks.

We assumed that there was going to be an extra seat in the Land Rover for Petros and we invited him to join us. He sighed with relief. Petros, a lover of Byzantine culture, was delighted to find out that I myself had been reading up on the history of the Holy Mountain[7] and I was urged, like a tourist guide, to deliver to my companions an impromptu lecture on the history of the place.

"The fame of Athos," I started, "goes back to ancient times, before the advent of Christianity. In 492 B.C. Mardonius, the king of Persia, in his attempt to invade and take over Greece, wrecked his fleet on the shores of Mount Athos and his expedition collapsed.

Twelve years later his successor, King Xerxes, learning from the mistakes of Mardonius, avoided the stormy tip of Athos by cutting through the neck of the promontory to create an isthmus for his new fleet. It took Phoenician engineers and thousands of laborers from the surrounding area three years to complete that task. The remnants of the isthmus are still there."

"You must have noticed it on your way to Ouranópolis," Petros pointed out.

"Unfortunately I did not," I said. In fact Antonis pointed out the isthmus to us as we were passing over it. But my mind was so absorbed with the beauty of the Aegean and the mountains of the Athonite peninsula that before I realized the historic significance of the place we had already left it behind. Akis the architect was driving, and he was not in the habit of staying within speed limits.

"According to Strabo and Plutarch," I continued, "an enterprising Greek engineer made a flattering offer to Alexander. The peak of Athos that rises to about six thousand feet at the edge of the promontory is very steep and made of pure white marble."

"There it is," Antonis pointed out. In the distance we could clearly see the white top of Athos looking like a snow-covered mountain.

"This engineer," I went on, "proposed to carve the peak of Athos into a colossal statue of Alexander as a timeless monument to the glory of Macedonia. But it is said that Alexander rejected the offer. According to these historians he remarked, 'Let the mountain stand as it is. It is enough that another king perpetuated his arrogance by having a canal cut through it.'"

"I wonder whether there were any ancient cities on Athos before it became a monastic retreat," Antonis said.

"From what I have read, yes. There were ancient settlements, but since the sixth century A.D. there are no records of any towns."

"The monks claim," Antonis added, "that God prepared the

Mountain to become *To Perivoli tes Panagias* [The Orchard of the Most Holy Mother of God]. This is how they refer to the area of Athos."

"How did monasticism come to Athos?" Akis asked.

"To answer that question," I replied, "we must look back to the early centuries of Christianity. Since the third century A.D. some Christians, disgusted with the corruption of the society in which they lived, have gone into the deserts of Egypt, leaving behind them the world of organized social life. They were probably influenced by the Stoic philosophers, who taught patience, acceptance of suffering, temperance, and so on. They must have also been influenced by the Neoplatonists and the Cynics, particularly the latter, who taught total rejection of material comforts. These hermits opened a new era for Christianity. They were called the *nyptic fathers*, meaning 'serene and wise.' "

"What did they do in the desert?" Akis the architect, who was generally unsympathetic to the whole idea of monasticism, asked.

"They cultivated *apathia*, meaning the overcoming of passions through continuous prayer," I replied. "You see, the early Christian mystics believed that the passions associated with the ego obstructed the full expression of the Spirit within. They thought they could silence the passions through various forms of *askesis*, or 'exercise,' by subjugating the body to all forms of deprivations, such as food, sleep, sex, and bodily comforts of all sorts. It was believed that these forms of spiritual exercises—or bodily mortifications, depending on how you want to look at it—would render the practitioner a vessel for the power and grace of the Holy Spirit. All that, of course, was done within the context of Paul's injunction of ceaseless prayer."

"And where did these practices actually lead them?" Akis wondered.

"For a few, at least, it led to some sort of mystical ecstasy, a direct experience of what they considered the 'Uncreated Light,' which they claimed was Christ Himself. It seems to me," I went on, "that these practices were analogous to the shamanic vision quest of native peoples. The difference is that the nyptic fathers embarked on their 'vision quest' from within the context of Christianity.

"Incidentally," I went on, "these nyptic fathers of early Christianity left a record of their experiences, which formed the basis not only of Orthodox theology but also of the ways and means of the Christian monastic tradition. They cautioned, mind you, that such *askesis* needed the assistance of an experienced teacher who could properly guide the neophyte. Furthermore, they warned of the need to examine the source of the experience, because for them, the forces of darkness could deceitfully imitate the Uncreated Light." I stopped and apologized for being carried away with lecturing as if I were in a classroom.

"No, continue, continue," Petros reacted, and the others nodded. Petros's excitement intrigued me. He must have felt good that someone, whom he assumed was an agnostic and a lost soul, was so engrossed with the Orthodox religious tradition.

"There was a time when as many as five thousand Christian hermits lived in the deserts of Egypt," I continued. "The most famous of them was Great Antonius, who lived a total of one hundred and five years between the middle of the third century and the middle of the fourth."

"The ascetic life did not, after all, take years from his life," Akis quipped.

"Actually," I added, "Saint Antonius was famous not only as a great teacher but also as a holy man endowed with spiritual powers, gifts of the Holy Spirit. In fact, I have here an interesting quotation about Saint Antonius."

I unzipped the pocket of my backpack and pulled out a book that I was reading called *The Orthodox Way*, by Cambridge professor Kallistos Ware, an Anglican turned Orthodox bishop. I read a quotation attributed to one Evagrius of Pontus. " 'There came to St Antony in the desert one of the wise men of that time and said: "Father, how can you endure to live here, deprived as you are of all consolation from books?" Antony answered: "My book, philosopher, is the nature of created things, and whenever I wish I can read in it the works of God." '8

"This seems to be," I continued, "the basic difference between the approach of the Eastern Church and that of the West. The Western Church followed a more scholastic approach to the issue of God, whereas the Eastern Church incorporated within its more esoteric practices the experiential approach of the desert fathers like the Great Antonius."

It was past midday and Antonis suggested that we eat something because it was not certain what time we would arrive. Once there we would be totally dependent on the Monastery and the monks to feed us. It was Holy Week, with austere proscriptions on diet and, as Antonis warned, the time schedule of the monks for eating and resting was very different from that of the rest of the world. None of us had had breakfast and the demands of our ascetically unschooled bodies were felt intensely by all of us. We settled for a bowl of plain bean soup, the only dish available in town.

"We are already getting a taste of the meaning of continence and renunciation," Akis quipped as he cleared the last traces of beans in his bowl.

"Incidentally," he went on to ask, "how did the monks come to Mount Athos?"

"Hermits," I replied, as I had the historical facts fresh in my mind, "had been coming to Mount Athos even before the ninth century, finding refuge here after the Arabs attacked their desert sanctuaries. These people made their homes in caves and led a life similar to that of their forerunners in the Egyptian deserts. That is why it is customary today to call hermits who live on their own in the Athonite wilderness as living in 'the desert of Mount Athos.' In A.D. 875 the emperor of Constantinople, Basil the Macedonian, issued a *chrysobull* [golden-sealed decree] proclaiming the Athonite peninsula an autonomous region after the first monastery was established. No outsiders were allowed to interfere with the affairs of the monks or to tamper with their lands. Subsequent emperors issued further *chrysobulls* reinforcing the independence of the peninsula as a retreat for hermits and monks and as occasional refuge for themselves. It is important to mention that the various Byzantine emperors interfered only when invited by the monks. So, from the ninth century until the fall of Constantinople in the fifteenth century the Athonite monks enjoyed political independence."

"I thought the Crusaders plundered the monasteries sometime during the thirteenth century," Antonis pointed out.

"Right. During the Fourth Crusade, which was supposed to liberate the Holy Land but actually struck Constantinople."

"That was after the schism between the Eastern Church and Western Church," Petros added.

"Yes, the Great Schism took place in A.D. 1054, when the patriarch of Constantinople and the pope excommunicated each other. The Crusaders captured Constantinople and the surrounding territories in A.D. 1204. It was disastrous for the monks of Mount Athos. The Crusaders considered the Greeks as heretics and there was plunder of the monasteries and persecution of the monks. The pope tried in vain to stop that. The persecutions and the plunders, however, went on until A.D. 1261, when the Crusaders left. Constantinople was liberated and Byzantium reestablished its authority in the area. Of course, throughout the history of the Holy Mountain there were always plunders and persecutions by pirates and marauding troops. That is why the monasteries are constructed like castles and that is why a tradition was established, lasting to this day, of closing the gates at sunset. It was to prevent pirates from sneaking in during the night."

"What happened after Constantinople fell to the Turks in 1453?" Akis asked.

"Well, the monks proved to be cleverly diplomatic. When the Turks captured Salonica in 1420, they knew that it was only a matter of time before Constantinople would fall also. So they quickly decided to submit officially to the Turkish governor of Salonica, Murad II. That saved Mount Athos from certain plunder and destruction. During the four and a half centuries of Ottoman rule the Holy Mountain was basically left alone. The sultan didn't care to bother with it.

"I should point out," I continued, "that it was during the nineteenth century that there was a large influx of Russian monks to the mountain. And in fact, when the Greek fleet took over the peninsula in the year 1912, the Russians actually outnumbered the Greek monks."

"Really?" Akis exclaimed, apparently not being aware that on Mount Athos there were not only Greek monasteries but also Russian, Bulgarian, and Serbian religious communities as well, not to mention the Rumanian monks who were dispersed among various monasteries and hermitages. "Where are the Russians now?" Akis wondered.

"After the Bolsheviks took over in 1917, most of the Russian monks left because they lost their sources of support. Presently, Saint Panteleimon's monastery is purely Russian. The majority of the twenty or so monasteries that exist today are Greek. The monastery of Chilandari is Serbian and that of Zographou is purely Bulgarian. But, as I said, there are also monks of various other nationalities living and carrying on their *askesis* in the other Greek monasteries."

"What is the status of the Athonite peninsula today?" Akis asked further.

"Under the treaty of Lauzanne of 1923, in the aftermath of the Greco-Turkish war, the Greek state was accorded sovereignty over the Holy Mountain. In turn the Greek state, with the cooperation of the Athonite authorities, set up a constitution that accords the Holy Mountain total local autonomy. That is why we need passports."

"There is the Land Rover," Antonis exclaimed, cutting short the impromptu seminar that we'd been enjoying on the history of Mount Athos.

# II

## CONFESSION

WE WALKED BEHIND THE COFFEE SHOP INTO THE OPEN FIELD where the driver, a tall, slender-looking monk, had parked. Petros followed us hurriedly, dragging along his oversized suitcase as Antonis embraced the ascetic and introduced him to us as Father Andreas, a deacon of the Monastery.

Antonis told us later that Father Andreas, a man in his early thirties, was a graduate in dentistry from the University of Athens. He gave up "the world" and in spite of the pleas of his unconsolable parents joined the large number of recent university graduates who had flocked to the Holy Mountain. Contrary to earlier epochs, where most of the monks on Mount Athos barely finished elementary school, in recent years, an extraordinary wave of college graduates began filling the cells, a "shattering" development according to a contemporary Greek theologian. When I heard of this unusual trend, that hundreds of young graduates from as far away as the London School of Economics, some with doctorates in science, had put on the "angelic gown," I thought of Sorokin's sociological prophecies, that Western civilization had reached the rock bottom of a "sensate" disintegration and was moving into a new, spiritual, or "ideational" integration of world order.

Father Andreas mentioned that he had some business to take care of at Daphnē and that we would be heading toward the Monastery in about an hour. Antonis suggested that in that case we could leave our luggage in the car and head on foot toward Karyes, the administrative center of Mount Athos which was on the way. The view was spectacular and the idea of hiking through the mountain paths above the sea was deeply appealing to me.

"I am really sorry," Father Andreas said, and shook his head, "My instructions are that I should drive you from Daphnē to the Monastery." He was very emphatic in the tone of his voice. No room for compromise. The plans were laid down by the abbot, his superior, who issued the directive on our behalf to have the extraordinary privilege of being driven to the Monastery.

I could not understand what that meant and I turned toward Antonis for clues. I signaled to him for some rational explanation of what was going on. He had been with the monks before and seemed to have a more experienced insight into their ways.

"You see," Antonis said, as we sat on a rock looking at the Aegean and waiting for Father Andreas to finish his chores, "a central part of the training of the monk is obedience. Obedience humbles the ego, which is the monk's most formidable opponent. It is the ego that prevents a person from seeing and experiencing God. Obedience is a virtue that one cultivates in the monasteries as a form of spiritual exercise. The stronger the ego the greater the estrangement from God. The monks believe that pride cultivated by the ego is a form of spiritual malady.

"Father Andreas," Antonis continued, "had clear instructions to drive us from Daphnē to the Monastery, not from Karyes. To fulfill that directive coming from his superior was part of today's exercise. I did not argue the point because we are guests here and I felt that we must honor their ways."

"Right," I said, as I threw a pebble into the sea. "Obedience of course has another purpose." I spoke as a sociologist employing the customary jargon. "It ensures the smooth functioning of a closely knit communal society. It seems that there is a convergence between the needs of the monk to find God, and the needs of the Monastery in maintaining itself as an ongoing social system, cut off from the rest of the world. The monks came from the outside world, a world that cultivates the opposite character qualities: competition, ego projection, self-centeredness, worldly ambition, individualism, consumerism, and so on. Such traits cannot easily be overcome. I suppose without the systematic cultivation of obedience as a virtue, cooperation under the rigid confines of monastic walls would have been problematic at the least. The resocialization of the monks into a radically different set of norms is imperative if monasticism is to be maintained.

"But," I went on to ask, "don't you think under such conditions there is room for abuses? I mean obedience no matter what the orders?"

"Impossible!" Petros who was sitting next to me retorted; his neck stiffened and eyes widened as his eyebrows were pushed upward. Being conventionally religious and a sympathetic traditional philologist he entertained a benign, "Panglossian" view of modern Greek culture and its varied traditional institutions.

"I am not aware of any abuses," Antonis responded, "at least not in the monastery that we are going to. But you know, the Orthodox monastic tradition works in such a way as to minimize the possibility of abuse of authority. For example, the abbot who is in charge of the administration of the Monastery is elected by the other monks. Incidentally, the new abbot has just been elected by the forty or so monks who live there. He won the position by one vote. To be elected abbot you must be a *hieromonk*, that is, you must be an ordained priest who can carry out confessions, offer communion, and administer all the other sacraments of the Orthodox Church.

And to be ordained a hieromonk you must reach a certain level of spiritual development as it is ascertained by other hieromonks and by the *gerontes* of the Monastery and of other monasteries."

"What is a gerontas?" Akis asked.

"The geron or gerontas [elder in Greek]," I interjected, "is the master of the monastery. He is the spiritual father of the monks, who guides them through their path and experiences. After he himself has attained a certain experiential mastery of the spiritual realms that is recognized by the others, he can function like a guru to the monks but without being worshiped as some kind of a god. In the Orthodox tradition only God, Christ, and the Holy Spirit are to be worshipped."

"How does one become a gerontas?" Akis asked again. "I mean, is one ordained as a gerontas, like being ordained as a bishop?"

"No. That is outside the official titles. A gerontas must be recognized as one by the other monks. So a gerontas is someone who has *charisma*," I said, and went on to explain what I meant by that term.

In spiritual texts, like the Bible, a charismatic person is one considered to be divinely gifted. It is someone who has become so cleansed from any traces of personal egotism and pride that he becomes a vehicle for the miraculous powers of the Holy Spirit. To the chagrin of theologians, the sociologist Max Weber borrowed the term and turned it into a political concept—that is, a *charismatic* leader is someone who is believed by followers to possess extraordinary gifts. Such a charismatic leader could deliver them from their personal and social troubles. According to Max Weber's definition both Jesus and Hitler could be listed as charismatic leaders along with Gandhi and Fidel Castro, Martin Luther King and Gautama the Buddha.

"From what I have read, the gerontes, or *staretz* in Russian," I continued, "are those monks who after many years of personal struggle to overcome their egotistical passions reach a certain stage of psychonoetic purification, of saintliness, so that the Holy Spirit can perform miracles through them. But they never take credit and certainly they would never boast that they have any powers. On the contrary, they present themselves in the most humble way and whatever miracles are performed in their presence they credit to the Holy Spirit, not to themselves. The gerontes of the Holy Mountain are the spiritual teachers and custodians of the Orthodox religion.

"Under such conditions, with a community of spiritually advanced teachers," I said further, "the possibility of abuse is reduced. It is a different situation when you have an unaffiliated maverick guru surrounded by uncritical devotees, who have no way of authenticating the level of his or her spirituality. Then abuses are more likely to take place. An abusive gerontas or staretz, on the other hand, will more easily be identified as such by other gerontes and may be either disciplined, or banished from the monastic community."

"Exactly," Antonis added. "That is why I am more inclined to trust gerontes like Father Vasilios and others that I have met on Mount Athos. I just feel greater security within the Orthodox spiritual tradition. I do not feel comfortable depending on a single master, regardless of how wise that master may appear to be, particularly if he is not affiliated with any long-established tradition or community of like-minded practitioners."

"What do you know about Father Vasilios?" I asked with surprise. Antonis was the third person in less than a month that mentioned him as a great holy man.

"I have never met him personally, but I have heard all sorts of stories about him," Antonis said, and without any further probing he went on to tell us some of them.

"Years ago there was a strange accident in Salonica. A twelve-year-old boy riding his bicycle was hit by a bus as he was trying to cross a street. Passengers and driver frantically rushed out of the bus expecting to find the boy crushed under the tires. Miraculously, the boy was saved and was standing in a state of shock on the opposite side of the street, while his bicycle was reduced to a bundle of scrap metal under the wheels. It was physically impossible for him to have jumped to the other side of the street. When asked how he ended up there he replied that at the moment when the bus was about to hit him a priest suddenly appeared, grabbed him and threw him on the opposite pavement. He could not tell them where the priest was. He somehow vanished the moment the boy was out of danger. Well," Antonis went on, "the father with his son began visiting various churches and monasteries hoping that the boy would identify the priest who so miraculously saved him. They went all over Mount Athos searching for this mysterious savior. After many months of searching they came before Father Vasilios. 'That's the one,' the boy said immediately."

Antonis paused for a few moments and then proceeded to narrate another story about Father Vasilios.

"A group of people went to visit him, not knowing that Father Vasilios was himself on a visit to the Orthodox monastery at Sinai, in Egypt. Yet they found him in his hermitage waiting for them, giving them lessons and blessings. The monks at the monastery were dumbfounded."

"So he is considered to have the ability that presumably very advanced souls have, that is, to be at more than one place at the same time?"

"Who knows?" Antonis replied. "But stories like this, about extraordinary feats by gerontes that are considered blessed by the Holy Spirit, you will hear in this place all the time. Here is another one," Antonis went on. "A group of Frenchmen visited Father Vasilios. When they returned to the monastery a monk asked them who their translator was, since Father Vasilios did not speak any foreign languages. The Frenchmen were amazed since they had no translator and Father Vasilios himself had spoken to them in fluent French.

"There are many more stories about Father Vasilios, but let us get ready. I see Father Andreas coming."

Antonis sat next to Father Andreas. Petros, Akis, and I took the back seats. We rode very slowly, not more than five to ten miles an hour, because the roads were not made for mechanized vehicles but for mules and hikers. We were impressed with Father Andreas's skill in maneuvering the Land Rover under the most adverse road conditions imaginable. On the way we were silent, not out of apprehension of the road conditions, driving at the edge of precipitous cliffs and ravines, but out of a deep feeling of awe, spellbound by the breathtakingly serene beauty that unfolded in front of our eyes. I could see why hermits had flocked to Mount Athos to find God and peace since the early decades of the Christian era. I could also partly appreciate the reasons why so many young, promising university graduates abandoned the cities and put on the "angelic gown" of monastic existence.

We reached our destination on the eastern side of the promontory at three in the afternoon. The Monastery was a massive Byzantine structure that once, as we were informed, accommodated as many as four thousand monks. But the "golden age" had passed, and until several years ago only seven elderly monks lived there, the structures beginning to fall apart all around them. But thanks to the recent influx of new blood, there emerged a renaissance in the Monastery, and in all the other twenty monasteries on Athos, for that matter. As many as fifty monks took charge, fixed a large portion of the ruined structures, cleaned up the magnificent church, and struggled for union with God with the guidance of their *gerontes*.

The moment we got out of the Land Rover a group of monks came along to welcome us. I was not certain whether all visitors were given the same kind of red carpet treatment. I knew, however, that in all the monasteries there was a legendary tradition of hospitality given freely to the pilgrims who took the time and trouble to reach that remote section of Greece. It was obvious that Antonis's contacts with the abbot and the gerontas of the monastery as well as with several other monks was crucial for our warm reception at this time when there were as many as two hundred and fifty guests staying over for the Easter holidays.

We were escorted to the *archondariki* (reception room) where we were offered the traditional *loukoumi* (Turkish Delight) and a shot of *raki*, a very strong liqueur concocted by the monks. I drank it all at once, as was the custom, and experienced a considerable widening of the pupils of my eyes. Father Maximos, a member of the welcoming committee and close friend of Antonis, looked at me, grinning with sympathy.

I felt an immediate liking for Father Maximos the moment Antonis introduced him to me. He was, like the abbot, a hieromonk, that is, an ordained priest who could administer the sacraments of the Church, including confession and Holy Communion. I don't recall ever meeting a Greek Orthodox priest who radiated as strong a spiritual presence as Father Maximos. In his mid-thirties, he was a graduate of the theological school in Athens. Rather than embarking on a career as a theologian, teaching religion in a gymnasium and periodically preaching in various churches, he had opted for the ascetic life on Mount Athos. We became friends immediately and I had the privilege of long discussions with him on theological issues and life on the Holy Mountain.

"We monks do not believe in philosophy," Father Maximos said to me the next day as we chatted inside the yard of the Monastery before the evening service. "We are after experience, the direct experience of God." He went on to say that studying the philosophical and theological writings of the Fathers of the Church was important, but in itself it was not sufficient for the direct experience of God.

His words were a not so indirect comment on my tendency and weakness as an academic to follow a more cerebral approach to the pursuit of Truth. "Parallel to the reading of the holy texts," he claimed, "we need to engage in spiritual practice." When I asked how that could be accomplished his response was, "Through, among other things, fasting, ceaseless prayer, confession, communion, and conscious and systematic participation in the liturgical services and sacraments of the Church. Through these practices we try," he said, "to empty ourselves of egotistical passions so that the grace of the Holy Spirit may freely flow within us."

We were assigned two rooms. A young monk whose task it was to see that guests were properly accommodated brought us clean white sheets and blankets. I was to stay in the same room with Antonis and his friend, the architect, who seemed to be the most secular member of our party. He had joined us primarily because Antonis had urged him to do so, luring him with descriptions of the extraordinary beauty of the countryside and the unparalleled architectural magnificence of the Athonite monasteries. A heavy smoker, he had to leave the Monastery every time he wished to satisfy the urge for nicotine. No smoking was permitted within the Monastery's walls, including the enclosed yard. And after 6 P.M. the heavy doors were firmly shut until sunrise. Akis learned the virtues of temperance.

"No showers?" I said with surprise as Antonis instructed me on the state of creature comforts.

"No," Antonis said. "The monks do not take showers. They only wash parts of their bodies, like feet and hands. And no hot water. That is why I asked you to bring baby wetties. It is one way of staying clean."

Antonis went on to say, as Akis was shaking his head, that the monks avoid any possibility of tempting themselves with sexual thoughts and stimulations. That would be a distraction from their exclusive focus on God through prayer. It is for this reason that they don't go swimming by the sea next to them, even during the hottest of months. Yet the Monastery was sparkling clean and

the monks themselves seemed quite washed and well groomed. The
only smell around was that of burning church incense.

Everybody present inside the walls of the Monastery feasted together, fifty monks and two hundred and fifty visitors. I felt uncomfortable being part of such a massive intrusion in the lives of these
ascetics. It was part of their tradition that they must never refuse a
visitor room and a sharing of their food. But that tradition was set
up in the tenth century when the first monastery of Great Lavra
was built at the edge of the Athonite peninsula. That was before the
invention of cars and airplanes, when only a few adventurous souls
dared travel or were capable of traveling outside of their villages.

Pilgrims and monks ate together in silence while a novice read
from a text of sermons written by the various gerontes and holy
men of Orthodoxy. The reading went on until everybody finished.
Then the reader came down from the rostrum and kissed the hand
of the abbot as the latter blessed the young monk and gave him a
piece of bread. Everybody stood up and the monks, headed by the
abbot, walked outside the *trapeza* (communal dining hall) chanting.
I felt uneasy. When we walked out of the trapeza and into the
churchyard the monks were lined up on both sides bending down
with a deep bow as the abbot, standing erect, kept his right hand
upward in a fixed position of the traditional Orthodox blessing.

"Don't be embarrassed," Antonis whispered at me as we walked
out. "It is part of their training in humility." I whispered to Antonis
that it was difficult for me. We were treated like emperors when in
reality we were more like intruders in their lives.

Before the Friday vespers we had a chance to walk around the
Monastery and talk with a few of the monks. A central topic of their
conversation was the miraculous powers of several ancient icons of
the Holy Virgin. One icon is said to have once saved the Monastery
from pirates. A monk was praying in church by himself when he
heard the Holy Virgin urging him to inform the other monks not

to open the gates because there were pirates waiting all night outside, ready for plunder. And that's how it was. The Virgin saved the Monastery and since that day that particular icon has been venerated with hymns and liturgies.

Another miracle that the monks reverently told us about was in reference to a small icon of the Virgin that they kept in the warehouse where they stored the barrels of olive oil, necessary not only for their cooking but most importantly for keeping the candles lit in front of the icons. To the despair of the monks the olive crop was a disaster one year and their supply of oil quickly reached bottom. All the barrels were empty and they were not going to have oil to light the candles the next day—the oil that they ordered from outside Athos had not arrived as yet. But the following morning they discovered that all the barrels were mysteriously filled to the brim with olive oil, without anyone taking credit for filling them up. The icon was declared miraculous and like other similar icons it was piously revered with litanies and special ceremonies on the site of the miracle.

Another icon of the Virgin, we were told, dematerialized in one monastery and was found in another. It was brought back to the first monastery and again it instantly disappeared and rematerialized in the other monastery. After several episodes of this type the two monasteries decided that the icon wished to be in that other monastery for some mysterious reason.

Phenomena of this type of instant dematerialization and rematerialization of icons are a common topic of conversation among monks and pious pilgrims. The first story we heard was from Father Andreas, who as we entered the Monastery pointed out to us a painted icon on the entrance wall over the gate. In 1822, one year after the Greek war of independence against Ottoman rule, a Turkish soldier drew his gun and fired at the icon, blasting a large hole in the painting that is clearly visible to this day. According to this story when he realized what he had done he rushed to the nearest tree and hanged himself. The next day the tree was found mysteriously dried up and dead.

Father Nectarios, a young monk, escorted us in front of an icon of the Madonna, ordinarily kept in the sanctum. Because of Holy Week, they had it displayed in the center of the church. The icon was gilded with gold and only the face of the Virgin holding a baby Jesus was exposed. The features were hard to identify due to the ravages of time. We were told the history of that icon: There was a time when the Monastery was finally ransacked by pirates and most of the monks were massacred. But a fifteen-year-old monk managed to escape. Before he ran away he rescued the icon of the Virgin from the church and threw it into a secret well. The young monk ended up in Crete and lived there for seventy years. Before he died at the age of eighty-five he paid a visit to the Monastery and told the monks what had happened to him seventy years earlier. Then he showed them where he had hidden the icon. They opened the well and to their amazement they found the icon floating on the water and on top of it there was a lit candle.

Such stories of miracles reinforced the faith of the monks that the way they carried on their lives, isolated as they were from "the world," was deeply meaningful and rationally sound. In their minds there was no question of the authenticity of such stories. Maintaining a keen sense of miraculous happenings and undergoing such experiences in their own prayers the monks substantiated within their own consciousness the validity of their faith in the ultimacy of spiritual realities as outlined within the context of Orthodox culture.

The supremacy of the Holy Virgin on Mount Athos is based on a legend that the monks like to tell to visitors. "It all started in the year A.D. 49," Father Andreas told us as we were being escorted to the various sanctuaries of the Monastery where special miraculous icons of the Virgin were housed. "The Mother of our God sailed with one of the evangelists from Jerusalem to visit Lazarus who was then bishop of Cyprus. It is not certain whether the evangelist who escorted Her was Mark or Luke. During their voyage there was a sudden change of the weather. A storm came over them and thick fog covered the sea. The navigator lost his direction and instead of Cyprus they ended up on the eastern shore of Mount Athos. When the Virgin stepped on land there was an earthquake and all the pagan statues were demolished. Gazing at the beautiful scenery the Holy Mother exclaimed, 'This mountain is holy ground. Let it be my orchard. Let me remain here.' Ever since that time the *Theotokos* [She who gave birth to God] is the ruler of the Holy Mountain."

We had been at the Monastery for two days already and it felt as if we had lived there for several weeks. We followed the life of the monks around the clock, waking up at four in the morning, going to church, listening to Byzantine chants and partaking in the mysteries of the Orthodox Church, and eating in the communal trapeza, twice a day.

In the Orthodox religious service the melodies of the liturgies during Holy Week lure into churches even atheists and agnostics that ordinarily hardly ever set foot in a church. It is said that a thousand years ago a delegation from Russia visited Constantinople and were invited to Saint Sophia, the great church of Byzantium. They were so enthralled with the liturgy and the hymns that on their return home they convinced the then ruling prince Vladimir of Kiev that Orthodox Christianity was the religion to introduce into Russia. Subsequently, one thousand years ago, the Russians, following the example of their prince, were converted to Orthodoxy.

The early fathers of the Church turned their religious poetry and prayers into music and song. In doing so not only did they facilitate religious experience, but they preserved Eastern Christianity throughout the one thousand years of Byzantium and the more than four hundred years of Ottoman rule. A basic training for any prospective monk or priest consists of the learning of Byzantine music and the ability to chant without dissonance.

"Father Andrea," I said as we were coming out of the Friday morning service, "your chanting is superb." Indeed, Father Andreas had an extraordinary voice. I was certain that had he chosen to make a career in the "world" he could have easily become a leading popular singer in Greece. "Oh," he exclaimed with a humorous grimace, "don't you know that whosoever praises a monk delivers him to the Devil?"

"I see what you mean," I said, and both I and Antonis, who overheard the conversation, laughed. I should have known better. The central aim of an authentic monk is to tame the ego, or rather to obliterate it. For it is a tenet of monastic life that the ego creates shadows obstructing direct vision and experience of God. Praise stimulates the ego's power and therefore it defeats the very purpose for which a serious devotee chooses the monastic life.

I went on to ask Father Andreas whether he would take up an invitation and return to his home town to become an archimandrite, a step that could eventually lead to a career within the hierarchy of the Church with prospects for a possible bishopric seat. I had learned about this from Antonis.

"I am not in a position to do that at this time," he said as he gazed toward the surrounding hills.

"Why not?" I asked.

"First," he said thoughtfully, "I must cleanse myself of egotistical desires. Only then would I be in a position to lead others on a spiritual path."

Not everyone who ends up on Mount Athos is attracted there because of spiritual yearnings. An elderly monk, for example, told me that in 1922 when he was fourteen he lost his parents during the destruction of the Greek community in Asia Minor, as a result of the Greek-Turkish war. Being an orphan, he found refuge on the Holy Mountain and became a hermit. At the age of eighty-three he had never experienced any other world except the world of Mount Athos. When I asked whether he regretted spending his life alone as a hermit he could not give me a clear answer because he said he had no other framework for comparison. On the other hand another elderly monk reassured me as to how happy he was there, not only because of the peace he found living by himself, but also because the Agion Oros was rich in game. He was a passionate hunter. When he learned that I was from Cyprus he proclaimed reassuringly that during the Turkish invasion of 1974 he had been ready to take up his gun and come to the island to fight the Turks.

I had read that in the past, on occasion, runaways from the law used to end up on Mount Athos.[1] The monks refused to turn them in to the Greek police because they believed that it was not accidental when a person ended up on Athos. They took it upon themselves to save the sinner.

One thing that was beginning to become clear to me was this: Irrespective of whatever social and personal contingencies were responsible for leading a particular monk to Mount Athos, once there he embarked on a radically new career often leading to spiritual and moral transformation radically altering his perception of reality and of himself. Entering into mystical states of consciousness, encountering various saints, and witnessing miracles were some of the transformative experiences common to the daily life of the ascetics and hermits. Their ceaseless spiritual practice heightened, among other things, their sensitivity to miraculous phenomena that from the vantage point of ordinary consciousness pass unrecognized. Billions of events and happenings are taking place continuously all around us but because of the conditioning that we have undergone throughout our lives such events remain unnoticed. It seemed to me that monastic existence, with all its excruciating deprivations, was aimed at deconditioning the self and resocializing it within a radically new set of norms so that alternate, or better, spiritual realities that were otherwise inaccessible to ordinary consciousness could be perceived.

I was sitting on a bench on the side of the courtyard next to the front entrance to the church when I saw Father Maximos with the usual smile on his face walking in my direction. Father Maximos was born and raised on Cyprus, an additional factor that facilitated our friendship. He told me how he was attracted to the Church very early in his life and how that led to the study of theology in Athens. He soon discovered that theology was not enough. Mount Athos was the place to engage in an uninterrupted spiritual practice where, with the help of the gerontes, he would purify himself and work for the salvation of others.

"Father Maxime, do you know of a gerontas by the name of Vasilios?" I asked as he sat next to me.

He smiled and remained silent for a few moments. "Well?" I persisted.

"Father Vasilios is my gerontas. I work with him."

It was one of those coincidences that makes you wonder whether they are in fact coincidences or the result of some ineffable cause hidden from ordinary consciousness. From the point of view of esoteric teachings, of course, nothing is coincidental. As Robin Amis, a student of the Eastern Orthodox tradition, said in an interview, "Mount Athos is a Byzantine survival, a part of an earlier civilization where they believe in miracles. There, gentle, almost invisible miracles actually happen, strings of coincidences that no statistician would believe. Sometimes these sequences follow one out into the world and change one's life."[2]

I had been led to understand, until that moment, that it would be impossible to meet Father Vasilios, "the Lion of the Holy Mountain," because of his inaccessibility and his avoidance of publicity even though he had become a legend in the entire Greek Orthodox world.

"Is it possible to meet with him?" was my immediate question.

"Yes, why not. We can visit him after Easter Sunday when most of the guests will be gone. But it will be a four-hour hike."

"I don't mind."

"Will you take Communion tomorrow?" Father Maximos asked pointedly.

"Well," I mumbled. "I guess everybody is taking Communion. Coming to Mount Athos without taking Communion would be an incomplete pilgrimage, wouldn't it?" I admitted that I rarely took Communion. I could hardly remember the last time I did—probably it was during my wedding, nineteen years ago, when I had no choice.

"Good," Father Maximos said. "When are you coming for confession?"

"Confession?" I asked, and my eyes widened.

"But you cannot take Communion without first going through the confessional," Father Maximos said matter-of-factly.

"Father," I said with a pleading tone in my voice, "is it necessary? The last time I went through confession was when I was twelve years old."

"So, it is about time. Don't you think?"

"Oh, Father!" I murmured, and shook my head not offering a straight answer. The secular skeptic in me was reacting. I had been trained as a modern social scientist and as such I assumed that when people wished to "confess" they would go to a psychiatrist or a clinical therapist, for a hefty fee. Religious confessions were for ordinary, "churchy" folks, not for academic professors.

"During the service tonight I will be confessing people in a small room right next to the church. Why don't you come?"

"I'll see," I said. I admitted that I wouldn't know what to say or do under such conditions.

"There is nothing to be afraid of," he reassured me.

The Holy Friday vespers on the lamentations for Jesus' burial began at seven o'clock. They were to last until eleven. I was absorbed along with the monks and the visitors with the beauty of the liturgy, the smell of the burning incense, the mesmerizing chants, and the light, emanating only from the candles made of pure beeswax that each one of us was holding.

I pretended that I had forgotten the conversation I had with Father Maximos when I felt someone gently pulling me by the elbow.

"Come," Father Maximos said softly, "let's go. It is your turn."

I offered no resistance. Oh well, it is hard to say no to Jesus, I thought half seriously. Academically, I justified my going along as "participant observation." After all, I rationalized, anthropologists would do all sorts of exotic things during their fieldwork, from participating in Native American "sweat lodges" to eating sacred mushrooms in the Amazon under the supervision of local shamans. The only obstacle to confession was my own pride which, within the context of Orthodox spirituality, was the greatest of sins.

We elbowed through the crowd as the chanters were singing a well-known hymn ordinarily sung on Holy Friday.

"When Thou, the Immortal Life, didst come down to Death, then didst Thou slay Hades through the dazzling brightness of Thy Godhead; and when Thou didst raise up the dead from the abyss, all the powers of Heaven cried aloud; Christ, our God, Giver of Life, Glory to Thee."

"How do we start?" I asked Father Maximos who sat in front of me in the dimly lit room under the shadow of several icons. His sympathetic smile was reassuring.

"Say whatever you want about yourself."

I sat there looking at him not knowing how to begin. How does one confess? I thought for a few moments and then I began. After a prolonged monologue during which time I revealed details of my life that until then had remained dormant in the recesses of my mind

I stopped and waited Father Maximos's verdict. He, like a good therapist, hardly spoke. I had described among other things aspects and episodes in my life that made me feel ashamed and others that made me feel proud, both forms of "sins." But contrary to my expectations, that the good father would pronounce me unfit for Communion, he passed no judgment on what I said. Instead he engaged me in a philosophical discussion on the nature of the "Uncreated Light" that one can experience with proper spiritual practice. He then revealed to me how he, as a confessor to other monks, had been learning of the rich spiritual experiences that they undergo during their prayers and spiritual practices. More than that he described to me how he himself, while engaging with Father Vasilios in an all-night vigil, experienced the Uncreated Light that is beyond description. "I was in ecstasy," he said, "everything was brilliant white and I felt the presence of Christ." He went on to say that at those moments even though he had his eyes closed he could see everything around him and with vastly greater clarity. "These are experiences that cannot be described," he said. "But once you experience the reality of Christ within you, then everything else pales by comparison." Father Maximos went on to say that after such an experience you become fully conscious of the utter misery of your present existence. It is this, he said, that makes many monks shed bitter tears during their vigils and prayers. They become aware of the vastness that separates them from God. Ordinary people do not shed tears because they are not aware of the nature of their miserable existence, being cut off as they are from their Divine source.

Later I understood that the meaning of "sin" in the mystical Orthodox tradition is very different from the pietistic notion of violating a particular taboo or social norm.[3] I learned that *amartia* (sin, in Greek) means in reality being "off your mark." That is, being off your true path for reunion with God. Therefore, when the monk prays ceaselessly the Jesus prayer—"Jesus Christ, Lord Savior, have mercy on me a sinner"—in reality it means "have

mercy on me who is cut off and alienated from You, my true nature." It is believed, therefore, that with repentance through the
practice of confession the individual gradually overcomes that which
keeps him or her ignorant, i.e., "sinful" vis-à-vis the God source.
Bishop Kallistos Ware puts it this way:

> If we are to see God's face reflected within us, the mirror
> needs to be cleaned. Without repentance there can be no self-
> knowledge and no discovery of the inward kingdom. When I
> am told, "Return into yourself: know yourself," it is necessary
> to inquire: Which "self" am I to discover? What is my true
> self? Psychoanalysis discloses to us one type of "self"; all too
> often, however, it guides us, not to the "ladder that leads to
> the kingdom," but to the staircase that goes down to a dank
> and snake-infested cellar. "Know yourself" means "know
> yourself as God-sourced, Godrooted; know yourself in God."
> From the viewpoint of the Orthodox spiritual tradition it
> should be emphasized that we shall not discover this, our true
> self "according to the image," except through a death to our
> false and fallen self. "He who loses his life for my sake shall
> find it" (Matt. 16:25): only the one who sees his false self for
> what it is and rejects it, will be able to discern his true self,
> the self that God sees. Underlining this distinction between
> the false self and the true, St. Varsanuphius enjoins: "Forget
> yourself and know yourself."[4]

"Come," Father Maximos said. "Bend down for a few moments."
He placed his stole over my head and read from a prayer book. He
then made the sign of the cross over my head and made an invocation for the absolution of my sins.

"Tomorrow come for Communion," he said as I walked out of
the confessional.

I must have spent close to an hour talking to Father Maximos.

When I reentered the church the monks were chanting the lamentations of Christ's burial, the kind of chants that for hundreds of years have nurtured the spiritual passions of the Eastern Orthodox, faithful and unfaithful alike.

"Both the Mind of Nature and the angelic hosts are at a loss to understand the mystery, O Christ, of Thine ineffable and inexplicable burial."

"O strangest of miracles! O latest of happenings! He, Who gave me breath, is carried away bereft of breath, and is buried by the hands of Joseph."[5]

The services ended around midnight. We walked to our rooms to get some sleep. The following day, the liturgy, we were told, would be much longer. I never could have believed what that meant. When the Easter services began at eight in the evening I assumed the Resurrection ceremonies would be over by midnight. Father Andreas grinned when he warned us that the services would take much longer. The service was in fact an all-night vigil that lasted until seven in the morning. Eleven whole hours. For some inexplicable reason I felt no fatigue and above all I did not get bored. "Just think," I told Antonis, "what would have happened had we been listening to lectures for eleven hours."

I came to understand that spiritual chanting does something to the body. When I mentioned that to Kostas he claimed that prolonged chanting may dissociate the psychonoetic body from the gross material body, open one's sacred centers, and cause oneself to enter a mesmerized state within the psychonoetic dimensions. Therefore, he would say, such an approach is not wise since the individual does not have mastery over such states. However, the spiritual practices of the monks aim precisely in that direction, though their vocabulary is different. For them it is the all-loving power of the Holy Spirit that takes possession of them. Therefore,

far from being exposed to any dangers they are graced by the energized force and protection of the Holy Spirit.

The experiences of spiritual visions, such as saints visiting the
monks to give them courage and advice, is common among serious
practitioners like Father Maximos. "Don't forget," Antonis had
pointed out to me, "that the liturgical services continuously construct benign angelic energies that act upon the participants. Don't
you feel the incredible vibrations in the church?"

In the past, Kostas showed me a photograph that a student of his
had taken of a church in Cyprus. In that church there was an icon
of the Virgin that had the reputation of miraculous healing powers,
similar to the icons on Mount Athos. This follower presumably used
an especially sensitive film. A clear, ghostlike image of the Holy
Virgin was hovering over the church. Kostas explained that the image was constructed by the believers themselves. "It is," he said, "a
humanly constructed image of the Holy Virgin which is, however,
connected with the Universal Mother. Therefore, it does all the
miracles that are attributed to that icon."

"If the theory of elementals is in fact a reality," I said to Antonis,
"then I can indeed imagine the power of angelic elementals that are
being constantly created by the prayers of all these monks, gerontes,
and other fathers."

It has been said in fact that the prayers of human beings like the
Athonite fathers keep the world together. If they stopped praying
the world would come to an end.

# 12

# GYMNASTS OF
# THE SOUL

EASTER CELEBRATIONS WERE COMING TO AN END WITH LITANIES
and feasts. During the Paschal meal, which took place right after
the eleven-hour service, we were offered generous portions of fish,
Easter eggs, and locally made tasty semisweet red wine. It was a
marked contrast to the tea, nuts, beans, bread and jam that was the
typical diet during the fasting period. Unlike other Orthodox believers and clergymen, the monks of Agion Oros, or at least those
at the Monastery, were basically vegetarian, eating fish only on occasion. Meat, I was told by a monk, stimulates the passions and
undermines a fully spiritual life. That is why the most serious and
dedicated monks and hermits avoid it.

By Tuesday most of the pilgrims had already left, relieving the
monks of the heavy burden of catering to so many guests while also
conducting the long services. Those of us who remained for a few
more days enjoyed the tranquillity of the place, took long walks and
visited nearby monasteries.

The Monastery was located at the base of a hill right by the sea.
It had its own natural harbor, ideal for boats and sailors. I often
walked there to be by the sea, reflect and write my notes. I was
sitting by the harbor on Tuesday morning after the liturgy when I

saw Father Maximos coming toward me. He was accompanied by Antonis and a visiting bishop from the monastery of the Great Lavra, situated at the tip of the promontory, the first and largest monastery established on Athos by Saint Athanasios during the tenth century.

"How about coming with us, Kyriaco?" Father Maximos asked me. "We are going to escort the father here back to his monastery by speedboat. Antonis is coming also."

The elderly father had come to the Monastery as a guest of honor to lead the ceremonies. It took him seven hours by land, whereas by boat it would take no more than an hour. The Greek coast guard, which had a station next to the Monastery, volunteered to spare the old father the ordeal of being driven to Great Lavra by Father Andreas. There was a rubber boat that could accommodate six passengers.

"I would love to come," I said. "But when are we going to visit Father Vasilios?"

"That's where we will go. The boat will drop us off at the monastery of Iveron and from there we will proceed on foot. That way we'll save ourselves more than an hour's walk." Father Maximos said that it would have taken us four hours' walking to get to him had we started on foot directly from the Monastery.

When Father Andreas heard that we were to go by boat he shook his head disapprovingly and warned us with a discouraging look on his face that "it will be rough." Once you are out of the harbor, he said, the sea is too turbulent and the boat too small. When Antonis heard what Father Andreas had to say he began having second thoughts. "I'll get stomach problems if the boat shakes too much," he complained, ready to quit the venture.

"Oh, don't worry," said Father Maximos. "Everything will be all right."

There were only two seats. In the front we accommodated the

bishop and behind him Father Maximos. Antonis and I sat on opposite sides at the edges of the rubber boat. The Greek sailor stood on the back maneuvering and guiding the craft. As it began speeding outside the harbor, both Antonis and I wished that we had listened to Father Andreas. The waves were too huge for a small rubber boat. There were no life jackets, and with every leap of the boat hopping from wave to wave I had the distinct sensation of riding a bull in a rodeo. I thought that at any moment both Antonis and I would be ejected at least twenty meters away into the very cold water. I held on for dear life as Father Maximos, who must have perceived our precarious situation, implored us to have trust in God, reassuring us that nothing would happen. Both he and the bishop, with their cassocks flying in the air behind them, seemed to enjoy the ride. Antonis turned pale but said nothing as he held fast.

After forty-five minutes of the most anomalous boat ride that I have ever experienced, during which time I hardly paid attention to the magnificence of the Athonite coast, we reached the monastery of Iveron safe and sound. The three of us, Father Maximos, Antonis, and myself, walked to the enclosed yard of the monastery and sat on a bench to get our breath back as the craft with the bishop continued the journey toward the Great Lavra.

"That was not too bad," Father Maximos said, as I sighed with relief and Antonis breathed deeply a few times to get his color back. At that point a man walked into the yard all soaking wet. He was a pilgrim from Athens. Water dripped from his jacket, his sweater underneath, his pants, his shoes, his hat. We assumed he must have slipped into the harbor somehow. There were no clouds around and the sky was brilliant. "No," he said with exasperation, "I was walking toward the monastery and suddenly a cloud came on top of my head and dumped all its water over me."

It was hard for us to control our laughter. "Such things happen on Mount Athos," the man said matter-of-factly. Still sloshing water out of his shoes with every step, he walked up the staircase to contact the abbot so that he would be given a room in which to change and dry his cloths.

"Time to go," Father Maximos said, after we were treated to the traditional refreshments by a novice, a thirty-year-old who, we learned, was a graduate from the London School of Economics. He was in charge of the library of the monastery and was trying to put in order manuscripts written by monks and others throughout the long history of monasticism on Athos.

Unlike the boat ride, we thoroughly cherished the long walk to Father Vasilios's hideaway. As we traveled we had a chance to engage Father Maximos in various theological discussions on the nature of monasticism, Orthodox theology, and other matters.

"What amazes me, Father Maxime," I said, "is the amount of cooperation and love that you people express to one another at the Monastery. At least this is the impression I have from these few days that we have been here with you."

Father Maximos smiled as he, holding a shepherd's cane, paced forward with determined steps, having Antonis on his right and myself on the left. "That is because," he said, "we practice real communism in the Monastery. We own nothing individually. We have nothing here to compete for, to create antagonisms. So we don't have the temptations that ordinary people have. You see," he said, and stopped for a few seconds as he placed his cane under his right arm and opened his palms facing upward. "I have not a single drachma to my name." Then after we began walking again he continued. "The communists in Russia failed miserably because they tried to bring about communism through force and violence. It cannot be done. Only through love and real compassion can communism work and flourish."

"The Marxist-Leninists," I added, "assumed that by simply changing the economic arrangements in society human beings would begin to behave like angels. Neither in the writings of Marx nor Lenin is there any concern with the issue of how to make human beings more loving and compassionate. Their cosmology and their theory of self as purely a product of social-economic conditions could not allow them to think otherwise. Therefore, a genius like Marx would entertain the absurd notion that once the proletariats came to power they would eventually let that power 'wither away' from their hands and full communism would then emerge, where people would have total freedom to pursue their creative potentialities."

"Only a theocentric form of communism can work," Father Maximos said authoritatively and moved on with such a fast pace that we could barely keep up.

"By the way," he went on to say, "please do not take any pictures of Father Vasilios. He does not like it."

"Why?" Antonis wondered.

"He objects to any kind of publicity for himself. And please don't ask him about the stories you heard about him. That would put me into a difficult situation." Father Maximos went on to clarify that publicity, photographs, and tape recordings go contrary to the hermitical life. The whole point is to overcome ego. Photographs and public attention are, according to the hermits, the means through which the Devil attempts to disorient them from their focus on God.

"No matter what he does to avoid publicity," I pointed out, "Father Vasilios's reputation has reached all the way to the other side of the Atlantic." Father Maximos shook his head as I went on to narrate another story that I had heard on the Monday after Easter. It was told to me by the abbot of the Monastery, who'd heard the story directly from Father Vasilios. It was night and the good father was praying in his hermitage. The door was closed and so was the window. Suddenly he heard knocks on the door. He looked out his window and saw the figure of a woman. He assumed that it was the Devil since there were no women on Mount Athos. Therefore, he refused to open the door. The woman persisted, claiming that she was not the Devil but Saint Ephemia, a woman saint who was martyred during the early years of Christianity. Father Vasilios still did not believe her until she began chanting the "Axion Estin Os Alethos Megalinin se ten Theodokon . . . ," a chant in honor of the Holy Virgin, the protectress of the Holy Mountain. Father Vasilios was then convinced that it was not the Devil and opened the door. Saint Ephemia stayed with him for a while giving him a lesson in theology and answering his questions. Then she suddenly disappeared.

"Is there truth in this story?" I asked. "I mean did Father Vasilios have such an experience?"

Father Maximos grinned but kept his pace. "Yes, it is true. But please don't ask him such questions when we meet with him."

We kept silent for a while as we continued our walk through a most spectacular passageway. On our left there was the northern Aegean Sea. On our right the mountains of Athos covered with thick, dark green vegetation. Nature was truly exuberant with color. I reflected for a while on the many unbelievable stories that I had heard, about events and happenings that were presumably taking place on Athos all the time, nurturing the faith and commitment of the monks. A dogmatic skeptic would automatically dismiss such stories as the fabrication of hermitical imagination. There is no room in modern secular minds for miraculous happenings. It would be easy to conclude that the old father, through ceaseless prayers, continuous fasting, vitamin deficiency, and sleep deprivation, began hallucinating. A psychologist friend of mine warned me once that if I were to confront a so-called supernatural or metaphysical happening I should do everything possible to explain it through physical means. Fair enough. But he, of course, rejected "metaphysics" with such passion that it often raised suspicions in my mind about the underlying subconscious motives for his intensity. He had once been a devout participant in the church. Subsequently, partly thanks to his educational training, he'd fallen under the spell of positivism.

"Spiritual things are caused by material things," he told me once, as if he knew a great secret. "It is material things, therefore, that we must try to understand." Indirectly he was telling me that I had gotten it all wrong.

The books I'd written led people with extraordinary tales to approach me, to unburden themselves of all sorts of experiences that they would not have revealed to persons like my dear psychologist friend, who dismissed a priori such stories as sheer nonsense. Modern secular intellectuals are by virtue of their beliefs cut off and insulated from a universe of human experience that I discovered after I had ventured beyond orthodox academic, positivistic boundaries. A French university professor, for example, who I will call Raymond, contacted me recently after reading my books. This tenured professor of languages revealed to me in all sincerity that while in India he was witness to a paranormal episode. "It just blew my mind," he said to me. Raymond was walking with a yogi on some mountain. They arrived at a point where they had to cross to the other side of a ravine. The yogi simply spread his hands upward and instantly appeared on the other side. The Frenchman, stupefied as he was with what had unfolded in front of his eyes, had to walk for another hour before coming to the point the yogi had reached through teleportation.

These thoughts and memories kept my mind busy as we paced silently. In a while we were to meet a person with a reputation for such wondrous abilities. What is the truth value of such stories, I thought to myself? Celebrated scholars have staked their reputations to propose views of reality that might accommodate such stupendous episodes. I thought of Huston Smith, the MIT philosopher of science and comparative religions. He put forth the argument that we as human beings can study scientifically only that which is below ourselves in consciousness, never whatever or whoever may be above us. To do science we must have controls. We can control rocks, mice, plants, and the like, and after appropriate scientific manipulations we can establish empirically validated truths. But science cannot study angels or archangels simply because the lower cannot control the higher, just as a dog could not control and manipulate a human being for study. In a published interview Huston Smith came out openly and provocatively in favor of the argument that there are beings higher than ourselves, by definition possessing unimaginable abilities and powers.

"I do believe," he said, "that beings greater than ourselves exist. I likewise believe that some of these may be in touch with us in ways we are not normally aware of. Regarding information that derives from them, I distinguish what has come to be called channeling from Revelation. Revelation proceeds directly from God, as to Moses on Mount Sinai. . . . In channeling as I would use the word, the source of the message is not God but a lesser spirit of some sort—a demigod, an angel, a departed soul, whatever."[1]

If we take seriously what these contemporary thinkers and explorers say, I thought as we continued our journey, then we must be open to the possibility that people like Indian yogis, Tibetan lamas, and some monks on Mount Athos may be in contact with realities inaccessible to ordinary people, who are focused on and attached to the preoccupations of daily living within the gross material world. Given these considerations the wise alternative is not to dismiss a priori the stories that the monks on Mount Athos tell us about miraculous happenings as nothing more than delusions or hallucinations. Rather we should just listen.

"Father Maxime," Antonis asked as we sat under a pine tree to get some rest, "from what we have been hearing about Father Vasilios my impression is that one day he will be considered one of the saints of the Orthodox Church."

"No doubt about that. In fact, I would dare say that he is now a living saint."

"Under what conditions is one declared a saint?" I asked.

"First of all," Father Maximos went on to say, "he must be recognized as a saint by the people. That means he must be known for an exemplary life not only in terms of morality and the way he conducted himself, but also in terms of miracles that happened because of him both during his earth life and afterward. In addition, we have noticed from experience that the remains of saints are different from ordinary people or ordinary monks. For example, the color of the bones is not white but dark brown and they often emanate a certain distinct fragrance. When all these signs are present, that is, reputation among the people, miracles during and after his earth life, and the color and smell of his remains, the Church comes and officially recognizes him as a saint. You see, it is not the decision of some committee of bishops that would declare one a saint and then the believers will accept him as a saint because of the decision of that committee. It is the other way around, from the bottom up rather than from the top down."

"So in the Orthodox Church," Antonis added, "the official definition of one as a saint is more or less the end product of a democratic process."

I pointed out, and Father Maximos agreed, that one may in fact be a "saint," that is, have all the characteristics of a saint, but remain unknown to his or her contemporaries. Furthermore, I said, my suspicion was that most saints are never known.

Among the treasures and relics of the Athonite monasteries important prominence is given to the skulls and bones of venerated saints. Usually the skulls of great saints are encased in silver boxes and kept in the sanctum. On special occasions the remains of such saints are brought out into the main church so that the faithful may pay homage. At the Monastery they held the skull of Saint John the Chrysostom, a most venerated saint of Orthodoxy. We were shown that one of the ears of the saint remained intact. The reason, we were told, was to symbolize the fact that John the Chrysostom, who wrote the main liturgy of the Orthodox Church, was simply writing what Saint Paul was dictating to him through that ear. I interpreted what the fathers told us to indicate that John the Chrysostom was "channeling" Saint Paul. The phenomenon of channeling, which is often thought of as a fad of the so-called New Age, is in fact part of the tradition of the heart of Christianity, as it is preserved on Mount Athos at least. Not to mention the phenomena of materialization and dematerialization, teleportation, and clairvoyance, which are an integral aspect of the Athonite culture.

We started walking again as Antonis opened another topic of discussion, the importance of the icons in the Orthodox liturgy. No service is possible in the Orthodox Church without the presence of icons. There is hardly a monastery on Mount Athos that does not have one or more icons of the Holy Virgin that have miraculous properties. No litany is possible without the carrying of icons by either monks or lay people. In fact we were expected as pilgrims to take part in the various processions, and we were invited to take a turn carrying the icons as a form of blessing and sanctification. By holding the icons we partook of their sanctity.

As we proceeded with our hike I mentioned an experience I had at the Stavrovouni (Mountain of the Holy Cross) Monastery in Cyprus while on a visit there with my friend Michael Lewis, a professor of art at the University of Maine. The day that we visited Stavrovouni there were monks painting religious images on the dome of the church. When they learned he was an artist they invited him to climb up the scaffold and observe their work. From below Michael noticed that they were using ancient techniques in their work. That fascinated him. He imagined for a moment, as he later told me, images of Michelangelo painting the Sistine Chapel at the Vatican. But he was shocked once he climbed up to see that the primary artist was simply copying images from a contemporary book. Later, in the monastery's basement workshop for icon painting, he noticed the same tendency of the monks to copy icons, with very slight variations. To him the process lacked "the vibrancy of originality," as he put it.

Father Maximos chuckled. "But the point of painting icons," he said, "is not the exercise on the part of the icon painter of his own individual creativity and personal imagination. You will never see on an icon, for example, the signature of the painter. Most of them have remained anonymous." An icon, he led us to understand, must be seen as a representation of a religious archetype that cannot be changed through the application of the painter's creativity and imagination. The icons are vehicles that connect this world with that of the Spirit. Icon painting, therefore, is not an outlet for the expression of individuality, for that stimulates egotism and fascination with one's importance. Furthermore, individual expression would distort the archetype which had been brought down through revelation. And the central aim of monastic life is the exact opposite—to silence egotism and self-absorption so that the Uncreated Light may come forward in the inner experience of the ascetic. In the same way that you can only minimally improvise on the liturgy, you can only minimally improvise on the icons.

The German scholar Ernst Benz admonishes the occidental observer to cast aside his or her preconceptions about art and try to understand the nature of icons from within the context of Eastern Orthodox culture. That means, among other things, to stop comparing icons to Western forms of painting and try to grasp the "peculiar nature of Eastern icon making in terms of its theological justifications." Once the mystical revelation of the images of the icons were imprinted in the original painters, then a tradition was established serving the spiritual aims of the Church.

"The art of icon painting," he wrote, "cannot be separated from the ecclesiastical and liturgical functions of the icons. . . . For the icon is a sacred image, a consecrated thing. This fact is present from the beginning, even as the icon is made. The procedure of painting itself is a liturgical act, with a high degree of holiness and sanctification demanded of the painter. The painter-monks prepare themselves for their task by fasting and penances. Brushes, wood, paints, and all the other necessary materials are consecrated before they are used. All this only confirms the theory that the sacred image has a specific spiritual function within the Eastern Orthodox Church, and that its tradition-bound form springs not from any lack of skill but from specific theological and religious conceptions which prohibit any alteration of the picture."[2]

The Catholic priest Henri J. M. Nouwen, after "discovering" how certain Russian icons opened for him the realm of spiritual experience, wrote: ". . . icons are created for the sole purpose of offering access, through the gate of the visible, to the mystery of the invisible. Icons are painted to lead us into the inner room of prayer and bring us close to the heart of God. . . . Icons are not easy to 'see.' They do not immediately speak to our senses. They do not excite, fascinate, stir our emotions, or stimulate our imagination. At first, they even seem somewhat rigid, lifeless, schematic and dull. They do not reveal themselves to us at first sight. It is only gradually, after a patient, prayerful presence that they start speaking to us. And as they speak, they speak more to our inner than to our outer senses. They speak to the heart that searches for God."[3]

It was only after my conversation with Father Maximos and after reading up on the nature of icons that I felt I understood their essence. My training as a sociologist conditioned me to look at icons in purely secular ways, particularly through the lenses of the most influential French sociologist, Emile Durkheim, who set the ground rules for the sociological study of religion.[4] The conversation with Father Maximos stimulated and brought to the forefront of my consciousness the Durkheimian arguments on the nature of religion and for a while, as we walked silently, my mind drifted to the sociological view of religion as developed by Durkheim, which shaped the thinking of sociologists on the nature of religion for generations. This kind of thinking, brilliant as it was, had perhaps cut us off from a deeper understanding of the nature of religion.

The essence of religion, Durkheim taught, is the dichotomous distinction that we find in every society between the "sacred" and the "profane." There are always certain things that are set apart from ordinary, profane things, toward which the faithful relate with special reverence. The artifacts of Christian worship such as icons, crosses, the Gospels, and the skulls of venerated saints are part of the sacred realm. But Durkheim, being a product of a "sensate age," secularized the sacred by suggesting that it can be just about anything that society decides to set apart, inducing its members to worship it. It could be an icon or a stone, the image of Stalin or the icon of Mao or the American flag or any political or religious ideology that can provide "social solidarity." Society, said Durkheim, needs religion for its own maintenance. Therefore, religion cannot die because society will always manufacture the religion it needs. In fact, he said, religion is society in disguise.

When people are worshiping their gods, said Durkheim, they are not aware that in reality they are worshiping their society. For example, within this context the biblical story of Abraham offering his only son as a sacrifice to God is nothing more than a myth concocted by a hierarchical, patriarchal society that expects its members to obey the rules handed from above without question. Durkheim believed that "traditional" religion, i.e., belief in "animism" or "supernaturalism" is on the way out but religion can live on in the form of secular religions. For most social scientists the notion that icons can be vehicles for an opening to another realm, a realm of spiritual experience, cannot be taken seriously. Such practices are useful superstitions that are functional for the maintenance of society.

I never felt comfortable with this definition of religion although, like most sociologists, I accepted it as fact. Yet, another leading contemporary French sociologist, Raymond Aron, objected vigorously to the reduction of the essence of religion to forms of social organization.

"Durkheim considers," Aron wrote, "that the science of religions presupposes the unreality of the transcendent as a matter of principle. The transcendent, being supernatural, is automatically excluded by the scientific method. Thus the problem is to rediscover the reality of a religion after having eliminated the supernatural from it."[5] Then Aron went on to state:

"It seems to me absolutely inconceivable to define the essence of religion in terms of the worship which the individual pledges to the group, for in my eyes the essence of impiety is precisely the worship of the social order. To suggest that the object of the religious feelings is society transfigured is not to save but to degrade that human reality which sociology seeks to understand."[6] Yet Aron does not go any further, to tell us how to approach the subject of religion.

The sociologistic notion that the essence of religion is the distinction between a socially defined "sacred" center and everything else, considered profane, is only a half truth. It is true only in terms of the exoteric manifestation of a religion, the way it is socially articulated and expressed within a particular time and a particular culture. Durkheim examined religion only in terms of its exoteric forms. Like most secular thinkers, he remained totally unaware of the reality of an "esoteric" core of religion that is grounded on direct experience of divine essences.

It was Rudolf Otto, in his classic work *The Idea of the Holy*,[7] writing a few years after Durkheim, who pointed out that the real essence of religion is in the direct experience of the Holy, what he called the *mysterium tremendum et fascinosum*. The Holy, or the "Numinous," is something beyond rational and ethical conceptions. Otto pointed out that rationalism had influenced religious thinking in the West by restricting and reducing the divine to those attributes of God which could be conceptualized and articulated in intellectual terms.[8] The essence of religion is not, as Durkheim argued, the distinction between the sacred and the profane, although this is true of the exoteric manifestation of religion, the socially constructed religion. The essence of religion is in reality the direct experience of the "Holy," the mysterium tremendum. And the experience of the Holy generates a sense of unworthiness on the part of the believer. It is this experience that leads the monks of Mount Athos to shed bitter tears once they have a taste of the numinous experience. By comparison, ordinary consciousness appears to be a form of damnation or at best a purgatory.

Apparently it was for these reasons that Father Maximos provoked me earlier with the statement "We do not believe in philosophy here. We believe in experience."

Father Maximos was an educated man and as we kept walking, absorbed with the beauty around us, I mentioned what was going on in my mind about the apparent contradictions I saw between the sociological approach to religion and that of Rudolf Otto. He grinned in his characteristic good-natured way. "The philosophers explain and elaborate without experiencing," he said. "The holy fathers experience and then they describe their experiences as best they can. So true knowledge is experiential knowledge. Because philosophers do not have experience they are off the mark. And I am talking about even great philosophers like Socrates and Plato." Then after a few more paces Father Maximos continued. "The problem with Catholicism is that they based their theology too much on the writings of Aristotle, believing that it is possible to know God through logic. They opened Pandora's box. You can only know God through direct contact with God. This is the greatness of Orthodoxy."

"And of all authentic mystical systems," I said softly. I had no desire to engage in some kind of debate between the merits of Orthodoxy and other spiritual traditions or the philosophy of God as contrasted with the direct experience of God. I have a deep appreciation of both what philosophy aimed at and what Father Maximos tried to convey to us about experience. I only pointed out that words may not bring us face to face with God but they can point the way.

After all, the early Greek fathers of the Church were themselves steeped in Plato. They employed the philosophical insights of Plato consistent with their own experiences to convey and articulate their theologies.

But I couldn't totally control myself. "Don't you think, Father Maxime, that it was a tragic moment when Emperor Justinian shut down the schools of philosophy in Athens because to him the Truth had been revealed through Jesus Christ and therefore there was no need for philosophy any more?"

"I am not against philosophy," Father Maximos tried to clarify. "I am only saying that it is not adequate as a vehicle to God. We must employ different methods for that." He then mentioned as a reference to what he was saying the work of a Russian staretz by the name of Silouan the Athonite, considered to have attained sainthood while still in this life. He died at the Russian monastery of Saint Panteleimon in 1938 leaving behind him, as I discovered later, a body of teachings considered to be one of the most profound in twentieth-century Christian mysticism. When I later read the book written by his disciple the Russian Archimandrite Sophrony, whom Stephanos had met in England, I was reminded of the conversation I had with Father Maximos. I was particularly struck by a passage on the inadequacy of even the most profound and enlightening philosophical contemplation as a vehicle to God.

The theologian who is an intellectualist constructs his system as an architect builds a palace. Empirical and metaphysical concepts are the materials he uses, and he is more concerned with the magnificence and logical symmetry of his ideal edifice than that it should conform to the actual order of things. . . . Many theologians of the philosophical type, remaining essentially rationalists, rise to suprarational . . . spheres of thought, but these spheres are not yet the Divine world. . . . People in this category . . . come to realize that the laws of human thought are of limited validity, and that it is impossible to encircle the whole universe within the steel hoops of logical syllogisms. This enables them to arrive at a supramental contemplation, but what they then contemplate is still merely beauty created in God's image. Since those who enter for the first time into this sphere of the "silence of the mind" experience a certain mystic awe, they mistake their contemplation for mystical communion with the Divine.[9]

We had been walking for more than two hours as we passed several *sketes* (hermitages, independent of monasteries, of small groups of monks who are guided by a gerontas) and a few hermits who lived all alone in the serenity of the Athonite wilderness.

"Christos Anesti, Father Savva," Father Maximos said to an old monk working in his small garden in a rugged black cassock. He responded with the traditional "Alethos Anesti Oh Kyrios" ("Christ is Risen, Father Savva"/"The Lord is Truly Risen").

It was hard for me and Antonis to fathom how old men like Father Savvas lived all alone in small shacks built by themselves in the middle of nowhere with no amenities whatsoever. At least the monks in cenobitic, or communal, monasteries, like Father Maximos, live in communities with the minimum necessities for their existence. But hermits like Father Savvas followed the strict traditions that the early fathers, like the Great Antonius, had inaugurated almost two thousand years ago in the deserts of Egypt.

"A couple of winters ago," Father Maximos said as we proceeded, "Father Savvas got lost one night. There was one meter of snow on the ground. He was delayed in reaching his hermitage because some pilgrims had stopped him on his path to ask all kinds of questions. By nightfall he was still far away from his place. It began to snow heavily again and the cold was extreme. He got lost in the darkness, got entangled in the bushes and did not know which direction to go. Exhausted, he sat down and began praying, feeling that the end was near. He prayed to the Holy Virgin. 'Mother of God,' he said, 'I have been in your Garden all these years praying and fasting. If I am to die please make it quick. If I am to live please show me the way to get to my place.' At that moment light began emanating from his heart like a flashlight, showing him the way. With the help of the light he found his way to his house. The moment he opened the door the light disappeared."

"It seems," Antonis remarked, "that nature favors the saint."

"Yes. Nature actually obeys the will of the saints."

"I have heard all sorts of legends about Athonite gerontes," I said. "That some of them presumably can befriend even wild beasts like wolves, boars, and poisonous snakes. They can pacify them and make them their friends. I was told by a pilgrim that he was a witness to a strange phenomenon. A gerontas, after seeing a poisonous snake that frightened a couple of other pilgrims on a path, walked next to the snake, patted it on the head and said, 'Now leave, my love, because you are creating terror in the hearts of these nice young men.' And the snake simply slid into the bush."

"You see what is happening," Father Maximos explained. "When someone reaches a certain state when one does not have any personal desires, when one becomes pure, clean of any egotistical yearnings, then what one asks is given because his will becomes one with the will of God. What the saint desires is exactly what God desires, therefore it is given. This is the purpose of *askesis*." Then Father Maximos went on to explain that the real meaning of *askesis* is the exercise of the soul. It is the exercise to overcome one's passions so that the Holy Spirit may flow through the person, emptied of any traces of egotism. I understood then that the word "ascetic" acquired a negative meaning in the West because it had become equated with masochism and bodily mortification. Father Maximos said that the authentic ascetic is no more masochistic than the

Olympic marathon runner who subjects himself or herself to excruciating exercises to attain a certain objective.

"So," I said, "the ascetics are in reality some sort of athletes or gymnasts."

"Precisely," Father Maximos replied. "They are gymnasts of the soul."

Months later Antonis, remembering the conversation on *askesis* that we had with Father Maximos, mailed me *The Way of the Ascetics*,[10] a book written by Tito Collianter, an Orthodox Finn. "Read this incredible book," he wrote in an enclosed note. "This author summarizes in a masterful way the method of *askesis* for lay persons, like ourselves, who wish to implement in their personal lives the insights on reality and existence discovered by the spiritually heroic work of the ascetics. Make certain you look up page 60."

I turned to page 60 and read: "With continuous *askesis* learn how not to have 'individual desires.' For him who has no individual, passionate desires, all things go in the direction that he desires them to go. This is what Abba Theodorus says. His will converges with the will of God and anything that he may ask in prayer is given." It is for this reason, I was led to understand, that when gerontes or staretzs like Father Vasilios pray for the welfare of the world their prayers are extremely important. And it is for this reason that they ceaselessly pray.[11]

We were told by Father Maximos to take heart because our long hike was soon coming to an end. He said we had about half an hour further to go. "Father Vasilios's hermitage is at the bottom of this valley," he said, and pointed ahead as we began descending from the high ground toward the base of the valley where a narrow river was flowing, concealed by thick vegetation.

"Last year," Father Maximos said as we began our descent, "there was this young fellow from Volos [a city north of Athens] who visited Father Vasilios imploring him to help his father, who was dying from cancer. Father Vasilios said he was going to do everything he could. In fact he promised to visit his father. The young man said, 'Well, let me write down the address for you.' 'Don't worry,' Father Vasilios said, 'I don't need it. I will find him.' 'But how are you going to find him without an address. Volos is a big city.' 'Don't worry, my son, I will find my way there. Here, take this little icon of the Virgin and place it under his pillow.' And Father Vasilios handed him a small printed icon he had in his pocket. The young man went back to Volos and did as Father Vasilios told him to do. He placed the icon under his father's pillow. The next day his dying father asked this young man, 'Son, who was that good priest who was here last night talking to me so nicely, giving me so much courage?' That fellow remained speechless. When his father died he wrote a letter to his mother telling her that he decided to become a follower of Father Vasilios and become a monk on Mount Athos. He sealed it and left it on the kitchen table without previously warning her about what he was planning to do. He left secretly. When Father Vasilios saw him he shouted at him, 'Oh you foolish lad! Go back to your mother. Go back. You are not meant to become a hermit, my son. Go back to your mother. She is desperate and is planning to commit suicide. Run immediately.'

"Well," Father Maximos continued, "when I saw that fellow he was in such a frenzy of a hurry. I asked him what was going on. He said he did not have time to explain because he had to rush to get the boat and go to his mother. He said, 'I will tell you over the phone.' He did go to his mother and, thank God, he reached her in time!"

"With all these stories floating around," Antonis asked, "does he find any peace? Don't people seek him out for all sorts of problems?"

"Yes. That is why he avoids publicity as much as possible. And he does not appreciate it when naive people ask him to perform miracles for them as if it is some kind of show," Father Maximos said with a grin on his face. Then he went on to tell us how a group of college students visited him and asked him to perform miracles. "He said to them, 'How about if I cut your heads off and then put them back again?' After that they stopped asking for miracles. That is why, please, don't raise the subject when you meet with him."

# 13

## RAINBOWS AND LIGHTNING

FATHER MAXIMOS'S WARNINGS ABOUT HIS GERONTAS INTENSI-
fied my anticipation even further. I was truly looking forward to
meeting Father Vasilios. I had no pressing personal problems to
discuss with him, and since my time with him was to be brief I
wanted to ask him in private certain theological questions. I thought
that since he was reputed to have divine charisma and since such
extraordinary tales were circulating about his spiritual feats and oth-
erworldly experiences, he might have insights to questions that official Church dogma could not deal with. I assumed that since I was
to see him in private he could tell me things that he could not say
in public or in the presence of others.

I was specifically interested in getting some direct or indirect
answers on the question of reincarnation. From my experiences with
psychics and spiritual healers I had arrived at the conclusion that
reincarnation may be a fact of life rather than a theological doctrine.
For example, an ordained Episcopal priest wrote to me on this subject claiming that he in fact remembered past lives and found no
contradiction between that belief and the fundamental teachings of
Christianity. He kept his experiences secret, however, for obvious
reasons. Similarly, an Anglican minister wrote to me along similar

lines only a few weeks earlier and expressed frustration that he could not speak about this publicly because of conflicts with the official doctrine of his church.

I assumed that Father Vasilios would have some important statements to make on the subject, either to reject it outright and categorically, or indirectly leave the door open for possible confirmation. I knew, of course, that he could not give me a clear "yes" answer to my question since this would have squarely contradicted the teachings of the Church and would have cast him into the role of "heretic." Erevna, which also works from within the Christian framework, takes reincarnation as a given. Kostas would claim that once an individual attained a certain level of spiritual development, then knowledge of past lives came naturally. If that were true, then I would assume that either Father Vasilios had such experiences himself but kept them secret in order to avoid possible unnecessary controversies with the Church, or that he simply had no such experiences.

The dominant doctrine of Christianity on the nonexistence of past and future lives may be so powerful as an "elemental" that it may prevent even saints from having such an experience. The other possibility of course may be that there isn't such a thing as reincarnation and that the whole idea is a clever distraction engineered by the Devil who has vested interests in keeping humanity away from the urgency of discovering God and uniting with Him in the here and now. Promises of future lives may lead one to a form of spiritual laziness and an overattachment to worldly things. The Catholic Church had to invent the notion of purgatory in order to cope with the obvious contradiction between the infinite love of God and the doctrine of eternal damnation. Presumably souls can evolve and find their salvation during this interim period between earthly life and heaven.

The philosopher and theologian Geddes MacGregor claims that from all ideas in the history of religion none is more universal in its appeal than the doctrine of reincarnation and that it is not in-compatible with the essence of Christianity. The absolute love and justice of God logically presupposes a doctrine such as karma and reincarnation, which is contrary to the official and cruel notion of eternal hell and damnation. He suggests that "The hospitality of the Christian Way to reincarnationist notions may turn out to be greater than we may have believed possible."[1]

MacGregor refers to the highly acclaimed and original Russian Orthodox thinker Nicholas Berdyaev who argued that the ultimate victory is not over death but over hell. Berdyaev alluded to the injus-tice of the traditional notion of hell where people are tormented in eternity for crimes they committed during one lifetime and admitted that the notion of karma and reincarnation is more just and logical. Yet, unable to break away from old habits of mind, he argued that it is impossible for Christian minds to accept reincarnation. It is revealing that immediately after that statement Berdyaev went on to say, "But it is essential to recognize that man's final fate can only be settled after an infinitely greater experience in spiritual worlds than is possible in our short earthly life."[2] MacGregor then asks, "If this be so, as seems to me an inescapable conclusion for Christians and one supported by the long and ancient tradition of 'an intermediate state,' why the re-jection out of hand of reincarnationism as something quite un-acceptable 'by the Christian mind'?"

"Look!" Antonis said with surprise. "Look at these signs," and he pointed at a couple of wooden signs indicating the direction "To Father Vasilios."

"Who put these up?" I asked.

"Certainly not him," Father Maximos said, laughing. "It was the other hermits around here who were constantly bothered by pil-grims knocking at their door in search of Father Vasilios."

As we came out of a heavily wooded pathway we faced a square, single-room stone dwelling with a roof made of brick tiles. "Here we are," Father Maximos announced. "I hope he is in." We walked into the yard, and behind the house there he was. Father Vasilios was sitting on a piece of wood supported by two rocks. Around him there was a group of university students who must have spent Easter in the nearby monastery of Simonos Petras.

Father Vasilios stood up when he saw us. He was a thin, "El Greco–looking" priest with a white pointed beard that reminded me of the iconographies that decorate Orthodox churches. It was as if he had just come out of the icon to greet us. Yet he was ordinary-looking at the same time. But being next to him one felt the presence of an extraordinary human being. I am not much of a reader of auras but in the case of Father Vasilios the feeling of warmth that his sheer presence radiated was unmistakable. Perhaps, I said to myself, I was predisposed to feel that way. But my "gut feeling" was telling me otherwise.

Father Vasilios was a smiling gerontas, hardly the austere-looking patriarch that one usually associates with the clerical role. He welcomed us with the "Christos Anesti," embraced Father Maximos and then kissed his hand as a gesture of humility, while the latter immediately did the same to his gerontas and master. Antonis followed suit and, bowing, kissed the elder's right hand. I did the same. It was the custom.

Father Vasilios invited us to make ourselves comfortable. There were some large rocks to sit on and a couple of old construction boards supported by two stones. Father Maximos sat on a rock. I sat next to Antonis on one of the boards. Father Vasilios had no amenities whatsoever. We were told earlier that his mattress was a piece of wood supported by rocks, and for kitchen utensils he had only one tin can where he boiled water for tea. For food he usually ate *paximadi* (hard roasted dried bread) after soaking it in his tea.

Whatever food he received was given to him by the nearby monasteries and by his disciples.

Father Vasilios's lifestyle reminded me of the ancient Cynic Di-
ogenis who lived in a barrel and had as his only possession a cup.
But when one day he saw a boy drinking from his palms he threw
his cup away. The hermits of the Egyptian deserts, who started this
tradition within Christianity, were in fact influenced by the practices
of the Cynics and the Stoics, and not by those of the Epicureans.
Father Maximos claimed that Father Vasilios hardly ate or slept,
since he spent most of his time in prayer and contemplation. Yet,
he appeared to us a very vigorous grandfather with piercing eyes
full of energy. His age was not easily determined. That is why speculations about his age ranged between sixty and close to a hundred.
Actually he did not appear more than sixty-five to me and the movements of his body were of a healthy man accustomed to mountain
hiking.

"Here, take some," Father Vasilios said as he passed around a
box of Turkish Delight that must have been brought to him by his
Easter visitors. "Take one, Kyriaco," Antonis whispered in my ear
in a light tone, "they are blessed."

Father Vasilios went back to the group of college students to
complete the discussions that we had interrupted. After passing
around some more Turkish Delight we heard him implore one to
complete his university education and forget about becoming a
monk. Apparently the lad entertained the notion of joining him on
Athos, and was asking Father Vasilios for advice. "Oh, my son," he
said with humor, "finish your education. I wish I listened to my
mother when she urged me to graduate from elementary school. I
wish I listened to her. At least I would have learned how to spell
correctly. So get your degrees, my lads, and send one to me. I could
put it to some good use."

"Monastic life is not for everybody," Father Maximos said to us. "It is a harsh life. If you are not made for it you can literally crack up."

It is for this reason that there is no attempt on the part of either the Athonite Monks or the Church to proselytize recruits into monasticism. On the contrary, potential monks are expected to spend at least two years as a trial period on the Holy Mountain, before they are formally accepted into the order.

There was plenty of laughter as Father Vasilios went on to crack a few more jokes after the group of students left. It was a pleasant surprise for me, to meet a venerated saint who had neither the serious heaviness that I associated with the traditional priestly functions nor the austerity of the desert fathers as they appear in the iconographies. His humor, I felt, was an expression of a very noble and loving heart, the type of person that once you meet him, you love him instantly. That was not necessarily the case with all the gerontes one met on Athos. I heard stories of some others who did fit the austere stereotype.

"When the sea is calm I am in trouble," Father Vasilios said, giggling as the students walked away. "When the sea is in turmoil I have peace and quiet here." Since the only way to get to Mount Athos is by boat the condition of the sea determines the extent of the influx of pilgrims and visitors like ourselves.

Father Vasilios opened the conversation by commenting on the predicament of the modern individual. He talked for some time on the foolishness of consumerism, which he himself, he claimed, found totally irrational and beyond his understanding. "People," he said, "kill themselves working in order to buy things that they don't really need. And after they buy what they think they need they work even harder because there are more things that now they think they need. And on and on. At the end they don't have a single moment even to pray."

"He is saying all these things for me," Antonis whispered to my ear.

"No," I whispered back, "it is for me."

Father Vasilios went on to point out the responsibility of educated people to be of service to their countries. Their education is a gift from God that should be put to good use, fulfilling Christ's commandments of loving one's neighbor.

Listening to the words of wisdom that Father Vasilios was offering to us, I began to realize that what was most important in meeting him was not so much to hear the verbal teachings of Christian wisdom but simply to be in his presence. I am not exaggerating in saying that even if only a fraction of what people said about him was true then Father Vasilios was the possessor of a certain secret knowledge impossible to be conveyed directly through oral communication.

Just before we arrived Father Maximos told us of one of Father Vasilios's ecstatic experiences when he was "shown" the entire Creation, the galaxies, the earth, the solar system, the oceans, everything. He was led to understand experientially that God is beyond all creation. It is an axiom that such experiential knowledge can only be metaphorically conveyed to those who don't have the experience.

"Father Vasilie," Antonis said, "may I see you privately for a few minutes?" It was customary for pilgrims to have a private audience with the gerontas and ask him for advice on a variety of personal issues. I have heard many pilgrims after consulting with a gerontas claim that they didn't really have to say much since the holy father simply knew everything that went on in their hearts and minds. In fact the abbot of the Monastery said to me, after he learned that I was a sociologist, that the greatest sociology is to reach a state through spiritual practice so that you can look at a person and know everything that is going on in the other's heart. I did not dispute the point nor did I comment on the possible mixing of sociology with psychology.

"You can be next, Kyriaco," Antonis said as he moved over with

Father Vasilios about thirty meters away and sat on a stone wall under a cherry tree.

"Father Maxime," I said, "look at Father Vasilios's profile. Isn't it impressive? May I take a picture?"

"No, please," Father Maximos said and, horrified, grabbed my hands as I pretended to open my bag. He relaxed and grinned when he realized I was only kidding.

For about fifteen minutes I chatted with Father Maximos while Antonis spoke privately with the gerontas on various personal matters. A group of seven pilgrims had already arrived, awaiting their turn for an audience.

The questions on reincarnation, karma, the notion of eternal hell and damnation spun in my head as I took my turn and sat face to face with Father Vasilios. I remained speechless for a few seconds, not knowing where to begin, while the good father kept looking at me, waiting with an understanding. I began by saying that I had no serious personal issues that I needed to talk about and that the few minutes that I was to spend with him I wished to probe some spiritual questions that were of great importance to me. I thought I should start with some more innocuous issue.

"Father Vasilie," I began, "what is your position on the phenomenon of healing? I hear that you are involved with this kind of work." I couldn't understand why that question came to my mind since I was preparing myself to discuss reincarnation. I immediately realized that I, the experienced interviewer, had made a foolish gaffe. I realized that that was the wrong question to ask when I saw Father Vasilios changing his facial expression, betraying a certain discomfort. I bit my lips since I was warned by Father Maximos that the gerontas does not entertain discussions about his work.

"Look, my son," he said with a serene tone in his voice, "all I do here is pray. Whatever happens to people that I pray for is the work of the Holy Spirit, not mine."

Father Maximos told me earlier that Father Vasilios constantly prays for others. He said that he spends his hours by focusing his prayers on various categories of people. For example, he would spend one hour praying for orphans, one hour for widows, one hour for people who are about to have accidents, one hour for the handicapped, one hour for the sick, one hour for the dead and wounded in various wars, and so on.

Father Vasilios told me that his *diakonia* is primarily to pray for others. I was told earlier that the meaning of the word *diakonia* means the way God has assigned you in life to be of service in a special way. For others the *diakonia* may be to work in the world or to be an abbot in the monastery or to run the kitchen. I understood the meaning of the word to denote the divine role or roles that one is expected to play in life. The *diakonia* of a hermit like Father Vasilios was to ceaselessly pray for others and be of service in a variety of ways, such as being a confessor to pilgrims, offering them advice, being a gerontas to other monks like Father Maximos, and even being the gerontas of a women's monastery situated at the edge of the Athonite peninsula. I learned that Father Vasilios periodically traveled to that and other monasteries playing the role of the gerontas to nuns and monks outside of Mount Athos.

I gathered my courage and was ready to probe Father Vasilios on the issue that I had prepared in my mind. "Father," I said, "will all human beings eventually attain their salvation?"

He looked pensive for a few seconds and then without hesitation said: "All human beings are given the opportunity to attain their salvation."

I pondered what he said but for some mysterious reason I did not follow up with further questioning on this subject as I had intended. I tried later to explore and understand my motives but I could not find a satisfactory explanation. Was it because I did not wish to put Father Vasilios in a difficult spot with my heretical questions? Was it because I did not want to take the risk and get an answer that I would find inadequate and therefore would undermine the image that I had created in my mind about Father Vasilios? Or was it because some force, perhaps Father Vasilios's own energy, prevented me from asking the question?

I thought to myself later that the most obvious and legitimate question that I could have asked would have been the following: Since according to the official doctrine of the Church salvation is only through Jesus Christ in what way does every human being have an opportunity to attain salvation? The greatest portion of humanity are neither born Christian nor have they necessarily heard of the doctrine of Christianity. In fact some of them in isolated tribal societies may not have even heard of the name of Jesus Christ. It was my understanding that the Church does not give any clear answer to this question and more often than not it evades it. When I asked a trained theologian and monk the same question the answer he gave was to the effect that it would be presumptuous for mere mortals to claim to understand how the unfathomable infinite compassion of God works. Therefore, the assumption was, that we must have faith in the ultimate justice and compassion of the Almighty and not be scandalized by problems that defy our intellectual understanding.

Instead of asking that and similar questions my conversation with Father Vasilios drifted around my own life and problems, exactly that which I thought I would not be spending time discussing. I had important theological questions that I wished answered by him, and my time was limited since there were others waiting in line for an audience with the gerontas. In a sense, I felt as if I'd blown it.

However, his answer was not disappointing to me. To say that all human beings have the opportunity for salvation leaves the door open for the workings of what Matthew Fox called the "Cosmic Christ." This celebrated and controversial Catholic priest and theologian makes the argument that in the early writings of the Greek fathers of the Church the idea of a Cosmic Christ permeating the entire universe was well established.³ Father Vasilios came out of that tradition, which is radically different from the Calvinist doctrine of a wrathful God that has sentenced the greatest portion of humanity to eternal hell and damnation, a motif that is electronically marketed by fiery fundamentalist preachers.

Karma works in mysterious ways, however. The answer I was unable to get directly from Father Vasilios I was given indirectly by accidentally coming across the text of a lecture delivered by a contemporary Greek theologian at the Orthodox Cathedral of the Holy Virgin in New York City on December 12, 1992. Dr. Constanine Cavarnos, unlike hell-and-damnation preachers, claimed that the great fathers of the Orthodox Church, such as Saints Gregory of Nyssa, John Climacos, Symeon the New Theologian, Gregory of Sinai, and Nicholas Cavasilas, taught that the individual's spiritual evolution achieved here on earth does not stop with death. They taught, according to Dr. Cavarnos, that in the afterlife there will be continuous progress, unending growth in perfection, in knowledge, and in love. It was for me a breath of fresh air when I began verifying what Dr. Cavarnos said in reference to the writings of the saints he cited.⁴

I found in this perspective an opening of a possible dialogue between the mystical philosophies of oriental and Western religions. For if the Soul continues to evolve after death, then the notion of eternal damnation is in reality a morbid and destructive Christian heresy presented as orthodoxy among fundamentalist Christian groups. It was neither part of the doctrine of Christ nor of some leading saints of the early Church. Furthermore, if the notion of evolution is a fact that reveals itself in the transpersonal ecstasies of leading saints, then it also implies that the Soul after death must be offered opportunities and experiences so that it *can* evolve—such as the freedom to make choices between good and evil and to transcend low desires. If such opportunities were not present, then it would imply that the Soul after death becomes some sort of a mindless automaton which evolves toward the Light mechanically without any engagement of the will and irrespective of the personal history of that Soul—sinners and saints alike would automatically evolve toward Theosis, an absurd notion. It seemed to me as I was familiarizing myself with the writings of these theologian saints that this was not what they implied when they taught that in the afterlife there will be continuous progress in perfection, in knowledge and in love. But then the question arises, why is it so scandalous to Christian minds to entertain the possibility that this evolution can unfold through experiences that the Soul undergoes not only after death but after being reborn time and again within the gross material worlds? I could have raised these issues with Father Vasilios but I lost my chance. Perhaps, I thought later, that was how things were supposed to be.

It was four in the afternoon when we bid farewell to Father Vasilios. There were still six people waiting around to have some time with him. Father Maximos told us that usually Father Vasilios is not that accessible. But it was the day after Easter, the greatest religious holiday in the Greek Orthodox tradition, and therefore he made an exception. Ordinarily, we were told, he would make himself unavailable so that he could totally focus on his continuous prayers, a preoccupation that for those of us unaccustomed to hermitical ways appeared difficult to comprehend. A disciple of a gerontas hermit explained graphically to a visiting priest why one must be extremely discreet on visiting a hermit.

"It is possible that you may interrupt his prayer. It is possible that at that moment he is in a state of ecstasy, divinely snatched to Mount Thabor and you may bring him down to this noisy earth. There is nothing worse that you can do to a hermit. He is not bothered by anyone's curses, only your invitation to come down from the mountain. But at the same time it is the best thing you can do to yourself, for at that moment he will fill you up with divine fragrance! He will blind you from the brilliance he had accumulated

. . . just like Moses emanating brilliance as he walked down from Mount Sinai and the Israelites could not lay their eyes on him . . ."⁵

The road back was long and would have taken us more than four hours of walking. We decided to spend the night at the nearest monastery, an hour away, and begin the hike the following morning. Hospitality was automatically offered to pilgrims but the presence of Father Maximos was an additional advantage as he was known among the other monks and was a friend of the abbot. Thanks to his presence we were shown the priceless relics of the monastery, from crowns of Byzantine emperors to bones of venerated saints to the girdle of the Holy Virgin encased in a silver box securely kept in the sanctum and brought forward into the main part of the church only on special occasions. The monk who showed us the Holy Girdle explained to us how it had ended up in the monastery after originally being given to Saint Thomas. The elaborate centuries-long adventure story was an epic on the scale of Steven Spielberg's *Raiders of the Lost Ark*. The Girdle, we were told, has miraculous powers and periodically is sent with an escort of monks and the Greek navy, for protection, to various communities out in the world. Only a year earlier the Holy Girdle was brought to Cyprus on a Greek navy vessel escorted by an entourage of abbots, gerontes, and bishops. A liturgy was conducted at the harbor and thousands of people, including the president of the Republic with his family, passed by, crossed themselves and kissed it.

We were told that women unable to conceive do so once they come in contact with the Holy Girdle. I asked whether it has been historically verified that in fact the Girdle was that of the Holy Virgin. The monk who showed us the holy relics smiled and gazed toward the ceiling as he spread out his arms and turned his palms upward.

"You don't ask such questions up here," Antonis whispered to me. "They believe that it is the Girdle and it has been sanctified with the prayers of monks and believers for two millennia. Miracles take place because of this Girdle. Therefore it is the Holy Girdle."

"I understand, I understand," I replied quickly, and I realized how silly my question had been.

We returned to the Monastery and stayed two more days, attending the services, talking to the monks, and reading in our rooms. Antonis had been reading a book given to him by the abbot of the monastery we had just visited and from the first page he never stopped externalizing his enthusiasm and interrupting my own reading.

"This is an incredible document," he said as he lay on his bed reading. "It is the biography of the life of a hermit by one of his disciples." He passed it on to me with eagerness. I took a quick look and without showing any particular zeal to read it, as I was engrossed into my own reading, returned it to Antonis. I did notice that it was written by a monk named Joseph.[6] His gerontas was also named Joseph. Antonis told me that the author is now himself a gerontas in one of the monasteries.

"Listen to this," Antonis said as he turned the pages to read a passage. "Here is where the hermit confided an experience to his disciple that took place during his youth. It was at a time that he felt he was being maltreated and oppressed by another monk, causing him great grief and disappointment. After an incident he withdrew into a corner and began praying to God with tears in his eyes. Here is how he describes it.

" 'I cried a lot that day as never before,' " Antonis read. I had no choice but to put down my book and listen. " 'I was complaining to God, so to speak, for not helping me out. I prayed and asked that I was not going to move until He would show me His mercy and to give me encouragement. At the same time I was also imploring the Holy Virgin. As I sat there, that clear day, gazing at the pinnacle of Athos, from where I could even see the little church of the Virgin at the top, I felt a sensation of joy and immediately I saw a brilliant irradiance move out of the little church and like a rainbow came and landed on my head. I was immediately transformed and forgot myself. I was filled with light inside my heart and outside and everywhere. I felt as if I had no body. And then the prayer began by itself inside me so rhythmically and beautifully (Lord Jesus Christ, Son of God, have mercy on me a sinner). I made no effort. I simply kept looking, listening, and marveled.

" 'It seemed to me,' " Antonis continued reading, " 'as if I had two selves. On the one hand I saw my internal condition filled with light and spiritual fragrance and joy as the prayer continued inside me uninterruptedly. At the same time my body was covered with light from top to bottom and I marveled at the greatness of Divine Mercy. I realized that that was Grace that heals the pain of those that It wishes, according to the Patristic tradition [the tradition established by the early fathers of the Church].

" 'I do not know how long that condition lasted after which the light withdrew to where it had come from. I came back to my former condition and saw that I was in the spot where I started. But a lot of time must have passed because it was close to sunset. Then I heard the old man [the monk that created the problems] calling me and telling me how much he regretted his former behavior and we walked together to our hut. Since then that condition of the prayer never left me. Without effort the prayer has stayed inside me, without however the same extraordinary energy that it had the first time that it came to me.' "

Antonis stopped the reading and waited for my reaction. I pointed out that the experience of the gerontas Joseph is typical of what various other saints had said about their ecstasies, which literally means "standing outside"—that is, standing outside of one's ordinary self.

"This is going to interest you," Antonis said, as he flipped the pages to a section he had already marked. "In this section," he said,

"Father Joseph [the author] talks about how Divine Grace gets energized for ordinary people and for those who have dedicated their life to the attainment of godliness. For ordinary people God is always there to offer solace and comfort. However, for the gymnasts of the Soul, those who have renounced everything for the love of God, Divine Providence, he says here, does not come to them periodically and unconsciously for solace or some healing. For these others Divine Providence looks after them with a system of motherly care and acts in a variety of ways. Here is what gerontas Joseph is saying on this point." Antonis went on and read.

" 'It reveals to them unknown and secret mysteries through supernatural interventions. It explains to them the duplicity and the ways of the demons. It reveals to them the secrets of nature and His kingdom. He heals them from illnesses and transports them instantly to faraway places and shows them various episodes of the past and the future. Above all he helps them out in their spiritual development and elevates them to a life consistent with their true nature.' "

Antonis stopped again and awaited my comments. "It is amazing," I said, "how we find these things right at the heart of Christianity. I mean the acceptance of phenomena that within the parapsychological parlance have been called with such names as teleportation, precognition, and so on."

"And out-of-body travel and clairvoyance," Antonis added. "Listen to this," he went on to read from another part of the book. ". . . 'I do not know how long my effort lasted to invoke with great humility the Divine Mercy. Suddenly I felt within me solace and I was filled with light, as it always happens in this state. My heart was filled to the brim with Divine Love and I went outside of myself. I was within an abundant light and in front of me there spread a boundless valley, like a sea without any sign of a horizon. It seemed to me as if I moved towards the East, but I was not walking on the ground, nor did I feel any weight or limitation. Only I was dressed,

as I saw, in my poor garments.' " Then Antonis went on to read on
the exosomatic experience of the hermit, who eventually entered a
temple where he was welcomed by the Holy Virgin, which caused
him another ecstatic and joyous experience.

" 'Our Gerontas,' " Antonis read on, " 'had depth. . . . He had
no need to ask questions to find out what problems we faced. And
I always wondered how did he know with such detail what was going
on inside me which even myself would have been in a difficult situation to describe? . . . He used to tell us that our central preoccupation should be Divine Grace and that without It a human being
can attain nothing. . . . One day after we ate, I made a prostration
in front of him as I was getting ready to leave for my cell. He held
my hand tight, and smiling said to me, "Tonight I will send you a
small package, and be careful not to lose it." I did not understand
what he meant and I did not discuss it further. After I rested I began
with other brothers an all-night vigil forgetting completely about
the small package. I don't remember how I started but I remember
clearly that as soon as I began to mention in my prayer several times
the name of Christ my heart filled with love. Suddenly it increased
so much that I was no longer praying but I was in a state of wonder
about this overflowing of love. I wanted to embrace and kiss all
human beings and the entire creation and at the same time I was
thinking so humbly. . . . I felt the presence of our Christ but I could
not see Him. I wanted to fall down to His immaculate feet and ask
Him how does He set fire to the hearts of people and yet remain
hidden from them. I was then given to understand that Christ is
inside every human being. I said, my Lord let me be in this state
forever and I need nothing else. This state lasted for some time and
when I came back to my original condition I couldn't wait until I
went to my gerontas to tell him all about it. . . . The moment he
saw me as he paced up and down outside of his cell he began smiling
and before I made a prostration in front of him he said, 'Did you
see how sweet our Christ is? Did you understand what you so per-

sistently asked for? Now be in a hurry to make part of you this Grace so that it is not stolen by negligence.' . . . When I told him exactly what happened to me and asked him for an explanation how it happened, out of humility he avoided telling me how. God, he told me, took pity on you and showed you in advance His Grace so that you may not have doubts.'

"This book is full of such miraculous stories," Antonis said, and turned to another section of the book where gerontas Joseph explains to his disciple and author how it is possible to know things that are hidden from ordinary awareness.

" 'When the mind of the person,' " Antonis read, " 'has been cleansed, purified and enlightened . . . it is given, in addition to its own light, the light of Divine Grace so that it remains permanently within him. Then it snatches him and exposes him to visions and perceptions true to Its own nature. However, such a person has the capacity, if he so wishes, to ask through prayer. Then Grace is energized and what he asks is given simply because he asks. But I believe the truly devout avoid such requests except in extraordinary circumstances.'

"Now here is something else that will also interest you," Antonis said as he turned to another section of the book that he had marked. "It is about psychic abilities that are signs not of Grace but of satanic conditions. He claims here that it is not difficult to recognize them, particularly in those who are characterized by pride and frivolity. 'Unfortunately,' he says, 'we have seen here on Athos, particularly in past years, these kinds of disoriented brothers that even in their external appearance the disturbance of their psychonoetic condition is clearly manifested. These are precisely the symptoms of diabolical energies. On the completely opposite pole one finds the truly gifted with Divine Grace whose spiritual vision is a manifestation of tranquillity, peace and total love. Divine Grace is offered to those predisposed to the love of their neighbor.' "

"It is very clear from the writings of the Orthodox fathers that psychic gifts may in fact be gifts of the Devil and not of Divine Grace," I added. "This is what many in the so-called New Age movement don't seem to be aware of. There is little discernment on this issue. You will see, for example, in a spiritual book shop in New York City next to a shelf of books on Eastern religions and Western mysticism works by Aleister Crowley and manuals on how to conduct black liturgies, and the like. And all that under the banner of New Age. No wonder both clergymen and scientists alike are stunned.

"One more quotation from this incredible book and I will let you sleep," Antonis said as he noticed that in spite of my yawning I was fair game as I was deeply fascinated by what he was reading. "Here is what he says about prayer. 'Our gerontas used to tell us that for those who pray with authenticity the sensation of the love of one's neighbor is revealed. When Grace is energized in the heart of the one who prays, then the love of God floods his entire being to such an extent that he may not be able to take more. Then this love is transferred to the love of the World and the human person. His love becomes so powerful that he asks to take upon himself all the suffering and unhappiness of the others so that they themselves may be relieved. He suffers with those who are in suffering even for that of animals, so much so that he sheds bitter tears when he becomes aware of their pain. These are attributes of Love. But you must keep in mind that it is prayer that energizes them and causes them. That is why those who have advanced in the prayer never stop praying for the World. To those it is even attributed the prolongation of life, regardless of how paradoxical and audacious this may sound. And you must know that if those who pray disappear then that would bring the end of the World.' "

As soon as Antonis completed his last sentence the lights went off. It was eleven in the evening, the time when the Monastery's generator was shut off. We talked for a few more minutes about our experiences on Mount Athos and then tried to get some sleep.

The next day I felt lucky to find an extra copy of Father Joseph's work at the Monastery's small bookstore. Based on what Antonis read to me the previous night I thought it was a unique document on the nature of the subjective experiences of Athonite gerontes, experiences that are interpreted as direct perceptions of realities beyond the five senses. Such an outlook, I thought, is completely foreign to the preoccupations of established, "exoteric" Christianity, which has repressed its mystical origins in its confrontation with rationalism and the scientific revolution. Experience in the West, in terms of its philosophies, sciences, and its religions has become totally suspect.

The following morning Antonis and I began our journey back to "the World." Father Andreas insisted on driving us to Daphnē in the Monastery's Land Rover and save us hours of walking with our backpacks. The weather looked ominous as thick dark clouds covered the entire area. Father Maximos joined us all the way to Daphnē where we were to take the boat back to Ouranópolis. On the way we passed by a section of the peninsula that had burned the previous year. A terrible fire lasting many days consumed thousands of acres of woodland and threatened some of the monasteries. We were told that that fire was known of ahead of time by some of the gerontes, who warned about it.

"We would have all burned here if it wasn't for the volunteers who came from Europe, particularly the Germans," Father Maximos pointed out. When I asked about the actions of the Greek authorities Father Maximos was not too enthusiastic. "The Greek workers," he scoffed, "were more interested in their coffee breaks. The mountain was burning and they insisted on having their coffee while the Germans worked around the clock nonstop."

We had barely approached Daphnē when suddenly heavy rain began pouring down, with hail, lightning, and thunder. Oddly enough the sea appeared relatively calm. Antonis, however, worried that we might not be able to leave in this kind of weather since the boat had not arrived as yet. He had urgent business appointments back in Cyprus and, unlike myself, had to work within rigid time schedules. Fathers Maximos and Andreas tried to reassure us that in spite of the heavy rain the sea was not rough to the point of preventing the ferry from approaching the harbor.

We tried to find cover at Daphnē as we waited anxiously for the boat to arrive. Father Maximos took me aside under the balcony of the customs office to chat with me in private for a while. As a farewell memento he offered me a *komboschini*, an assortment of knots for prayer, that he himself created.

"I will pray for you, Kyriaco," he said, "so that God may one day bring enlightenment to your mind. I am thankful that God spoke to your Soul and that you have begun to taste of the sweetness of the presence of Christ within you. The study of the works of the Fathers and their practical implementation, as much as that is possible, will reveal such mysteries in your heart so that you will continuously remain in a state of enchantment of the wonders of God. When you will compare these experiences with whatever other knowledge and theories you may have, then you will be able to arrive at your own conclusions.

"Allow me to add, within the context of my own limitations and weaknesses," he went on to say, "that what the Holy Fathers have written are infinitesimal in comparison to the depth and width of reality. And this is what the Fathers of Orthodoxy are saying themselves—that in the end everything is done and expressed through silence, including the very communion of God with human beings. Even when we describe reality it remains beyond description, a mystery unexpressed and ineffable."

I nodded with appreciation as the familiar words of Taoism, "The name [the Tao] that can be named is not the eternal Tao," came to mind. I have read the same aphorism that Father Maximos was articulating in the mystical Orthodox teachings: "God," said

Evagrius of Pontus, "cannot be grasped by the mind. If he could be grasped, he would not be God."[7]

The thunderstorm stopped as suddenly as it started. The dark clouds began to move toward the east on the other side of the peninsula and the sun was beginning to illuminate patches of the mountain. At that moment a fabulous rainbow appeared, arcing from one side of the peninsula to the other, and under it in the distance we could see, to the great relief of Antonis, the ferry boat approaching.

"One more thing, my dear Kyriaco," Father Maximos said as we were getting ready to leave. "I want to underline that which you yourself are already aware of. That the practical implementation of the teachings of Christ and participation in the sacraments and mysteries of the Church is a presupposition for spiritual development. Therefore, beyond the study of the patristic teachings of Orthodox spirituality, which is of course necessary, you must struggle on the practical road. From the very beginning you should set up the right foundations that will pave the way to essential results and authentic fruition of the Divine Grace of our Christ. I wish wholeheartedly that through experience your heart will be informed that the fruit of true spirituality is the Christ Himself in a personal communion with each one of us."

I remained speechless and deeply moved by Father Maximos's eloquence and his concern for my enlightenment and salvation. Remaining silent I embraced him and bid him farewell. I was certain that I was bound to meet with him again. "Your contact with the Holy Mountain, Kyriaco, will mark your life forever." Those were the last words that I heard from Father Maximos as I picked up my backpack and walked with the others toward customs.

# 14

## BEYOND THE
## SHADOWS

THE CUSTOMS OFFICIALS EXAMINED OUR BACKPACKS WITH UN-
usual zeal before allowing us to board the ferry back to Ouranópolis.
Too many thefts of priceless religious relics by robbers imperson-
ating pilgrims had prompted the Greek government to impose strict
controls. The only objects that we were allowed to take along were
souvenirs hand-made by the monks, such as carved wooden crosses,
*komboschinia* for prayer, incense, and painted icons of no archaeological value.

We had stayed at Agion Oros for two weeks, one week longer
than what we were formally allowed. Akis, the architect, had stayed
for only four days as he had work to attend to in Athens. Besides,
he said, he was not made for the cloistered life of a monastery. Yet
even he was deeply affected by the experience and promised the
abbot that on his next trip to Mount Athos he planned to bring
along several of his workers to repair the dome on one of the shrines
of the Monastery.

I realized that I too was not made for the monastic life when I
saw women for the first time as they stepped into the bus we
boarded at Ouranópolis on the way to Salonica. It was a refreshing,

reassuring sight. Life seemed more balanced in the presence of the other half of humanity.

Antonis flew to Cyprus directly from Salonica in the company of Petros the philologist, who was beaming with a beatific look on his face from his Athonite adventure, in spite of the hardships he suffered from wearing the wrong shoes, wrong clothes, and dragging along the wrong luggage.

Before I left Greece I decided to spend a few more days on an Aegean island and try to sort out my thoughts and feelings about my formidable encounter with the Holy Mountain. I carried with me a heavy load of books I bought from the bookstores of the monasteries and from Salonica as well as the voluminous material passed on to me by Father Maximos. I wished to delve further into the Eastern Orthodox mystical tradition while experiencing the legendary delights of the Aegean archipelago.

From Salonica I took another bus, heading south toward Volos, and from that coastal city I boarded a ferry to the nearby island of Skiathos, its name literally and appropriately meaning "Under the Shadow of Athos." It was late April and mercifully the tourist season had not as yet begun. I found a clean, inexpensive room near the harbor and center of town, a spot where I could work and enjoy frequent breaks at the coffee shops and waterfront tavernas. Not far from where I stayed there was the house, now a museum, of the celebrated early-twentieth-century Greek writer Alexandros Papadiamantis, a literary preference of mine during my high school years and himself deeply influenced by the mystical traditions of Mount Athos and Eastern Orthodoxy.

I sat on the balcony going over my material. In front of me I could see a portion of the harbor through the narrow street opening. Fishermen were preparing their small boats loaded with nets while other islanders, having finished the day's work, gathered at the harbor's coffee shops. Many paced up and down the promenade. It was

a scene that I had seen innumerable times not only on Aegean islands but in the coastal towns of Cyprus. I felt at home.

My mind was on Athos and what I had experienced and learned
about the Holy Mountain and Eastern Orthodoxy. What is the
meaning of Mount Athos? What is there other than just a medieval
cultural preserve? Is there something in the life and practices of the
Athonite monks of relevance to contemporary life and civilization?
Those were the questions that kept swirling in my head as I settled
at Skiathos and began perusing my notes and the published and
unpublished material that I brought along with me. I felt cold sweat
over my body when I remembered what a Greek parliamentarian
once proposed in the early sixties, that Athos and its monasteries be
turned over to businessmen who could develop them into profitable
casinos.

Obviously, I thought, the path of the monk, as Kostas would have
argued, is not a path for ordinary people like myself. It could not
be my way of attaining higher states of spiritual consciousness. Few
individuals could cope with its hardships and rigors. The fathers of
Agion Oros themselves know that and would discourage someone
from following their ways who is not cut out for that lifestyle. There
are many examples of monks gone mad, as Father Joseph pointed
out in his book. Yet, I felt profoundly indebted to those few ascetics
and gymnasts of the Soul like Father Maximos and Father Vasilios
who, like Prometheus or heroes "with a thousand faces," renounced
the pleasures and comforts of the world to reach God and bring
knowledge of ineffable spiritual realms inaccessible to the rest of us,
who live within the routines and distractions of daily life. The monk,
said Christos Yiannaras, a contemporary Greek theologian, is a
tragic hero, just like in ancient tragedy. He removes himself from
ordinary life in order to see things more clearly.

A modern individual could dismiss the whole monastic tradition
as an anachronistic leftover of medieval times and pity those who
"waste" their lives in the wilderness. Yet we honor and celebrate

scientists as benefactors to humanity when they devote their lives with equal zeal by isolating themselves for years in sterile laboratories, in treacherous corners of the earth, in the Antarctic, in the rain forests of Africa and Latin America, and perhaps eventually in space, to pursue their scientific work. Obviously not everybody could or should become such a self-denying scientist. Yet the few who do play a pioneering role in our civilization.

Those individuals who devote their lives to the pursuit of the knowledge of God, I thought, deserve analogous honor, although they themselves would neither seek nor care for it. The monks of Athos also, I thought, have preserved for us a living tradition of mystical practices that would have been lost to those of us living in the midst of contemporary urban secular civilization. Many of them not only pray ceaselessly for the good of the world but have also written down their spiritual experiences and discoveries. Their writings help those of us who cannot live our lives as monks to at least indirectly benefit by studying the sacred texts and testimonies they left behind.

Without the records of their experiences there wouldn't be any information for us on mystical Christianity as expressed through the patristic writings. It was my friend Stephanos who first introduced me to this written tradition that I had been unaware. Names like Maximos the Confessor, Symeon the New Theologian, Saint Gregory Palamas were all new to me. I did not know that there was such a spiritual treasure as the *Philokalia*,[1] a collection in several volumes of the writings, aphorisms, and methods of spiritual practice of these mystical witnesses and fathers of the Eastern Church. I did not know that the *Philokalia* as a spiritual guide was unmatched for those serious in their search of a Christian mystical experience. It was Stephanos who pointed all that out to me. Christos Yiannaras, in an autobiographical work,[2] bitterly complained that in his university years as a theology student in Athens the living mystical tradition was not taught at all. The theology he was exposed to was imported from the rationalistic, scholastic, and Protestant West. He castigated the official establishment of theologians for ignoring and even repressing the mystical tradition that springs from within Eastern Orthodoxy, a tradition that to this day continues to be a living reality on Mount Athos. With a group of other theologians they began a struggle to rectify the problem and bring this esoteric and experiential form of mystical Christianity back to the forefront of the Eastern Church.[3]

I left my room and walked down to the harbor. I paced back and forth at the promenade a few times, constantly thinking of Mount Athos and trying to figure out what of that experience was of relevance to the modern world and contemporary Christianity. Obviously its cloistered medieval social context could not be the basis for the enticement of the modern mind. Yet within that very cloistered setting of continuous prayer, paranormal events such as out-of-body travel, clairvoyance, extraordinary healing phenomena, psychokinesis, and even levitation and teleportation may in fact be taking place. These are parapsychological happenings, or miracles that the New Age has identified only within the context of oriental religions, Native American shamanism or early "primitive" Christianity. The stories of such events happening on Mount Athos are no different than similar stories within the yogi tradition of India, Tibetan Buddhism, or Native American spirituality. One can of course dismiss all such stories as nothing more than folklore. This has been the approach of mainstream social science—a reductionistic, rationalist approach that dismisses the miraculous as nothing more than superstition. Yet no serious and open-minded student of such phenomena would dismiss them a priori as superstitions, given the massive evidence of such episodes that have been studied by serious researchers during the past hundred years.[4]

What distinguishes the practices of the Athonite monks from other metaphysical systems is the centrality and power of prayer as the vehicle for the experience of spiritual realities and eventual attainment of Divine Grace and union with God at Theosis. It seemed to me that for the Athonite fathers human beings were created for the sole purpose of prayer and nothing but prayer. And this prayer must be ceaseless and uninterrupted. As Father Maximos told me, "We ought to take literally Saint Paul's admonition that we must pray continuously."

The first time I heard of the "Jesus prayer" and the notion of continuous prayer was when a friend passed on to me the nineteenth-century Eastern Orthodox classic *The Way of the Pilgrim*, written by an anonymous Russian peasant who was searching to figure out the meaning of Saint Paul's words. With the help of teachers of Orthodox spirituality and the discovery of the *Philokalia*, that Russian pilgrim learned the technique of how to repeat: "Lord Jesus Christ, Son of God, have mercy on me a sinner." As he reports in that autobiographical work his life was radically transformed through that prayer.

I became interested in learning more about that mystical Christian prayer as I met several people who confessed to me that it, as in the case of the Russian peasant, had radically transformed their lives for the better. I learned that not only monks employ that prayer, but also people who live in as cosmopolitan a place as Manhattan, and the prayer has had extraordinary effects on their lives. A woman in New York City told me, for example, that at one point in her life she reached the rock bottom of depression and had it not been for the practice of the "Jesus prayer" she would have committed suicide. The prayer saved her sanity and her life. Yet I also heard stories of people going mad from excessive indulgence in the prayer combined with a lack of experience and lack of a spiritual teacher to guide them through the prayer. When I mentioned such possible complications to Father Maximos his response was: "You don't offer a baby a bowl of beans. A baby needs milk. It is only when the infant grows up that you begin to feed it with a bowl of nutritious beans." Likewise the "Prayer of the Heart," as it is often

called, must be engaged in only at a certain point of spiritual mat-
uration and only under the guidance of an elder or a gerontas.

"Father Maxime," I had asked him one afternoon as we were
about to take a walk outside of the Monastery, "tell me about the
Jesus prayer and how to do it." Before leaving the grounds of the
Monastery Father Maximos borrowed a book from the bookstore
which was at the gate of the Monastery. "This," he said as we paced
toward a nearby hill, "will tell you a lot about the method of the
prayer and its meaning."

The book, written in Greek, was a conversation between an
anonymous visiting priest and a hermit gerontas on the very issue
that I wanted to discuss with Father Maximos.[5] I raised with him
the fact that the Jesus prayer reminded me of the practices of Eastern religions, particularly of mantra yoga, since the technique employed is to repeat over and over the name of Jesus and chase away
all other thoughts. "Not so," Father Maximos claimed, and turned
the pages of the book to read the answer given to that question by
the elderly gerontas. It was the standard set of replies to a question
that many others had apparently been raising.

"First of all," Father Maximos said as he pointed out several
passages of the book, "with the prayer we express our intense faith
in God who has created everything and cares for and loves His
creation. We plead with Him and say, 'Have mercy on me.' We
cannot attain salvation by ourselves as some other systems maintain.
Only through the Grace of God can we do so and of course after
a lot of struggle on our part. But strictly by ourselves we can accomplish nothing.

"Second," he continued, "we are not struggling to unite with
some impersonal God. Our prayer is focused on the personal nature
of God, the God-man Jesus Christ and therefore we say, 'Lord Jesus
Christ, Son of God.' And we try to follow his injunctions."

Among the many symbolic meanings of the Trinity, I was given to understand, is the implied notion that God is neither an absolute impersonal principle nor is He a lonely God. In Orthodox spirituality God is three in one, linked together by the bonds of total and infinite personal love. That implies that in the very heart of the universe there reigns a personal reality, a personal love. Is this the reason perhaps, I thought, that in reports of mystical experiences as well as in near-death experiences when people report of encountering divine entities they always describe them as personal and loving?

The early fathers of the Church, who were thoroughly versed in Platonic philosophy, incorporated a great amount of that philosophy into Christian doctrine. They differentiated, however, their theology from Plato in one important respect. Plato believed that the ultimate reality is the world of the perfect ideal forms, the archetypes that lie beyond the shadows of gross material reality. The fathers of the Church on the other hand insisted, based on their own understanding and experience, that the archetypes themselves are caused by an even higher reality, the reality of a personal God. The destiny of the human person therefore is not to align himself or herself with these spiritual archetypal forms but with that higher reality, the personal God that created them.

"Third," Father Maximos read on, "by means of the prayer we try to attain humility and avoid pride. We consider ourselves worse than anybody else and plead to God to have mercy on us. Without humility we can attain nothing. Pride is the greatest enemy of the spiritual life.

"Fourth, salvation for us does not mean the obliteration of our individuality. We are aiming at uniting with the Triune God but we maintain our uniqueness and personhood.

"Fifth, the prayer itself helps us to differentiate and recognize the machinations and movements of the demons from the energies of Christ. You see, often demons present themselves as angels of light. Some people who are not experienced often think they are surrounded with angels and carry on conversations with them when in reality they are carrying on with demons. The prayer helps us distinguish the two.

"Sixth, for us there is no such a thing as indifference. We are constantly praying for the world. We are not trying to save ourselves alone. Joy that is only ours is not real joy." Father Maximos stopped there and passed on the book in the event that I wished to pursue the matter further. He thought that the anonymous hermit in the text clearly identified the salient ways of Orthodox practices in contrast to those of oriental yogis. Since my aim was to understand the methods of Orthodox spirituality I was not predisposed to engage Father Maximos in an academic discussion about the similarities and differences between Athonite practices and yoga meditations with their great diversity and varieties. What for example are the similarities and differences between Eastern Orthodox mysticism and Mahayana Buddhism as practiced by the Dalai Lama and the Tibetans? In fact a group of Tibetan monks visited Mount Athos, Father Maximos informed me, and when the former told the Athonite monks that they were doing essentially the same things the Orthodox fathers strongly disagreed.

After our walk with Father Maximos that day I went to my room for a couple of hours to examine the text written by the anonymous priest, a text that set down in detail how one should systematically employ the "prayer of the heart" as practiced on Mount Athos. The heart, according to the patristic teachings of Eastern Orthodox spirituality, is the center of the spiritual life and the aim is to "join together mind and heart" through the prayer so that eventually the individual becomes graced with the Holy Spirit and attains "Christification," which is considered, according to some interpreters of Eastern Orthodox spirituality, the birthright of every human being.[6]

There are instructions on how to concentrate on the heart while repeatedly saying the Jesus prayer and even on how to breathe, how to inhale by saying the first words, and how to exhale as one completes the prayer and then repeat the process again, over and over for a certain period of time. One can even shorten the prayer by simply saying, "Jesus, Jesus, Jesus . . ." preventing any other thoughts from entering the mind.

The time allotted to the prayer would increase gradually and always under the careful guidance of an experienced gerontas. For there are grave dangers if one indulges excessively into this spiritual practice, as I was often warned. According to the fathers the demons will do everything possible, through all sorts of interferences, to prevent a person from reaching God. Therefore, one who begins such a practice must be guided on the ways and means to neutralize the power of these demons, who get enraged every time someone embarks on the Divine journey. There are instructions on how to concentrate on the prayer and how to prevent any other thoughts from interfering during the prayer, and there are instructions on how, before starting the Jesus prayer, to first engage in certain practices to "warm the heart," such as reciting standardized prayers from the liturgy or reading a few pages from a sacred text. With advanced practice the prayer will eventually become self-activating and even while the individual is asleep the prayer will remain active within the subconscious. When the visiting pilgrim asked, "How is it possible for a person to be asleep and his heart to continue praying?" the hermit gerontas gave the following explanation.

All the episodes, all the impressions of daily life and all the preoccupations of the mind penetrate the depths of the heart, enter the subconscious, as we say today. Usually then with whatever a human being is preoccupied during the day, it is with that which the heart is preoccupied at night when the mind is silent and human energies and powers are resting. As the Great Vasilios [early father of the Church, eleven hundred years before Freud] said, the fantastic representations during dreaming are echoes of our daily experiences. The devious thoughts and devious preoccupations of the day generate devious dreams. The same happens with good works and good thoughts. The ascetic and the lay practitioner keep in mind ceaselessly the memory of God through the repetition of the prayer. They repeat this with every other activity, be it eating, drinking or working. Therefore, it is natural that during the few hours of nightly rest the heart continues to think and pray to God. It remains awake.

Advancement in the methods of the prayer and continuous purification of the heart would lead the individual to "Christification" and to be graced by gifts of the Holy Spirit. These would include clairvoyant sight and many other paranormal powers including the ability to exorcise demons. I was fascinated to discover, in addition to Father Joseph's account, more written documents of extraordinary feats allegedly performed by other gerontes. For example, a contemporary gerontas named Father Paisios wrote about his gerontas, named Father Arsenios (canonized as a saint by the Church), and described in great detail his master's extraordinary healing gifts and his clairvoyant and other ESP abilities. His reputation apparently spread not only among the Greeks but also among the Turks, who sought him out and benefited from his healing interventions in a place with no medical doctors. Witnesses were reportedly terrified when they saw gerontas Arsenios levitating inside the sanctum during a liturgy in the Asia Minor village of Farasa (a Greek village in the middle of Turkey before the expulsion of the Greeks after the Greek-Turkish war of 1922), where he served as the village priest. He was also credited with the ability to cause rain during droughts by simply praying and to cause other paranormal phenomena similar to those some Indian shamans are said to be capable of.[7]

I almost forgot that I was walking the promenade in Skiathos. My mind was still transfixed on Athos. I wonder, I thought to myself as I sat at the edge of the harbor watching the fishermen motor out of the harbor, how the American bishop in Needleman's *Lost Christianity* would have reacted had he learned of the spiritual practices and experiences that I have come across in my exposure to Athos, and the reputed psychospiritual results of these practices. Would he still have resorted to Zen?

After half an hour of walking on the promenade I sat at a coffee shop for refreshments and some reading. I carried with me a thirty-page manuscript that had been passed on to me, just before I left Maine, by my friend Demetrios, the acupuncturist from New Bedford. He had mailed the manuscript with the categorical injunction, "You must read this. It is about Charalambis."

Demetrios had been telling me about Charalambis for several years. "No guru or psychic healer could ever impress me," Demetrios told me, "after having known Charalambis." He jokingly said once, "I am not worried about death. I know that when I die Charalambis will be there to welcome me and show me around."

It was through Demetrios that I first learned that within the Greek Orthodox mystical tradition there is another category of hermits, the more rare case of the *saloi* (*salos* singular), literally meaning "the fool in Christ." None of the fathers and hermits that I met on Athos would qualify as a salos. Charalambis was reputed to be such a salos among the people of Kalamata and the surrounding areas of the Peloponnese. Demetrios grew up in the area and met with Charalambis on many an occasion. The stories he told me about Charalambis sent me to the library a few times to find out about this strange human phenomenon. Kallistos Ware, a professor of religion at Cambridge and an ordained Orthodox bishop, formerly an Anglican, wrote about the salos:

"He is a living witness to the truth that Christ's kingdom is not of this world. . . . He practices an absolute voluntary poverty, identifying himself with the humiliated Christ. As Iulia de Beausobre puts it, 'He is nobody's brother, nobody's father, and has no home.' Forgoing family life, he is the wanderer or pilgrim who feels equally at home everywhere, yet settles down nowhere. Clothed in rags even in the winter cold, sleeping in a shed or on a church porch, he renounces not only material possessions but also what others regard as his sanity and mental balance. Yet thereby he becomes a channel for the higher wisdom of the Spirit." Professor Ware points out that the salos is an extremely rare vocation and that it is not easy to distinguish the counterfeit from the genuine, the "breakdown" from the "breakthrough." Yet, he goes on to say, it is still possible to distinguish the two. "The false fool is futile and destructive, to himself and to others. The true fool in Christ, possessing purity of heart, has upon the community around him an effect that is life-enhancing. From a practical point of view, no useful purpose is served by anything that the fool does. And yet, through some startling action or enigmatic word, often deliberately provocative and shocking, he awakens men from complacency and pharisaism. Remaining himself detached, he unleashes reactions in others, making the subconscious mount to the surface, enabling it to be purged and sanctified. He combines audacity with humility. Because he has renounced everything, he is truly free."[8] Ware gave the example of the Russian salos (*iurodivyi* in Russian) Nicolas of Pskov who placed into the hands of Czar Ivan the Terrible a piece of meat dripping with blood. The salos, Ware pointed out, can rebuke the powerful of the world with a boldness that others lack. He is the living conscience of the community, provoking and scandalizing the conventionally pious. Klitos Ioannides, a Cypriot researcher of Byzantine and Eastern Orthodoxy, described the phenomenon of the salos in a local Greek periodical as follows: "The saloi in Christ are gifted with clairvoyant sight and perform miracles. They often mock the weaknesses and sins of their fellow human beings in such subtle ways so that only those who are affected become aware of the implicit criticism. Yet the salos appears more sinful than the person he mocks. For example although in a provocative way and in front of the eyes of others he would indulge in meat eating during times of

fasting he in reality fasts continuously. Even though he would publicly appear as if he visits prostitution houses in reality he goes there
to offer solace and advice to the prostitutes trying to liberate them
from their predicament. . . . The life of the salos in Christ is a real
mockery of this world, the most extreme form of *askesis*. It is the
ultimate rejection of the self, the total overcoming of ego."⁹

The author then describes the case of the medieval salos Saint
Symeon Eméses, who one day was "called by Heaven" to become
a salos. He told his fellow hermits and monks, "In the name and
power of Christ I am going out to mock the world." He then went
into the towns causing healing miracles, at the same time committing outrageous acts to provoke the public and prevent at all costs
any social honor from being bestowed upon him. He would, for
example, throw stones at people who were going to church or scandalously enter a public bath for women, after which he was beaten
and chased out by the enraged patrons. Ioannides writes: "This form
of scandal of the pious is reminiscent of Jesus' provocative cancel-
lation of the Sabbath when He healed the lame. . . . Christ, however,
does not destroy the law. Rather He reveals the transcendence of
the law at the border of the Kingdom. Likewise Saint Symeon is a
citizen of the Kingdom and in his person he manifests the transcendence of the law which is a scandal only for those of us who
still live under the necessity of conducting our affairs within the
context of the law's authority as we have not as yet reached, or we
are unaware of, the 'end' of the law where one encounters the freedom of the saints."

That was how Demetrios remembered his compatriot, the modern salos Charalambis from Kalamata. All the writers that have referred to this phenomenon list names and examples from previous
centuries. Charalambis was the only case I have come across of a
salos who lived and died in modern times. Being true to his calling
as a salos he was hardly known outside the town of Kalamata and
the surrounding region. The manuscript passed on to me by De-

metrios was written by a fellow who knew Charalambis personally and felt the urge to rescue his memory in a typed and privately distributed brief biography.[10] Demetrios knew the late author and discussed with him the case of this Christian salos. When Demetrios showed me pictures of bearded Charalambis with his long and scruffy hair, dressed in ragged clothes, carrying a wooden cross in one hand and symbolically offering a blessing with the other in the traditional Orthodox way, I was reminded of the Old Testament prophets descending upon the towns of the Hebrews, preaching about the One and only God and thundering against injustice. It was hard to believe that in a contemporary society a man could behave in analogous ways without being thrown into an asylum. Perhaps, I thought, thanks to the "underdevelopment" of Greek society, the strong presence of Orthodox Christianity and the Athonite tradition, it was still possible for people like Charalambis to roam the streets and mountains without being arrested or otherwise abused by well-intentioned health workers.

One Sunday morning, Demetrios told me, during the Divine Liturgy and in the presence of a visiting bishop, Charalambis rushed into the center of the church and began dancing provocatively, scandalizing the pious and the various dignitaries. When the bishop asked him privately why he did that Charalambis whispered in his ear, "My dear bishop, let the people think that I am crazy. I reserve my sanity only for God."

Most people took pity on Charalambis, thinking of him as simply a harmless fool who had lost his wits and lived like a wild beast. He had no place to stay and no property other than the rags he was dressed in. Yet others, particularly women, knew him as a miracle worker and considered his passing through their town a blessing. Never asking for food, Charalambis was always given food whenever he would pass by homes that considered him a prophet, a healer, and a witness to the Holy Spirit. Stories like the following established Charalambis in the minds of some as a divinely gifted saint, not a madman as he was perceived because of his outward appearance. Three women who Demetrios knew were about to visit a remote chapel on the top of a hill. As they made their approach at dusk they heard beautiful chants coming out of the little chapel, which seemed all lit up even though there was no electricity. Surprised, they peeked through the half-open door and saw a sight that made their knees tremble. Charalambis was kneeling in front of the Holy Altar with his face and hands upward in a state of ecstasy, radiating light that illuminated the entire chapel. The chants, the women felt, were coming from a legion of angels that surrounded Charalambis. Without disturbing him they rushed to town to tell everybody what they saw.

This Greek biographer reports case after case of episodes of paranormal happenings surrounding Charalambis, which the author himself experienced firsthand. They were identical to the lore about the yogis and rishis of India and Tibet that I had read about, such as those on Nityananda[11] and what Yogananda reported in his autobiography about his teachers and gurus.[12] Charalambis, for example, according to this biographer, was seen by many eyewitnesses levitating and walking off the ground. Presumably only yogis of India can accomplish such paraphysical happenings. Yet there are also reports that the monastic brothers of Saint Ignatius Loyola, concerned about the official clerical establishment and the Inquisitor, had a hard time keeping him grounded and resorted to pulling his robes down during his ecstasies. We tend to forget, of course, that Jesus Himself was, according to the Gospels, seen walking on water and trying to teach his reluctant and fearful Apostles how to do the same, telling them that what He can do they can do also, and more.

Story after story of Charalambis's ESP abilities are reported in this obscure and unknown biography that I held in my hands. There are episodes of prophecy, clairvoyance, and even teleportation. A woman, for example, was shocked by an incident that took place when Charalambis stayed for the night in her cellar. There were no windows. For some strange reason Charalambis told the woman to lock the cellar from the outside while he was spending the night there. In the morning when she unlocked the door she was horrified to discover that Charalambis was nowhere to be found.

There are in the manuscript stories of Charalambis healing the sick by simply praying over them, and an episode during the Italian occupation of Greece in the early part of World War II that bewildered a group of Italian soldiers. After ordering Charalambis to stop, when he failed to obey, they opened fire at close range. Yet no bullet hit him. They never bothered Charalambis again. He was the only Greek in the area who could walk the streets during hours of curfew.

Charalambis never begged. The only thing he asked was to have his bottle of olive oil filled. His apparent mission was to journey on foot from remote chapel to remote chapel (Greece is full of them) and fill the candles in front of the icons with oil so that they would remain lit. Yet, as his biographer pointed out, nobody knew what Charalambis's real mission in life was.

Charalambis Papayianne from Kalamata, Greece, died in 1974 at the age of ninety after more than sixty years as a salos. As a young man Charalambis had prepared to practice medicine, completing his education in France. He was considered a lively and likable fellow full of energy and zest for life. As was the custom at the time, a marriage had been arranged for him and the engagement celebrations were being prepared. But it was not to be.

According to his biographer, to whom he confided his story, just before the ceremonies Charalambis heard a voice inside him saying, "My son you shall not go to church. You shall not be married. The way of your life will change drastically if you choose to follow us." Charalambis was confused. He stepped out onto the balcony to get some fresh air. The voice followed him. "Do you see straight ahead of you that tall mountain?" When Charalambis looked at it, in a split second he found himself on top of that mountain. Before he had time to recover from the shock he was back on the balcony. He turned yellow. "It created within him a tremendous earthquake that shattered his worldly ambitions," wrote the author. Then the voice spoke to Charalambis again. "You see, the will and power of human beings compared to mine is nothing, insignificant. Whatever I Will, it happens. Everything is possible. That is why I transported you to the top of that mountain and then returned you to your original position in a matter of seconds. I did so in order for you to appreciate better my words and decide for yourself on your new mission. The road that I have set out for you is very difficult, treacherous I should say. But I will always be with you to support you and give you strength. At the end of your tribulations My Father who is in Heaven will prepare for you your own heavenly home. Pray to Me and to my Mother and to Saint Charalambos, your name-saint. Fear nothing, for we shall always be protecting you."

After that shattering experience Charalambis kneeled down, weeping uncontrollably. "Through his tearful eyes," wrote the author, "Charalambis saw a brilliant light and within it he clearly distinguished the figure of Christ blessing him while Saint Charalambos stood by. In a state of utter enchantment Charalambis held his breath as his soul soared within the abundant light of saintliness and the atmosphere emanated an exquisite fragrance. Gathering his courage he slowly made the sign of the cross and murmured 'Thy Will Be Done.'"

Feeling empowered, Charalambis then went to his room, put on the oldest clothes he had and told his bewildered parents that there would be neither an engagement party nor a wedding. Without explaining to them what had happened he disappeared into the mountains and spent the first night inside a chapel, thinking things through. And that was how that well-bred, prosperous young man who was being groomed for a medical career ended up as a hermit and a salos. According to my friend Demetrios there was an ongoing

effort by a few clergymen and lay people, who either knew Charalambis personally or knew of him, to persuade the Church hierarchy to formally anoint him as a saint of the Eastern Orthodox
Church.

I placed the manuscript back into my folder as I rested my eyes
on the local crowd that was pacing back and forth on the promenade. "What am I to make of all this?" I mused to myself. My
sociological impulse was to reduce all these stories to just folklore,
collective fantasies, or simply "social constructions of reality." But
it was no longer so easy for me to do that. I had come to appreciate
the ongoingness of the miraculous in everyday life. My exposure to
healers and psychics and to literature on psychical and "mind/body"
research, the recognition of the reality of ESP phenomena, the
breathtaking implications of research at the frontiers of science[13] or
"paraphysics," and the metaphysical implications of the recent empirical support of the "Big Bang" theory of the creation of the universe gradually chipped away the rationalistic, sensate view of reality
that I had inherited from my formal training as a modern sociologist
and academic.

Speaking of the "Big Bang," I reasoned that the greatest miracle
of all was the mystery of the original explosion that created the
universe. Since the universe was born out of such a spectacular miracle, then the miraculous, contrary to our popular scientific and
materialistic beliefs, must have remained an integral and inherent
property of the created cosmos. It is the emergence of that peculiar
agnostic and atheistic view of reality still dominating our cultural
life that is the historical and social construction requiring a sociological explanation, not the ever-present miraculous in the world
and our everyday lives.

Once I suspended my a priori academic disbelief about miraculous phenomena, and followed a more open-minded approach that
was nonjudgmental, nonreductionistic, and phenomenological in in-
vestigating these phenomena, then things began to open up for me.

It was as if the universe was somehow rewarding me for simply being ready to listen without the usual debunking mind-set reducing everything to materialistic explanations characteristic of mainstream modern and postmodern intellectualisms. Previously, Demetrios would not have talked to me about Charalambis, nor would he have entrusted me with that unknown little manuscript circulated among friends.

Antonis would also not have urged me to join him on Athos to meet the gerontes and spiritual masters of the Orthodox religion nor would he have brought to my attention the extraordinary phenomena that were beginning to unfold on the island of Lesbos and Cyprus had I remained a rigid skeptic.

"After you read this book," Antonis told me the previous year, "no trace of doubt will remain in your mind on the objective truth of spiritual realities." The book he passed on to me was written by a well-known writer and artist from the island of Lesbos[14] who documented with great care and convincing detail the extraordinary happenings that began taking place on his island in the late fifties. These paranormal phenomena and healing miracles were attributed to three saints who until the early sixties were totally unknown. Yet today, in the early nineties, the miracles attributed to the newly discovered Saints Raphael, Nicholas, and Irene have captivated the imagination of thousands of Greeks in the same way that Lourdes has captivated the religious imagination of thousands of French and other Europeans. Yet the spectacular story of Saints Raphael, Nicholas, and Irene is not known outside of the contemporary Greek world.

"Today, in the year 1962," wrote the author Kontoglou in the opening paragraph of his meticulously documented and extraordinary work, "I begin to write down a true story which is not only inconceivable for non-believers but difficult to believe even for the most pious among us."

During the late fifties something very unusual and dramatic be-

gan to happen to a number of people in the town of Thermi on
Lesbos, a Greek island off the coast of Turkey. These people, whose
names and photographs Kontoglou provides, began seeing for many
days and weeks vivid dreams of a monk who introduced himself as
Raphael, an uncommon name for a Greek monk. He also introduced
his companions, another monk by the name of Nicholas and a young
girl called Irene. When the people began talking to one another
about their experiences they discovered that indeed they were seeing
identical dreams. They pieced them together and wrote down what
this monk was telling them. Raphael dictated to them his biography,
a most detailed and convincing story—where he was born, how he
ended up in Lesbos, and so on. Most importantly he claimed that
he and his companion Nicholas had been monks in a local monastery when the Turks captured Constantinople in 1453. When the
island fell to the Turks that year they were tortured and killed along
with the young girl Irene. Raphael told them in fact that the soldiers
sawed his cheekbone as they were killing him. Furthermore he told
the people where they could dig and find their remains.

The people visited the regional religious authority, the metropolitan, and implored him to help them get permission to begin
excavations to find the remains of these martyrs as they were instructed to do in their dreams. After tremendous and frustrating
efforts were made to convince the skeptical government officials,
permission was finally granted. After several months of digging, the
remains of the three were discovered exactly as they were described
in the local people's collective visionary dreams. They even identified the sawed cheekbone of Saint Raphael and the young skeleton
of the tortured girl.

But the story did not end there. Saint Raphael and his companions continued to appear not only in people's dreams but in a materialized form, right in front of ordinary people in their ordinary
state of consciousness. Healing phenomena began to happen to vis-

itors at the shrine built in honor of the newly discovered saints. People with incurable cancers and other chronic illnesses began getting cured after Saint Raphael appeared in their dreams. The Church, convinced of the authenticity of their sainthood and based strictly on the dream stories and the continuing healing miracles, declared all three of them the latest saints of the Greek Orthodox Church. Fotios Kontoglou, the artist who first wrote about this extraordinary and paranormal phenomenon, painted, on the basis of descriptions by people who experienced the visions of these saints, an icon of the three that has been copied repeatedly, decorating churches all over Greece and Cyprus.

Saint Raphael, through further dreams and apparitions, asked that the monastery that was about to be set up in their honor be a women's monastery. And so it happened—an interesting development, I thought, when one considers that Lesbos is the birthplace of Sappho, the celebrated poetess of the ancient world and a central symbol of the women's movement.

Episodes of reported miracles and materializations of the saints began to spread all over Greece, stirring the faith of the faithful and scandalizing the skeptics and the secularists. But nowhere perhaps, besides Lesbos, was the impact of the saints as powerful as it has been on Cyprus. Based on dreams and visitations two new churches were set up on the island in honor of the saints, one on the east coast and the other on the west coast facing the sea. Hundreds of Cypriots claimed that Saint Raphael had miraculously healed them. A local researcher carefully collected these stories and published them in a book,[15] further reinforcing the conviction, by an increasing number of people, that the story of Saint Raphael is an authentic story and not make-believe or a collective fantasy. Of course a local psychologist trying to explain the phenomenon dismissed the claims of saintly visitations. "They are all phenomena of autosuggestion," he authoritatively announced through the local media, offering the conventional explanation. He dismissed the protests of people who insisted that they had witnessed the saint next to their bed, promising to heal them. And they had been healed.

So much had Saint Raphael become a popular saint on Cyprus that the local airline scheduled weekly flights to Lesbos for the many pilgrims that wished to visit the monastery on that island. In the meantime the mother superior, the nun in charge of the monastery, kept careful records of the hundreds of cures that have been attributed to miracles of Saint Raphael and his companions.

When I visited Cyprus after my ten-day stay on Skiathos one of the dominant discussions among people interested in metaphysical issues was the increasing healing phenomena attributed to Saint Raphael. My friend Yiannis gave me a taped conversation that had aired on the local public radio about a most spectacular episode of contact with Saint Raphael. A taxi driver was riding by himself late at night from Larnaca, the southwestern town, to Limassol where his home was. As he told the interviewer, he reached a point where he had to turn left to enter the main road between Larnaca and Limassol. But the steering wheel would not go left. Thinking that there was something wrong he proceeded a little further and turned right. The steering wheel had no problem turning right. At the corner he saw two monks waiting by the road and a young girl standing next to them. Usually, he claimed, he was not in the habit of volunteering to give free rides or picking up hitchhikers. Yet he stopped, asking the monks whether they needed a lift that late at night. With a trembling voice the man began to describe what happened after they entered the car. The girl sat in front and the two monks in the backseat. The moment they entered, he said, the car was filled with a strange, brilliant light even though he had not turned the inside light on—and, besides, it could not have generated so much luminosity. The teenage girl and one of the monks remained silent. The other one told him to inform his cousin who was in the hospital (he mentioned the name of the woman) not to worry, and that she will become completely well. Saint Raphael will cure her.

The taxi driver was in a state of shock. That monk, he said, could not have known about his cousin in the hospital nor about her desperate and incurable condition. When he came out of his amazement his passengers disappeared along with the light. He then discovered that his steering wheel was now turning left as well. The man broke down during the interview and went on to explain what happened to him after that episode. His taxi emanated a peculiar beautiful fragrance for several days after the encounter. His cousin miraculously got well as he was told she would. And he himself was never the same person again. He told Klitos Ioannides, the interviewer, that from that day on he became deeply religious and more devoted and loving to his wife and family than he had ever been before.

The transformation of that taxi driver reminded me of what usually happens to people who undergo a near-death experience—a radical transformation of the self in the direction of greater spirituality and expression of love and affection to people around them, particularly members of the immediate family.[16]

"I don't know of a single Englishman who either saw Saint Raphael, or Saint Nicholas or all the other saints that the Greeks keep seeing," Akis, my brother-in-law, who lived most of his life in London, exclaimed with his characteristic humor and debunking irreverence after he heard of such stories. "Do the Greeks, perhaps, have a monopoly on the saints?" he retorted with a foxy smile dripping with humorous irony.

His reaction was right on the mark. Indeed, what answer to this obvious question would effortlessly come to any modern mind? To his question I added many of my own. One that I jotted down on the plane coming back to Maine at the end of the summer of 1991 was the following: Why all these appearances, miraculous healings, and apparitions that have reached epidemic proportions in the last twenty years? Why did Saint Raphael, Saint Nicholas, and Saint Irene wait five centuries since their martyrdom to make their appearances, first in the dreams of the people of Thermi and then to all those believers and nonbelievers within Greek Orthodox culture? Those were questions that I carried with me when I returned to Maine.

# 15

## LIFTING THE
## VEIL

DURING THE SUMMER MONTHS OF 1993 WHILE THE UNIVERSITY WAS
in recess, I decided not to collect any more data for my book. I
stayed instead in Maine, working on the material that I had gathered
during the last few years, trying to find answers to the questions on
the reality of paranormal phenomena I had posed for myself during
the aftermath of my visit to Mount Athos.

Most social scientists, of course, would have assumed that the
phenomena I described had no metaphysical source and could be
explained by natural factors. For example, a mainstream sociologist
would have guided his or her critical eye to explore the social conditions that had given rise to such experiences and discount a priori
the objective reality of such allegations. Within the context of social
science such reports must be explained not on what people themselves say about their experiences but strictly and solely on the basis
of what happens to them either as groups or as individuals due to
factors beyond their awareness. For example, a sociologist may hy-
pothesize that such reports are collective forms of escapism resulting
from the pressures of modernization, the decline of traditional institutions, and the confusion and alienation that people experience
when they find themselves drifting away from the security of their

traditional moorings. Or in the case of Cyprus, in addition to the above factors, a sociologist may convincingly propose that people resort to these collective beliefs because of the asphyxiating pressures produced by the presence of a threatening Turkish army occupying the northern part of Cyprus. It would be analogous to a thirsty person hallucinating an oasis in the middle of a desert or a lost sailor seeing nonexistent shores on the horizon.

Within the context of such a perspective the apparitions of saints and similar phenomena can be described as projections of collective yearnings for Divine intervention at a time of a hopeless sense of powerlessness, when practical or rational ways of confronting the perceived threat are sorely absent. Fair enough. The sociologist can draw from a powerful repertoire of anthropological studies that would tend to confirm and reconfirm such an approach. For example, the sociologist or the social anthropologist might make interesting comparisons between the appearance of the saints in Cyprus and the emergence of the millenarian movement known as the Ghost Dance among the Plains Indians. This phenomenon occurred toward the end of the nineteenth century among desperate Native Americans who could not militarily defend their lands against the encroaching settlers. They believed that the spirits of their ancestors would come to rescue them.

Such explanations may give some partial insight as to why phenomena of this nature emerge on such a widespread scale at certain historical periods. But it would remain a partial insight at best. In fact it may turn out to be a grossly misleading insight, only a half truth.

I have personally learned to respect people's claims of miraculous happenings because I, as a social scientist, have long recognized the inherent and often misguided mainstream scientific paradigm in explaining away such phenomena. I have learned to allow room in my thinking for the possibility of authentic miracles, objectively and continuously taking place at all times and in all places, miracles that defy our conventional understanding of the world. They may be real happenings only open to the awareness of those who have "eyes to see and ears to hear."

The critical and legitimate questions raised by my brother-in-law about the reported miracles by Saint Raphael and his two co-martyrs were raised again by my friend Demos when he and his wife, Maria, visited us in Maine while I was steeped in the process of writing this book. They arrived from New Jersey to spend a few days with us and escape the excruciating heat wave hitting the New York area. The first thing Demos reminisced about, with his characteristic humor causing uproarious laughter all-round, was our experiences in Astoria just prior to my trip to Greece in the spring of 1991. But unlike previous years, he now showed a keen interest in what I was doing and what I had to say—even though he remained, as he reassured us, a skeptic.

Far from being a distraction from my work Demos's presence offered me the opportunity to air out some tentative, unconventional conclusions based on the research I had been doing. It presented me with an opportunity to suggest tentative answers to the questions I so intensely posed for myself.

With Demos the discussion was always easygoing as he had no fear whatsoever that listening to yarns like mine would "undermine the foundations of rational Western civilization," as a die-hard scientist and colleague once accused. I was able to bring up issues that most academics would shy away from, such as the miracles of Saint Raphael, Filipino psychic surgeons, and the so-called UFO abductions that have reached epidemic proportions lately in America. Those were topics that came up as we sat on our balcony facing the Stillwater River during that hot Saturday afternoon. The shade generously offered by the thick vegetation and the opening toward the river cut the heat to comfortable levels. Demos, Maria, Emily, and I were joined by a colleague from another university, a psychologist, who happened to be in Maine that day and who was beginning to open to the issues that had preoccupied me for some time now. Her husband, who also joined us, was an engineer who entertained the novel view that spiritual principles could be applied to mechanics.

I told Demos how grateful I was to him for inducing me to focus my ideas with his pointed questions. In doing so he was assisting me to bring closure to my present work. I brought out from my study a pile of books, several files of notes, clippings, and photocopied articles so that I could easily refer to them during our discussions if need be.

"To answer your question about these so-called miraculous happenings," I said to Demos as we munched on various goodies that Emily and I had prepared, "I will have to propose reversing all of the key assumptions upon which modern science is founded."

"That's pretty presumptuous," Demos quipped.

"I know it is. And risky I may add. But keep in mind that modern science is founded on certain unexamined, mechanistic metaphysics that are taken for granted by practicing scientists."

"Unexamined metaphysics are bad metaphysics," Roger, the engineer, interjected.

"Definitely. So let me offer a set of assumptions about reality that diametrically contradict the current scientific worldview, a set of assumptions that mainstream scientists will have a hard time swallowing," I said, laughing.

"Assumption number one is the following," I went on: "The world of the five senses is not the only world there is."

"All right," Demos interrupted, "but on what basis do you make such a claim?"

"This is what I plan to do later. I will come to that. But to briefly answer your question, on the basis of my own experience, of course. It is based on my involvement with Erevna, the contact with Mount Athos, Plato's philosophy, the theoretical work of such physicists as David Bohm (with his notion of the 'implicate order'), of biologists like Rubert Sheldrake (and his notion of 'morphogenetic fields'), and of course with the phenomena that we are exploring today, which cannot be explained within the prevailing assumptions of science.

"Assumption number two: Other worlds exist that interpenetrate our own. These worlds are layered—that means they relate to each other in a hierarchical manner. The world of the five senses is at the bottom of this spiritual totem pole. These layers are not only out there in nature, objectively speaking, but they are also part of the structure of human consciousness itself.

"Three, the various worlds are in ongoing communication with one another. But most often the communication moves in a conscious way from top to bottom, rarely from bottom up. The higher realms constantly influence the lower realms in ways that the lower realms are not aware of. At all levels of this hierarchy there are conscious beings. Those above us are on a superior, more evolved vantage point in reference to consciousness and knowledge than ourselves. Some members of our own reality make contact with these higher realms. We have called them shamans, psychics, prophets, saints, and so on. Their reports of what they find always are couched within the language of the culture that these gifted people happen to live in. Therefore, knowledge of these higher worlds is always colored, filtered, and distorted in varying degrees through the cultural constructions of time and place. Even living saints are subjected to this law.

"Fourth, if the above assumptions are true, and I believe they are, then it logically follows that we as a species and as individuals are never alone. The universe or, better, universes are peopled by higher intelligences than ourselves, and perhaps lower than ourselves.

"Fifth, contrary to Sartre, Camus, and Beckett the world is utterly meaningful. This meaning is derived from the fact that Creation is not an accident but the product of a Divine Plan. The project of Creation and the existence of all the hierarchy is for the sake of the unfoldment and evolution of consciousness. This consciousness has as its destiny the transcendence of the hierarchy itself and the conscious reunification with the Absolute Spirit or the Personal God out of Whom we come and within Whom, like fish in the ocean, we constantly are. This means that history is not drifting aimlessly but is inherently purposeful like the individual lives that compose it. It is, as Hegel would have said, the autobiography of God. That means, also, that everything is related to everything else in the cosmos. It is for this reason that mystics have proposed the seemingly preposterous notion that a single thought disturbs the entire universe.

"I can go on and on," I said, "setting down the details of this 'holographic paradigm' that contradicts head-on the existing scientific paradigm, but I'll stop here. It will suffice for the purpose of our present discussion. But, I would like to add that there are always individuals among us who have not only reached the top of this consciousness hierarchy, if in fact we can speak of a top, but have gone beyond it right into the radiant light of the Christ Logos or the Absolute Spirit. These are the true saints that most probably, I dare say, are hardly known to the rest of us." I waited for reactions but before anyone said anything else I added another point.

"In these critical times in which we happen to live this inherently purposeful historical process is leading humanity to a point where the veil that has kept separate this world of the five senses from the higher, more numinous worlds is gradually being lifted. The lifting of this veil appears to be the reason of the mushrooming manifestations of paranormal realities that utterly confound us, forcing us to reexamine our cherished and flawed materialist assumptions about the nature of the world. I would also like to add that the lifting of this veil is absolutely critical if we are to survive as a species.

"What I am suggesting here," I added, "is not mine. It is the conclusion that many concerned scientists, philosophers, ecologists, religious people, and poets have come to and been reporting for many years now."

"I think I need an aspirin. You have turned my mind around and around with your assumptions. I need time to digest them," Demos blurted out.

"I would like to know how you have come to your conclusions. What kind of evidence can you offer that would convince a skeptic like myself about the truth value of these assumptions," Demos said.

"I really don't think it is possible to convince anybody with arguments and so-called evidence. You have to look at this whole thing as a gestalt. I have come to these conclusions over a long period of time and reflection. So when someone tells me, 'prove it to me' I feel very frustrated. It can't be proven in traditional ways.

"But for someone who is sincerely looking for answers and is open to other possibilities I usually start by suggesting books to read, a kind of 'bibliotherapy,' if you will. For somebody who is scientifically inclined I usually suggest some hard-core scientific works and authors who have legitimacy in the eyes of the reader. The first task for opening up to other possibilities presupposes letting go of one's faith in the absolute validity of the present worldview. Deconstructionist and postmodernist thinkers in the social sciences, philosophy, and art have done a tremendous job in knocking down the certainties of positivistic science. At first this work creates chaos, confusion, and uncertainty."

"And you suggest that out of this confusion a new worldview will come about?"

"Yes. The confusion is necessary. This 'dark night of the Western mind' is a precondition for opening up to new possibilities. We are witnessing now the disintegration of what Sorokin called the 'sensate phase' of Western civilization and the emergence of a world that will be hospitable to spiritual realities. We may finally witness the end of the war between science and religion that started about three centuries ago. The wall that separated them into two hostile camps is, I believe, finally being brought down by the 'peace work' that goes on in both camps, by enlightened scientists and enlightened members of the religious community. The lion and the lamb will finally lie down together in peace."

"These are big words," Demos responded. "But can you be a little more specific, please. How can I, a person who has not been exposed to the things that you have been talking and writing about, how could I start? What evidence do I have at my disposal that could prove to me that there are worlds beyond the material universe that we apprehend with our five senses."

"Okay," I said. "You can start by familiarizing yourself with the voluminous literature that has accumulated during the last hundred years about psychical research. Scientists tend to ignore that work because it does not fit their preconceptions about reality. But they cannot ignore it forever. It is now creating cracks in the established dogmas."

"But can you be more specific? A hundred years is too great a period to explore. Where can one begin without years of library research?"

I thought for a few moments and then suggested to Demos that perhaps he could start by looking up the current work related to near-death experiences. "Read, for example, the work of Dr. Raymond Moody," I said, and went on to elaborate on why research in that area suggests the existence of other realities beyond the material world.

"Throughout history people have had near-death experiences and reported what they went through during their 'death' to their friends and relatives. But it was only recently that it has been possible to verify scientifically that there is such a thing as a near-death experience."

"Briefly tell me what you understand by the near-death experience so that we all know what we are talking about," Demos asked.

"These are people who have been pronounced clinically dead by doctors using modern, up-to-date medical instruments. Then somehow miraculously they are brought back to life and can describe their experience in great detail. Modern medical technology is making it possible for us to confirm the reality of such an experience—and not only can we now verify an episode of a near-death experience, but it is technologically possible to bring back from 'death,' so to speak, an increasing number of people, who in previous eras would have simply died, permanently. So here we have technology in the service of spiritual awakening. Perhaps, I would dare to suggest, it is science itself, long considered the enemy of religion, that may in fact rescue religion in the coming centuries."

"But how does the near-death experience prove the reality of other worlds?" Demos asked after pondering for a while what I had just said.

"It does not in a strictly scientific way, of course. The reality of other worlds is simply suggested on the basis of what these people report after they return from such a journey. When someone is clinically dead one presumably does not feel or know anything during that state. The body is in a coma. Yet the startling reports coming from these studies is that patients not only tell in great detail what they have encountered during their comatose state but knew what was going on in other parts of the hospital (or other parts of the city) and what the doctors were saying when they were writing up the death certificates of these people. These stunning, well-documented reports simply suggest that the consciousness was out of the body and the individual was fully alert in another dimension with what Erevna would call their psychonoetic bodies. Moody reports, for example, the case of a woman who, after being revived, told the doctors not only what they had been saying while trying to revive her but that outside, over the roof of the balcony of the operating room there was a shoe. The doctors were stunned when they discovered it exactly as she described it. This is just one among many cases of this nature.

"But what is most significant with these cases," I went on, "is what happens to people during the near-death episode and how it affects their lives after they recover from it. Typically people report that during their near-death they find themselves speeding through a tunnel and entering another world."

I pulled out one of Moody's latest works and read: " 'This world is attended by deceased relatives bathed in glorious light and ruled by a Supreme Being who guides the new arrival through a review of his life before sending him back to live longer on earth.' "[1] What these people uniformly report is that once they are in the presence of that Christ-like figure they want to stay there, as if they had gone home to a loving mother or father that they had missed for a long time. This is precisely the way some Athonite gerontes talk when they describe their mystical contact with the Christ Logos."

I then went on to mention that I'd met a medical doctor at a conference organized by the National Institutes of Health who had a near-death experience himself and described it in ways identical to the subjects of Moody's studies. He told me that his fear of death was totally gone after the experience and that in reality he couldn't wait until he reunited with the Christ Being that he encountered.

"But to repeat what I just said, the most amazing thing about the near-death experience is what happens to people after they went through it. This is what fascinated Moody. 'Upon return,' he wrote, 'the persons [who had a near-death] are never the same. They embrace life to its fullest and express the belief that love and knowledge are the most important of all things because they are the only things you can take with you.'[2]"

"It is very comforting to know that love and knowledge are the most important things in life," Lydia, the chemist, pointed out.

"Exactly. That is why, according to Moody and other researchers who have studied this issue, when people return from that trip they become more loving, and begin to study and read in cases when they had not done so before. We as human beings are really created for love and knowledge. That is why we always crave these two."

I picked a little book from my pile and passed it on to Demos. "Here is a book that you may find both entertaining and enlightening. You will not be able to put it down once you begin reading it. It is the personal story of Dr. George Ritchie, a practicing psychiatrist from Virginia describing his spectacular near-death experience."[3]

Demos flipped its pages and promised to look at it later in the evening. "What else?" he asked, referring to my suggestion that we may be witnessing the lifting of the veil that separates this world from the others.

"By the way," I interjected, "the notion that we may be witnessing a lifting of the veil that separates our world from other worlds is not mine. It is being suggested by serious philosophers, scientists, and researchers in general who are engrossed in the study of phenomena that cannot be explained from within the conceptions of reality that are prevalent today in our sciences and dominant philosophies. Take for example the UFO phenomenon. . . ." I paused for a moment as I saw Demos making a funny disapproving grimace. I laughed.

"Demo," I said. "I would have reacted the same way a few years ago upon hearing stories about UFOs. I thought that only people who read the kind of papers at the checkout points in grocery stores would be interested in what I thought was sheer nonsense. Lately I realized that I was just prejudiced. I discovered that large numbers of people in the U.S.A. and elsewhere, but particularly in the U.S.A., claim that they have been abducted by UFOs either during sleep or during their waking period, and subjected to various tests by extraterrestrial beings. The amazing thing about this phenomenon is the similarities of the stories people report, and the number of people that claim to have been abducted. According to a recent poll that was conducted between July and September 1991 on "unusual events" it is suggested that hundreds of thousands if not millions of individuals in the United States may have undergone abduction or abduction-related experiences."[4]

"I know this sounds preposterous but let me read you some passages from the conclusions of a formerly skeptical Harvard researcher about this topic." I then pulled from my pile of material an article written by Harvard psychiatrist and Pulitzer Prize winner Dr. John E. Mack, director of the Center of Psychology and Social Change, who has been conducting research and therapeutic sessions among abductees.

"What impressed Professor Mack was not only the fact that these people were ordinary, normal human beings who did not suffer from any symptoms of mental pathology, but that there was internal consistency of the detailed accounts they reported in spite of the fact that they had no way of communicating with one another. Their stories, he claimed, had emerged only with difficulty, followed by distressing emotions."

"So what are his conclusions?" Lydia asked with urgency in her voice.

"Well, here are some," I said, and began reading.

" 'The abduction phenomenon confronts us with an authentic and disturbing mystery. . . . For there is no way, I believe, that we can even make sense, let alone provide a convincing explanation, of this matter within the framework of our existing views of what is real or possible. Our psychological theories do not include a way of accounting for the simultaneous occurrence among thousands of people, unacquainted with one another, including small children, of complex, elaborate, and sometimes overwhelmingly powerful experiences that resemble one another in minute detail, accompanied by a variety of equally peculiar physical phenomena. At the same time our understanding of physical reality cannot explain the technology whereby a population of beings from some other space/time realm can enter our world with such limited detection and affect so many people.' "[5]

I tried to see Demos's reaction. Then I proceeded. " 'We may learn from further research a great deal about the nature of the human psyche and expand our notions of psychological and physical reality. The phenomenon may deliver to us a kind of fourth blow to our collective egoism, following those of Copernicus, Darwin and Freud. For we may be led to realize that not only are we not physically at the center of the universe, transcending other life forms and rational masters of our psyches—we are not even the preeminent or dominant intelligence in the cosmos, in control of our psychological and physical existences. It appears that we can be invaded or taken over, if not literally by other creatures, then by some other form of being or consciousness that seems able to do with us what it will for a purpose we cannot yet fathom.' "[6]

I passed the article to Demos who, shaking his head in disbelief, seemed to check for himself that I had accurately read what the esteemed Harvard scholar had to say. "There are others, Demo," I said, "who have studied this phenomenon and have come to similar conclusions." I then pulled another book from the stack I had in front of me. It was Dr. Kenneth Ring's[7] latest work, where he compared a sample of individuals who'd undergone a near-death experience with a sample of abductees.

"Kenneth Ring is professor of psychology at the University of Connecticut who, like John Mack, dared to study these taboo subjects. His conclusions are extremely interesting and similar to Mack's. He discovered that both groups are composed of ordinary people without any mental pathologies. They are, however, characterized by greater than average sensitivity. Both groups of individuals became radically transformed after their corresponding experiences. Individuals become more spiritual and more concerned about the fate of the earth, for example. Kenneth Ring proposes the startling idea that both the UFO phenomenon and the near-death experience serve a fundamental evolutionary purpose in awakening humanity to other realities beyond the gross material mechanistic worldview that is leading our planet down the path of self-destruction. He argues in fact that we are at the point of a major and radical transformation of human consciousness, what he calls 'the shamanization of humanity.' Here is what he said about this lifting of the veil that I mentioned before: 'Indeed, the world of the dead and the world of the living are ones between which there may eventually no longer be a sharp distinction. Veils will be lifted from the face of the nonphysical, and we ourselves will become diaphanous beings, with bodies of light.' "[8]

"Kenneth Ring," I went on, "like many other researchers, has come to the conclusion that phenomena such as UFOs are monitored by an intelligent reality or realities that are beyond the physical universe. These encounters are happening today because there is a general recognition that our planet is in peril and there is an urgent necessity for a drastic and radical transformation of human consciousness. This transformation cannot take place until we collectively transcend our materialist superstitions. Ring quotes another explorer of the UFO phenomenon, Carl Raschke, who claims that the UFO experience is thrust upon humanity 'to loose it from the fetters of its encrusted habits of thought and action.' Raschke considers the project of the UFO as that of 'cultural deconstruction.' Here is a quotation: 'The UFO is an idea whose purpose is to confound science, because science has begun to threaten the existence of the human species and the entire ecosystem of the planet. And at this point a shock is necessary for the culture—a shock equivalent to the shock of the Resurrection on Roman imperialism.'[9] And here is what Ring himself considers the principle lesson that is derived from the UFO experience: '**We are meant to be baffled!** Only by confronting and yielding to the unknowable—by rigorously avoiding both the temptation to deny, or explain away, these phenomena or to try to find some conventional explanation for them—can we, as a species, evolve in consciousness to the point where we may be able to take the steps necessary to avert the grim planetary fate . . . [that we have been warned about].' "[10] I closed the book.

"I am just as baffled by all these as you are, Demo," I said after a pause. "There are so many other truly extraordinary phenomena, such as psychic healing in the Philippines[11] and Brazil, that are reaching our attention thanks to modern technologies. These phenomena are now being videotaped by seasoned scientists who are as stunned by what they observe as you and I. Many scientists are bewildered when they become aware of the reality of these phenomena. Some plunge into the study of these realities and become agents of transformation within their disciplines. Others, terrified for their reputation, shun any further involvement, or become, like religious fundamentalists, crusaders against anything that disturbs the established materialist worldview. I was told, for example, by Henry Belk, a longtime investigator of paranormal phenomena, that on several visits to the Philippines, where he videotaped over forty hours of psychic surgeons at work, there were American doctors who were witnessing what was going on. Yet upon their return to the U.S.A. they avoided talking about it because they were afraid that the American Medical Association would revoke their licenses. And there are reasons for a doctor to be concerned about his or her reputation. I was told of a physician who lost his license because he was interested in nonmedical healing. I met a pilot of a major airline who told me that he almost lost his job because of his interest in UFOs. A flight attendant with a masters degree in psychology had complained to her superiors that since this pilot was interested in UFOs he was mentally unbalanced and therefore unfit to fly a plane.

"But things are changing," I went on to say. "Even the American Medical Association is beginning to open up as a result of the revolution that is taking place within medicine itself, brought on by the pioneering work of physicians who have broken through the materialist fortifications. Who would have believed even a few years ago that the National Institutes of Health would have set up an office for the study of 'Unconventional Medical Practices.' Yet it has happened." I paused, awaiting a reaction from Demos and the others.

"So how does all this connect with the miracles of Saint Raphael that you talked to me about, Mount Athos, and Erevna?" Demos asked after we had a brief break.

"I believe the appearance of the saints among so many Greeks is not unconnected to what is happening to Americans, either with the abduction phenomenon or the near-death experience, or what is happening globally at this point with reports of similar baffling phenomena from other countries and regions of the earth. These experiences may have as a common result the radical transformation of human consciousness toward a spiritual, sacred understanding of the cosmos. This is perhaps the underlying reason that connects all these seemingly unconnected phenomena. If we accept that there is a spiritual reality beyond the material universe—the set of assumptions that I suggested at the beginning—then it is logical to assume that there is a connection between what is going on in the various societies and cultures of the world. Spiritual realities are manifesting themselves within various cultures in the specific ways that the people within these cultures will understand and respond to. That is why Britons do not see Saint Raphael. Likewise it would be incongruous for a Hindu believer or a Chinese peasant to have visions of Greek saints and Christian madonnas. Kenneth Ring suggests that the abduction phenomenon is relevant to modern culture because of its materialist focus and its technological obsession with space travel and the like. It is easy for Americans to connect with UFOs and ETs—as it is easy for Greeks to connect with Orthodox saints.

"What I am suggesting is this: spiritual realities will always present themselves from within the meaning context of a given culture and civilization. To put it in ecclesiastical language, it is as if God in His infinite love and compassion for humanity is sending His saints, messengers, or the Holy Spirit to alert us to the reality of His presence as a precondition to save Creation from the disastrous course that we are presently heading toward. To the Greeks God sends saints like Raphael, Nicholas, and Irene, and to industrialized and secularized Americans God sends UFOs and ETs. The impact on human consciousness is similar: an opening to spiritual realities.

"Now the question that was raised before was why now? Why does it look as if it is somehow a worldwide epidemic during the last twenty to thirty years, an epidemic that creates so much animosity, confusion, and angry reaction on the part of the scientific fundamentalists, who have erroneously concluded that what is happening is a global regression into prerational superstitions? A possible answer to that has been suggested by some, in my estimation, enlightened thinkers, scientists, and philosophers."

I went on to elaborate on the extraordinary work of some contemporary transpersonal theorists and neo-Hegelians like Ken Wilber[12] and Richard Tarnas[13] who have convincingly argued that the development of scientific reason and rationalism was in fact not a wrong turn in the evolution of human consciousness, as some have suggested, but rather an essential step in its unfoldment toward transrational and translogical states of consciousness. That the alienation, secularism, and seeming antispiritual posture of Western thought during the last three hundred years was a necessary stage that humanity had to go through in order to develop its rational, critical faculties. That secularization itself was in reality a hidden process of spiritual unfoldment.

"So what these people are saying," Demos said, "is that in order to develop our rational faculties we had to forget our gods and demons."

"That's right."

"This is what I always believed," he quipped.

"Yes, but what these contemporary thinkers are saying is that the time has come to reestablish a spiritual understanding of reality now that we, as a species, have developed our rational faculties. Let me put it differently. Before the advent of rational thought humanity operated almost exclusively by the activity of the 'right brain,' our intuitive side. The rational analytical 'left side' remained atrophied and undeveloped. Tarnas, Wilber, and others are saying that in order for the left side of the brain to develop humanity had to repress the dominance of intuition and right brain activity. Tarnas went so far as to argue that the emergence of patriarchal culture, with all the negative implications that feminists have brought to our attention, was an inevitable and necessary development from a spiritual point of view. It created the conditions for human consciousness to develop its autonomy and individuality out of its originally undifferentiated relationship to nature. But this process was accompanied by all the painful consequences of alienation and estrangement of human consciousness from its ground of being, from the spiritual. Now, Tarnas says, the conditions are ripe and urgent for the reawakening of our intuitive faculties at a higher level of synthesis, where the right brain and left brain, like the Chinese yin and yang, will be reunited and balanced. This would presuppose 'the embrace of the feminine,' and the equalization of the masculine and feminine principles within each one of us and within civilization itself. This will happen, Tarnas says, because 'the deepest passion of the Western mind has been to reunite with the ground of its being.' It is the passion of the Prodigal Son who yearns to return to his father's palace."

I went on to suggest that this metaphor is not only applicable for every human soul, for the microcosm, but also for the entire civilizational process, for the macrocosm. If the meaning of the descent into the worlds of Creation, as Erevna suggests, is to acquire experience for the sake of enhancing individual autonomy within the oneness of God, then Western civilization is the sociocultural matrix within which this process unfolds.

I stopped and asked my friends whether I was making them tired with all of this theorizing. Since I heard no complaints I continued.

"The survival of our species and life on earth is not guaranteed, however. We live in extremely perilous times. The masculine principle embodied in the analytical, rationalist left brain has in a way gone amok, threatening the very existence of the planet. Hence the urgent signals that we are getting from the spiritual realms. Humanity since the Second World War and Hiroshima is at a turning point, and is living on borrowed time, as Arthur Koestler warned us before his death.[14] Unless there is a speedy and radical shift in human consciousness, to bring about a 're-enchantment of the world' and the return of the sacred to the center of our personal and collective life, the human enterprise on Planet Earth most probably will come to a catastrophic end. The paranormal events that we have been discussing may be the wake-up calls coming from the regions of the Holy Spirit, or what Kenneth Ring calls 'Mind at Large,' to overcome our morbid entanglement with materialism in all its forms and manifestations and help us become aware of our Divine origins and our destiny as beings in the process of deification. Once that understanding, now buried down in the recesses of our individual and collective subconscious, comes to the surface, then we will feel, think, and behave in ways that will render us custodians of Creation and not its mindless destroyers."

Demos was silent after my prolonged monologue. I was not certain that it made any sense to him but my words kept his attention. "Conventional scientists," I added, "sooner or later will have to recognize that what is happening today is not regression to pre-rational states of superstition but a quantum leap into super-rational states of awareness. It is not the reversal of the Enlightenment, as they are worried, but its fulfillment through the development of a new science that will incorporate the spiritual at the center of its preoccupation."

"On the basis of what you have just said, where do you place Mount Athos and the Erevna work?" Lydia asked after a while.

"That's just what I was going to ask," Demos added.

"Let's look at mainstream Christianity for a moment and then I will respond to your question," I said, and proceeded to outline some of my concerns.

"One of the problems with Christianity as represented by the organized churches and the various denominations is that they have become so secularized they have banished that which is at the very core of religion—the reality of miracles, of mystery and faith in the potentiality of every human being to attain union with the Divine through systematic methods of spiritual practice. Most Western theologians, utilizing only the left side of their brains, have bought totally into the mechanistic view of reality, and they have transformed Christianity into nothing more than a system of ethical rules for social and political action. Jesus of Nazareth is no longer the historical embodiment of the pan-Universal Logos,[15] the miracle worker pointing out to humanity its Divine origin and destiny, but simply a great teacher of moral philosophy."

"They do so because they don't want to be embarrassed in front of secular scientists. They are afraid of being perceived as premodern and superstitious," Lydia said.

"Exactly," I replied. "But it is for this reason that there is such a surge of interest today, on the part of so many people, particularly among the educated and the young, toward new religions that emphasize experiential knowledge of spiritual realities.

"Just as conventional science needs to make drastic changes in its conception of reality, organized, established religions will have to make appropriate changes too if they are to be relevant in the decades to come."

"What changes do you have in mind?" Demos asked.

"The reincorporation of the miraculous, the mysterious, and the experiential as part of the central concerns of religion. It is for this reason that, remarkably, I think Mount Athos may be relevant for Christians today. For there the experiential tradition that was characteristic of early Christianity has been preserved."

Demos reacted as if what I was saying was incomprehensible to him, since Mount Athos represented a medieval order that was completely out of tune with the ways of the modern age. I agreed that there was a thousand-year-old gulf separating the social context of Mount Athos and modern America and Europe. I agreed too that the ways of Mount Athos may not be exportable to peoples and cultures outside of the Eastern Orthodox world.

"Yet I do believe," I said, "that the Eastern Orthodox mystical theology and practices that have been preserved on Mount Athos can play an important role in the regeneration of Christianity, once that theology is freed from its medieval context and adapted to the needs and ways of the modern Christian West. Already I see a growing interest among some Protestant and Catholic theologians and priests who, like myself, are discovering the wealth of mystical practice that is found in the *Philokalia* and other works by Eastern Orthodox mystics."

I then went on to read a passage from the work of Dr. John Rossner.[16] As an Episcopal priest and professor of comparative religions, Father Rossner discovered the spiritual wealth of Eastern Orthodox mysticism as a repository of the primordial tradition that is manifested in all the esoteric practices of the great religions. Commenting on the Orthodox saint Gregory Palamas, Rossner wrote:

" 'The great medieval . . . saint, Gregory Palamas, developed a Christian theology of human sanctification and transformation which is thoroughly consistent with the yoga traditions of the East and the Primordial Tradition. . . .

" 'Palamas' theology held that man's knowledge of God could not be purely intellectual, but rather must be direct, intuitive, and experiential. Such direct experience of God is possible because man is not an autonomous being in himself but an 'image of God' which is 'opened upward.' However, no man could experience such a birth-right in actual practice unless he was first restored to his 'natural state.' Such a restoration to the natural state of 'wholeness in being,' from which man has fallen through conformity to the existing social and cultural world, could only be attained through ascetical detach-ment, self-discipline, and an ethical process of de-egotization or self-transcendence. . . .

" 'Here, then, is a recognition within classical, Eastern Orthodox Christian theology of the legitimate place and the indispensable need for various technologies of the mind and spirit. . . . These must be found and used in order to open the soul 'upwards' to the Divine Spirit before man can be restored to his truly natural, human state. In such a higher state alone can man be reached by God. Only in such higher modes of functioning of the human consciousness, or more spiritually attuned states, can man indeed hear the . . . voice of God speaking from within him.' "[17]

"You see, we are witnessing today," I said after I placed Rossner's book back on the table, "a revolutionary movement toward a spir-itual interpretation of reality, as the sociologist Pitirim Sorokin pre-dicted several decades ago. In science it is happening thanks to the assault, on the part of rebel scientists, against the positivistic, mech-anistic notion of reality that has dominated science for three cen-turies. It is happening in religion by a similar process resulting from the works of religious functionaries and thinkers like fathers John Rossner and Matthew Fox and by the pressures generated by an increasing number of people who report having psychic and mystical experiences. These developments are radically changing our world. And they are necessary changes if humanity is to survive. We may be heading toward a point in history when the traditional conflict between religion and science will come to an end. It will do so through a deeper understanding of nature and reality, resulting from the lifting of the veil separating ordinary three-dimensional con-sciousness from super-sensible realities."

"And you think the mystical theology and practice of the Eastern Church can play a role in this lifting of the veil?" Lydia asked.

"Yes, assuming, as I said, that it is freed from its medieval social context. Or, and this seems to be more plausible, the insights and methods of spiritual purification and practice of the Athonite tradition as expressed in texts like the *Philokalia* are creatively adapted for use within the context of modern industrial and postindustrial civilization."

"Where does your involvement with Erevna fit here?" Roger asked.

"You see, Roger," I said, "the philosophical insights and rational clarity of the Erevna work that I have been involved with for so many years has been of crucial importance in helping me comprehend and appreciate various mystical traditions such as that of Eastern Orthodoxy. In fact it was the former that opened my mind and heart to the latter. So, as far as I am concerned, the two complement one another within my own understanding of reality."

I then mentioned how I often wondered whether the mystical part of Eastern Orthodox Christianity was for me the appropriate aesthetic and cultural context within which I could have, perhaps, an actual experience of the higher spiritual truths and realities that Erevna speaks about. After all, I was born and raised within that tradition. It would be as natural for me to follow an Eastern Orthodox path as it would be for a Tibetan to follow the way of Tibetan Buddhism and a Hindu to follow the way of the Vedas and Upanishads.

"Well, have you resolved your wonder?" Roger asked jokingly.

"Not yet, not yet," I said, laughing. "I need more time, perhaps. My rational academic ego has been busy constructing mighty fortifications. I am reluctant to give up everything and begin the hike full-time, systematically, and without distractions. So far I have confined myself to walking around and around the Mountain, contemplating, exploring, and inspecting the various trails that lead to the top."

"But what really keeps you stranded at the foothills?" Lydia asked teasingly.

"Like I said, most probably my long-established academic ego that needs time to gradually fade away," I quipped.

"But perhaps there is another reason," I went on to say. "I have realized that quite a few of those who enter one of the several paths often assume that the path they are on is the only legitimate path. And there emerges in their minds a certain intolerance for the validity of alternative paths. By virtue of being on a path they undergo transpersonal experiences and breathe the clean air as they climb higher and higher. The path they are on does work and it will eventually lead them to the top. But on both sides of each path there are tall trees that prevent hikers from seeing that others are moving toward the summit through different pathways."

"Perhaps this is necessary so that the hikers are not distracted from focusing on the path they have chosen," Lydia interjected.

"That may be so," I added. "Only those who have reached the top of the Mountain, beyond the trees, are in a position to recognize that there are other paths besides the one they have chosen themselves. And these God-realized beings are the only ones who could also evaluate which of the paths are the truly most effective and most appropriate for the hike to the top. No one else."

"Therefore, we who carry on an existence at the foothills of the Mountain can legitimately claim only that there are different paths. This is what we have learned by going round and round the Mountain," Lydia said.

"Exactly. It is the contribution of secular education and secular culture to the spiritual advancement of humanity."

"I don't get that," Demos reacted.

"When we finally enter a path, Demo," I said, "we will do so in full recognition and respect for the reality of other paths beyond the trees. We will recognize more readily that the infinite love and compassion of the omnipotent, omniscient, and omnipresent personal God, in order to accommodate our great diversity, offered us many paths to the summit. Our modern, secular education made us more aware of this diversity of the human condition and the relativity of all socially and culturally constructed worldviews. Therefore, a thinking person exposed to this diversity cannot but become more understanding and accepting of others who worship God in different, and from our point of view, strange ways."

It was getting dark. We became aware of how time had flown when we saw the moon rising over the trees on the opposite bank of the Stillwater River. Emily lit two special candles to keep the mosquitoes away and we carried food out onto the balcony. Over some Cypriot wine and beer that Demos brought from New York we continued our spiritual symposium until the late evening.

# NOTES

## 1. SECRET KNOWLEDGE

1. See the thirteen-volume work of Yogi Ramacharaka published by the Yogi Publication Society, Chicago, Ill.
2. Alan Watts, *Psychotherapy East and West* (New York: Vintage Books, 1975).
3. Huston Smith, *Forgotten Truth: The Primordial Tradition* (New York: Harper & Row, 1976).
4. P. D. Ouspensky, *A New Model of the Universe* (New York: Alfred A. Knopf, 1931), pp. 11–14.
5. Fritjof Capra, *The Tao of Physics* (Boston: Shambhala, 1991).
6. For a fascinating discussion and debate of this issue read David R. Griffin and Huston Smith, *Primordial Truth & Postmodern Theology* (Albany: State University of New York Press, 1989).

## 2. PERENNIAL QUESTIONS

1. Ken Wilber, *Eye to Eye: The Quest for the New Paradigm* (New York: Doubleday/Anchor Press, 1983).
2. Jim Hunter, "The Guru Visits Peoria," in Barbara Blazej, *Noetic News* (Orono, Me., 1990).

3.  Yogi Ramacharaka, *Fourteen Lessons in Yogi Philosophy* (Chicago: Yogi Publication Society, 1903), p. 78. See particularly the chapter "Thought Dynamics."

4.  Ibid., pp. 84–85.

5.  Matthew Fox, *The Coming of the Cosmic Christ* (San Francisco: Harper & Row, 1988).

6.  Ramacharaka, *Fourteen Lessons*, pp. 89–90.

## 3. MYSTERIES

1.  Carl Jung, *Memories, Dreams, Reflections* (New York: Vintage Books, 1989).

2.  The Catholic as well as the Eastern Orthodox churches have ritual procedures on how to exorcise demons. These practices are apparently preserved within monastic sanctuaries. It is reported that the pope himself is skilled in carrying out exorcisms. Dan Rather of the American television channel CBS reported in August of 1993 that in 1981 the pope had in fact carried out an exorcism right inside the Vatican of a woman thought to be possessed by demons. When the pontiff read the specific prayers it was reported that the "demons" instantly left her and the troubled woman found peace of mind.

## 4. DEVOTEES

1.  Carl Jung, *Memories, Dreams, Reflections* (New York: Vintage Books, 1989), pp. 155–156.

2.  David Ray Griffin and Huston Smith, *Primordial Truth & Postmodern Theology* (Albany: State University of New York Press, 1989).

3.  Colin Wilson, *Beyond the Occult* (New York: Carroll & Graf, 1988).

4.  Paramahansa Yogananda, *Autobiography of a Yogi* (Los Angeles: Self-Realization Fellowship, 1987).

5.  Howard Murphet, *Sai Baba Avatar: A new journey into power and glory* (San Diego, Calif.: Birth Day Publishing Co., 1977).

## 5. SKEPTICAL INQUIRERS

1.  Robert Basil, ed., *Not Necessarily the New Age: Critical Essays* (Buffalo, N.Y.: Prometheus Books, 1988).
2.  Pitirim A. Sorokin, *Social and Cultural Dynamics*, 4 vols. (New York: American Book Co., 1937–1941).
3.  Oswald Spengler, *The Decline of the West* (New York: Alfred A. Knopf, 1962). Originally published in 1918.
4.  Julian Jaynes, *The Origin of Consciousness in the Breakdown of the Bicameral Mind* (Boston: Houghton Mifflin, 1976).
5.  Pitirim A. Sorokin, *Fads and Foibles in Modern Sociology and Related Sciences* (Chicago: Regnery, 1956).
6.  Pitirim A. Sorokin, *Society, Culture and Personality* (New York: Harper, 1947).
7.  Basil, *Not Necessarily the New Age*, p. 18.
8.  Anonymous, *Course in Miracles*, 3 vols. (New York: Foundation for Inner Peace, 1977).

## 6. PIONEERS

1.  Paul Edwards, "The Case Against Karma and Reincarnation," in Robert Basil, ed., *Not Necessarily the New Age: Critical Essays* (Buffalo, N.Y.: Prometheus Books, 1988), pp. 87–129.
2.  Wilder Penfield, *The Mystery of the Mind* (Princeton, N.J.: Princeton University Press, 1975).
3.  *New York Times Book Review*, January 18, 1976.
4.  Larry Dossey, *Recovering the Soul: A Scientific and Spiritual Search* (New York: Bantam Books, 1989).
5.  The methodological details of their research appeared in the *Journal of Scientific Exploration* 3:43–63.

6. Dossey, *Recovering the Soul*, p. 47.

7. John G. Fuller, *Arigo: Surgeon of the Rusty Knife* (New York: Thomas Y. Crowell Company, 1974).

8. Ibid., pp. 18–19.

9. Quoted in Fuller, *Arigo*, pp. 185–186.

10. Colin Wilson, *Beyond the Occult* (New York: Carroll & Graf, 1988), pp. 242–43. For a recent comprehensive review of the scientific literature on paranormal phenomena read Richard S. Broughton's *Parapsychology: The Controversial Science* (New York: Ballantine Books, 1991).

11. Ted Schultz, "A Personal Odyssey Through the New Age," in Basil, *Not Necessarily the New Age*, pp. 337–60.

12. Alan M. MacRobert, "New Age Hokum," in Basil, pp. 373–85.

13. Barbara Ann Brennan, *Hands of Light: A Guide to Healing Through the Human Energy Field* (New York: Bantam Books, 1988). Also by the same author: *Light Emerging: The Journey of Personal Healing* (New York: Bantam Books, 1993).

14. Thomas Kuhn, *The Structure of Scientific Revolutions* (Chicago: University of Chicago Press, 1970).

15. Ken Wilber, *Eye to Eye: The Quest for the New Paradigm* (New York: Doubleday/Anchor Press, 1983).

16. Ken Wilber, *A Sociable God: Toward a New Understanding of Religion* (Boulder: New Science Library, 1984).

17. Frits Staal, *Exploring Mysticism* (New York: Penguin, 1980).

## 7. FILTER OF AWARENESS

1. Deepak Chopra, *Quantum Healing: Exploring the Frontiers of Mind/Body Medicine* (New York: Bantam Books, 1990).

2. Ernest Becker, *The Denial of Death* (New York: Free Press, 1973).

3. Peter Berger, *The Sacred Canopy: Elements of a Sociological Theory of Religion* (New York: Doubleday/Anchor Press, 1969).

4. Huston Smith, *The Religions of Man* (New York: Harper & Row,

1986). Reprinted and revised as *The World's Religions* (San Francisco, Harper, 1991).
5. William Rodarmor, "The Secret Life of Swami Muktananda," *Co-Evolution* 40 (Winter 1983), pp. 104–11.
6. Rick Fields, "Perils of the Path," *Co-Evolution* 40 (Winter 1983), pp. 124–29.

## 8. FALSE PROPHETS

1. William Rodarmor, "The Secret Life of Swami Muktananda," *Co-Evolution* 40 (Winter, 1983), pp. 104–11.
2. Baba Muktananda, "The Dharma of Ashram Life," *In the Company of the Saints* (South Fallsburg, N.Y.: Darshan, July 1988).
3. Colin Wilson, *The Occult* (New York: Vintage Books, 1973).
4. See Rodarmor, *Secret Life*, p. 111.
5. Anonymous, *Course in Miracles*, 3 vols. (New York: Foundation for Inner Peace, 1977).
6. Jane Roberts, *The Coming of Seth* (New York: Pocket Books, 1976). A series of "channeled" monographs followed this publication.
7. Jon Klimo, *Channeling: Investigations on Receiving Information from Paranormal Sources* (Los Angeles: Jeremy P. Tarcher, 1987). A recent fascinating work on the subject is that by Arthur Hastings, *With the Tongues of Men and Angels: A Study of Channeling* (Chicago: Holt, Rinehart and Winston, 1991).
8. Quoted in Keith Thompson's, "The UFO Encounter Experience as a Crisis of Transformation," in Stanislav Grof, M.D., and Christina Grof, eds., *Spiritual Emergency: When Personal Transformation Becomes a Crisis*, (Los Angeles: Jeremy P. Tarcher, 1989). pp. 121–34.
9. Herbert Benson, M.D., *The Relaxation Response* (New York: William Morrow, 1975); see also by the same author, *Your Maximum Mind* (New York: Avon Books, 1987).
10. Dean Ornish, *Reversing Heart Disease* (New York: Random House, 1990).

11.   See Brian Weiss's recent work *Through Time Into Healing: Discovering the power of regression therapy to erase trauma and transform mind, body and relationships* (New York: Simon & Schuster, 1992).

12.   Roger J. Woolger, *Other Lives, Other Selves: A Jungian Psychotherapist Discovers Past Lives* (New York: Bantam Books, 1988).

## 9. TRANSITIONS

1.   Archimandrite Sophrony (Sakharov), *We Shall See Him As He Is* (Essex, England: Stavropegic Monastery of St. John the Baptist, 1988).

## 10. PILGRIMS AND SCHOLARS

1.   Jacob Needleman, *Lost Christianity* (New York: Bantam Books, 1980), pp. 1–2.

2.   Nikos Kazantzakis, *Report to Greco* (New York: Bantam Books, 1966).

3.   Ken Wilber, *A Sociable God: Toward a New Understanding of Religion* (Boulder: New Science Library, 1984).

4.   Max Weber, *The Sociology of Religion* (Boston: Beacon Press, 1963).

5.   Max Weber, *The Protestant Ethic and the Spirit of Capitalism* (New York: Scribner's, 1958).

6.   I must not reveal the real name of the monastery where we stayed. Therefore, from now on I will simply refer to it as "the Monastery."

7.   Phillip Sherrard, *Athos: The Mountain of Silence* (London: Oxford University Press, 1960; Michael Choukas, *Black Angels of Athos* (Brattleboro, Vt.: Stephen Daye Press, 1934).

8.   Bishop Kallistos Ware, *The Orthodox Way* (London and Oxford: Mowbray, 1979).

## II. CONFESSION

1.  Michael Choukas, *Black Angels of Athos* (Brattleboro, Vt.: Stephen Daye Press, 1934).
2.  Merrill Badger et al., "Gnosis: Robin Amis Discusses Historian/ Philosopher Boris Mouravieff's Writings on the Christian Esoteric Tradition." Interview in *Earth Star* (December/January, 1992).
3.  Christos Yiannaras, *Alfavitari tes Pistis* [in Greek, "The Abc of Faith"] (Athens: Domos Publications, 1988).
4.  Kallistos Ware, *The Orthodox Way* (London: Mowbray & Co., 1979).
5.  *Greek Orthodox Holy Week & Easter Services* (Daytona Beach, Fla.: Patmos Press, 1990).

## I2. GYMNASTS OF THE SOUL

1.  Jon Klimo, *Channeling* (Los Angeles: Jeremy P. Tarcher, 1987), p. 172.
2.  Ernst Benz, *The Eastern Orthodox Church: Its Thought and Life* (Chicago: Aldine Publishing, 1963), p. 5.
3.  Henri J. M. Nouwen, *Behold the Beauty of the Lord: Praying with Icons* (Notre Dame, Ind.: Ave Maria Press, 1987), p. 14.
4.  Émile Durkheim, *The Elementary Forms of the Religious Life* (Glencoe, Ill.: Free Press, 1954). Originally published in 1912.
5.  Raymond Aron, *Main Currents in Sociological Thought*, vol. 2 (New York: Doubleday, 1970), p. 51.
6.  Ibid., p. 66.
7.  Rudolf Otto, *The Idea of the Holy* (New York: Oxford University Press, 1958). Originally published in 1923.
8.  Thomas O'Dea and Janet O'Dea Aviad, *The Sociology of Religion* (Englewood Cliffs, N.J.: Prentice Hall, 1983), p. 23.
9.  Archimandrite Sophrony, *The Monk of Mount Athos: Staretz*

*Silouan, 1866–1938* (New York: St. Vladimir's Press, 1975), pp. 100–
101.

10.   Tito Collianter, *Asketernas Vag* [in Finnish]. Trans. in Greek as
*Oh Dromos ton Asketon* [The Way of the Ascetics] (Athens: Akritas,
1990).

11.   I was fascinated when later I came across an almost identical
passage from Buddhism. According to Mahayana Buddhism the Buddha, or the person who attains Buddhahood, also has power over
nature. "Possessing to a superior degree the miraculous powers attributed to all saints, the Buddha can at will create, transform and
conserve external objects, shorten or extend his life-span, move
through solid bodies, travel rapidly for long distances through the air,
reduce the size of material bodies. . . ." See Edward Conze, *Buddhist
Thought in India* (Ann Arbor: University of Michigan Press, 1967).
Quoted in Marco Orru and Amy Wang, "Durkheim, Religion,
and Buddhism," *Journal for the Scientific Study of Religion* 31 (March
1992), p. 53.

## 13. RAINBOWS AND LIGHTNING

1.   Geddes MacGregor, *Reincarnation in Christianity* (Wheaton, Ill.:
Theosophical Publishing House, 1989), p. 23.

2.   Nicholas Berdyaev, *The Destiny of Man* (London: Geoffrey Bles,
1937), p. 336. Quoted in MacGregor, *Reincarnation in Christianity*, p. 16.

3.   Matthew Fox, *The Coming of the Cosmic Christ* (San Francisco:
Harper & Row, 1988), pp. 107–9.

4.   Reported in the Boston Greek-American weekly *The Hellenic
Chronicle*, August 12, 1993. See Nicholas Cavasilas, *The Life in Christ*,
trans. by C. J. de Catanzaro (Crestwood, N.Y.: St. Vladimir's Press,
1974); Panayiotis Nellas, *Deification in Christ: The Nature of the Human Person*, trans. from the Greek by Norman Russell (Crestwood,
N.Y.: St. Vladimir's Press, 1987).

5.   Anonymous, *Mia Vradia Sten Erimo tou Agiou Orous* [in Greek]

(Livadia, Greece: Holy Monastery of the Birth of Theodokos, 1990), pp. 35–36. Translated into English as *A Night in the Desert of the Holy Mountain* (Crestwood, N.Y.: St. Vladimir's Press, 1991).

6. Monk Joseph, *Geron Joseph Oh Hesychastes* [in Greek] (Daphne: Agion Oros, 1984).

7. Kallistos Ware, *The Orthodox Way* (London: Mowbray & Co. 1979), p. 12.

## 14. BEYOND THE SHADOWS

1. The many volumes of the *Philokalia* are gradually being translated into English. See volume 1, *The Philokalia: The Complete Text.* Compiled by Saint Nikodimos of the Holy Mountain and Saint Makarios of Corinth. Translated from the Greek and edited by G. E. H. Palmer, Philip Sherrard, and Kallistos Ware (Boston: Faber and Faber, 1990). Also *Early Fathers from the Philokalia: together with some writings of St. Abba Dorotheus, St. Isaac of Syria and St. Gregory Palamas.* Translated and selected from the Russian text *Dobrotolubiye* by E. Kadloubovsky and G. E. H. Palmer (Boston: Faber and Faber, 1981). Also see a recent collection from this voluminous work in *Prayer of the Heart: Writings from the Philokalia,* trans. by G. E. H. Palmer et al. (Boston: Shambhala, 1993).

2. Christos Yiannaras, *Katafygio Ideon* [in Greek, "A Refuge of Ideas"] (Athens: Domos Publishers, 1987).

3. See, for example, the work of Panayiotis Nellas, *Deification in Christ: The Nature of the Human Person,* trans. from the Greek by Norman Russell (Crestwood, N.Y.: St. Vladimir's Press, 1987).

4. A recent summary of this work is presented in Richard S. Broughton's *Parapsychology: The Controversial Science* (New York: Ballantine Books, 1991).

5. Anonymous, *Mia Vradia Sten Erimo tou Agiou Orous* (Livadia, Greece: Holy Monastery of the Birth of Theodokos, 1990). Translated into English as *A Night in the Desert of the Holy Mountain* (Crestwood, N.Y.: St. Vladimir's Press, 1991).

6.  Nellas, *Deification in Christ.*

7.  Monk Paisios of the Holy Mountain, *Oh Agios Arsenios Oh Kappadokis* [in Greek, "Saint Arsenios the Kappadokian"] (Salonica, Greece: Holy Monastery of Monazouson, 1991). A recent case of another contemporary gerontas with reputed extraordinary gifts was that of Father Porfyrios who lived and practiced in a church right at the heart of Athens, at Constitution Square. He died in 1991.

8.  Kallistos Ware, *The Orthodox Way* (London and Oxford: Mowbray, 1987), pp. 131–32.

9.  See Klitos Ioannides, *Oh Geron Porfyrios* [in Greek] (Nicosia: Saint Marina Monastery, 1992).

10.  Menelaos Leventis, *Oh Eremites Charalambis: Mia megale physiognomia tou Christianikou pneumatos* [in Greek, "The Hermit Charalambis: A great physiognomy of the Christian Spirit"] (Athens: Unpublished manuscript, 1982).

11.  M. U. Hatengdi, *Nityananda: The Divine Presence* (Cambridge, Mass.: Rudra Press, 1984).

12.  Paramahansa Yogananda, *Autobiography of a Yogi* (Los Angeles: Self-Realization Fellowship, 1987).

13.  The work of the physicist Paul Davies is of great importance in this respect. See his latest work, *The Mind of God: The Scientific Basis for a Rational World* (New York: Simon & Schuster, 1992).

14.  Fotios N. Kontoglou, *Semeion Mega: Ta Thaumata tes Thermes* [in Greek, "A Great Sign: The Miracles of Therme"] (Athens: Aster, 1964).

15.  Klitos Ioannides, *Thaumata tou Agiou Raphael se Kyprious* [in Greek, "Miracles by St. Raphael to Cypriots"] (Nicosia: Saint Marina Monastery, 1991).

16.  Raymond Moody, *Life after Life* (New York: Bantam Books, 1976); also *The Light Beyond* (New York: Bantam Books, 1988).

## 15. LIFTING THE VEIL

1. Raymond Moody, *The Light Beyond* (New York: Bantam Books, 1988), p. 2.
2. Ibid.
3. George G. Ritchie (with Elizabeth Sherrill), *Return from Tomorrow* (Tarrytown, N.Y.: Fleming H. Revell, 1978).
4. John E. Mack, "The Alien Abduction Phenomenon," *Noetic Sciences Review* (Autumn 1992), p. 5.
5. Ibid., p. 10.
6. Ibid., p. 11.
7. Kenneth Ring, *The Omega Project: Near-Death Experiences, UFO Encounters, and Mind at Large* (New York: William Morrow, 1992).
8. Ibid., p. 239.
9. Ibid., p. 245.
10. Ibid., p. 246.
11. See, for example, Jaime T. Licausco, *The Magicians of God: The Amazing Stories of Philippine Faith Healers* (Philippines: Metro Manila Publishers, 1982).
12. Ken Wilber, *Up from Eden* (New York: Doubleday/Anchor Press, 1981); also *A Sociable God: Toward a New Understanding of Religion* (Boulder, Colo.: New Science Library, 1984).
13. Richard Tarnas, *The Passion of the Western Mind: Understanding the Ideas That Have Shaped Our World View* (New York: Harmony Books, 1991).
14. Arthur Koestler, *Janus: A Summing Up* (New York: Vintage, 1978).
15. See Matthew Fox, *The Coming of the Cosmic Christ* (San Francisco: Harper & Row, 1988).
16. John Rossner, *In Search of the Primordial Tradition and the Cosmic Christ* (St. Paul, Minn.: Llewellyn Publications, 1989).
17. Ibid., pp. 121–22.